THE BOUNDARIES OF
OUR BEING

Paul Tillich was born in the province of Brandenburg
in 1886, and after his university studies served as a
chaplain with the German army during the 1914-18
war. After the war he held various academic positions, teaching theology and philosophy, but one of
his main interests was in the movement of 'Religious
Socialism', attempting to avert a repetition of the
conditions that had led to war. He was forced to
leave Germany on Hitler's rise to power, and found
a home in Union Theological Seminary, New York.
When he retired from his Chair of Philosophical
Theology there in 1955, he was invited to become a
professor first at Harvard University and then at the
University of Chicago. He gave many lectures in
other universities, including the Gifford Lectures in
Aberdeen, and received several doctorates and other
honours. He was the author of many books. He died
in 1965, and was buried at New Harmony, Indiana.

By the same author

in the Fontana Library of Theology and Philosophy

THE COURAGE TO BE

MORALITY AND BEYOND

PAUL TILLICH

THE BOUNDARIES OF
OUR BEING

*

A Collection of His Sermons
The Eternal Now and *The New Being*

with His Autobiographical Sketch
On the Boundary

COLLINS
LIBRARY OF
THEOLOGY AND PHILOSOPHY

This collection first issued in the Fontana Library 1973
The Eternal Now first published 1963 by SCM Press, London
The New Being first published 1956 by SCM Press, London
On the Boundary first published 1966 by Charles Scribner's Sons,
New York.

Printed in Great Britain
Collins Clear-Type Press
London and Glasgow

Contents

Acknowledgment

PREFACE

This paperback edition combines three books by Paul Tillich: *The Eternal Now*, 1963; *The New Being*, 1956; *On the Boundary*, an autobiographical sketch which originally appeared as the first part of *The Interpretation of History*, 1936, and which was published separately in London in 1967. The new title was suggested by a passage in the first chapter of *The Eternal Now*, where Tillich speaks about penetrating 'to the boundaries of our being, where the mystery of life appears'.

The sermons that were collected under the title *The Eternal Now* are printed first because they were preached between 1955 and 1963 and show Tillich at the height of his power to communicate with non-theologians. As a reviewer in the London *Church Times* commented, here Tillich 'seems to have achieved a new and most impressive simplicity in his discussion of many of the cardinal points of man's relationship with God. It is a simplicity which reveals a wealth of reflection and understanding.'

Next come the sermons collected as *The New Being*. They were preached (like the other series, mostly in university and college chapels) in the United States between 1947 and 1955. Bishop John Robinson, the author of *Honest to God*, wrote that in this book Tillich 'has provided an entry into his deepest mind which requires in the reader no technical theological knowledge. In these addresses the great words and symbols of the Bible speak with healing power to our modern need, at the same time as they convict us of our frightening superficiality.'

The earliest volume of Tillich's American sermons to be published was *The Shaking of the Foundations*, 1949. In Britain this has been available as a Pelican paperback since 1962. Tillich himself wrote that '*The New Being*

is, so to speak, the answer to the questions developed in
The Shaking of the Foundations.' But in this edition it has
been thought useful to include some brief reflections on
his life up to the age of 50. Tillich wrote these reflections
when he had been exiled from his native Germany by
Nazism and when he had not yet built his second,
American career; and *On the Boundary* shows the conflicts which had shaped the preacher who was to win
such influence throughout the English-speaking world.
About it, R. Gregor Smith wrote: 'As an introduction to
Tillich it is unparalleled.' But *On the Boundary* is more
than a background to the sermons and the theology.
Tillich preached and taught in America at a time of
widespread churchgoing, and several of these sermons
reflect his prophetic disquiet about the ease with which
God's name was being used. In comparison, the Germany which he recalls in *On the Boundary* was less
ecclesiastical, and his chief concern in those days was to
develop a 'religious socialism', about which he writes:
'It is more than a new economic system. It is a comprehensive understanding of existence . . .' This concern
unites Tillich with the generation arising after the decline of the religion of the Eisenhower years.

Tillich was very conscious that he was a German, and
in particular that he had to learn how to use idiomatic
English. He took great trouble. He dedicated *The New
Being* to Miss Mary Heilner, who 'helped me to eliminate
Germanisms and other stylistic shortcomings and ad-
vised me in the organization of the whole book.' *The
Eternal Now* was dedicated 'to the memory of Hermann
Schafft, friend for more than half a century', but he also
offered thanks 'to Mrs Elisabeth Wood, who did the
hard and necessary work of stylistic correction'. The
original translation of *On the Boundary* from the German was revised in 1964 under Tillich's direction, and
R. Gregor Smith justly observed: 'this final version with
its stripped unflashy English testified further to his ability
to cross the boundary of language and of poetry.'

As a preacher or autobiographer, Tillich was always serious. His recollections are not amusing, and church-goers would not be delighted if all preachers were to imitate his style. But he was in private life a genial man, fond of humour, travel and parties, and it is possible that he might not object to a comparison between this book and a ride in a funfair. The reader's journey begins quietly. For a paragraph or two, the only unusual feature may seem to be that not a word is wasted. Tillich is never sentimental or trivial. He never exhibits his humanity or his learning. He never flatters or woos the reader; he assumes that the reader is concerned for the mystery of his own life. He calmly takes a biblical text or a common experience, as other preachers do. But suddenly the reader finds himself shot into the heights. This book lifts the heart up because it expresses the power of one of the noblest and most religious minds in the history of Christianity. And then, as suddenly, the reader is brought down into utter realism, almost into the abyss; and he realizes how profoundly Tillich is aware of the limitations of religion, of the enigmas of nature, of the tragic power of evil in the real world, and of the loneliness, anxiety and doubt which are the human condition. Two typical Tillich sentences come in his sermon on the 'Spiritual Presence'. 'We live in an era,' he says, 'in which the God we know is the absent God. But in knowing God as the absent God, we *know* of him; we feel his absence as the empty space that is left by something or someone that once belonged to us . . .' It is only after – or, rather, through – such an acknow-ledgment of the character of the twentieth century that Tillich makes his Christian affirmation, as in the sermon on 'The New Being': 'We want only to communicate to you an experience we have had that here and there in the world and now and then in ourselves is a new cre-ation, usually hidden, but sometimes manifest, and cer-tainly manifest in Jesus who is called the Christ.' Our own lives are, as Tillich shows from his own life, divided into different spheres or periods, as if by boundaries. For most of us, this means that our lives are broken into fragments. But for Tillich the mystery that surrounds all existence is the mystery of Being, the mystery traditionally called God, and the source of our lives in the Eternal gives them wholeness and meaning. Tillich never forgets, and never lets us forget, the feeling of being a boy by the sea, with 'the experience of the infinite bordering on the finite'.

He wrote many books which give his teaching more fully, most notably his *Systematic Theology* in three volumes (James Nisbet and Co., Ltd.) and his Terry Lectures at Yale in 1952, *The Courage To Be*, available as a paperback in the Fontana Library of Theology and Philosophy since 1962. But many who have made a careful study of Tillich's thought agree that his sermons are the most powerful summary of its relevance, while a leading commentator on Tillich, Dr J. Heywood Thomas, wrote when introducing the British edition of *On the Boundary*: 'Anyone who comes across this book and has never read any of Tillich's works can quickly and easily form for himself a clear picture of Tillich's achievement and gain a real appreciation of his peculiar style of theological thinking.'

Tillich travelled far from the parsonage where he was a boy, but he often recalled the text which his father gave him at his Confirmation: 'You will know the truth, and the truth will make you free.' He did seek God, the Infinite Being, with all his heart and mind and strength, and that was why he was able to persuade his hearers that every sermon should 'awaken infinite concern'. And he found God; which was why he, the professor familiar with the culture of two continents, spoke so often and so movingly about being arrested, blessed and healed. And with this he found a freedom to leave the conventions and to witness to the reality with honesty, tact and awe.

1973   DAVID L. EDWARDS

THE ETERNAL NOW

*

PART ONE

THE HUMAN PREDICAMENT

*

1. Loneliness and Solitude

And when he had sent the multitudes away, he went up into a mountain apart to pray: and when the evening was come, he was there alone.

MATTHEW 14:23

I

'He was there, alone.' So are we. Man is alone because he is man! In some way every creature is alone. In majestic isolation every star travels through the darkness of endless space. Each tree grows according to its own law, fulfilling its unique possibilities. Animals live, fight and die for themselves alone, confined to the limitations of their bodies. Certainly, they also appear as male and female, in families and in flocks. Some of them are gregarious. But all of them are alone! Being alive means being in a body – a body separated from all other bodies. And being separated means being alone.

This is true of every creature, and it is more true of man than of any other creature. He is not only alone; he also *knows* that he is alone. Aware of what he is, he asks the question of his aloneness. He asks why he is alone, and how he can triumph over his being alone. For this aloneness he cannot endure. Neither can he escape it. It is his destiny to be alone and to be aware of it. Not even God can take this destiny away from him.

In the story of paradise we read: 'Then the Lord God said, It is not good that man should be alone.' And he created the woman from the body of Adam. Here an old myth is used to show that originally there was no bodily separation between man and woman; in the beginning they were one. Now they long to be one again. But although they recognize each other as flesh of their own flesh, each remains alone. They look at each other, and despite their longing for each other, they see their strangeness. In the story, God himself makes them aware of this fact when he speaks to each of them separately, when he makes each one responsible for his own guilt, when he listens to their excuses and mutual accusations, when he pronounces a separate curse over each, and leaves them to experience shame in the face of their nakedness. They are each alone. The creation of the woman has not overcome the situation which God describes as not good for man. He remains alone. And the creation of the woman, although it provides a helper for Adam, has only presented to the one human being who is alone another human being who is equally alone, and from their flesh all other men, each of whom will also stand alone.

We ask, however – is this really so? Did not God accomplish something better? Isn't our aloneness largely removed in the encounter of the sexes? Certainly it is during hours of communion and in moments of love. The ecstasy of love can absorb one's own self in its union with the other self, and separation seems to be overcome. But after these moments, the isolation of self from self is felt even more deeply than before, sometimes even to the point of mutual repulsion. We have given too much of ourselves, and now we long to take back what was given. Our desire to protect our aloneness is expressed in the feeling of shame. We feel ashamed when our intimate self, mental or bodily, is opened. We try to cover our nakedness, as did Adam and Eve when they became conscious of themselves. Thus, man and woman remain alone even in the most intimate union. They cannot penetrate each other's innermost centre. And if this were not so, they could not be helpers to each other; they could not have human community.

This is why God himself cannot liberate man from his aloneness: it is man's greatness that he is centred within himself. Separated from his world, he is thus able to look *at* it. Only because he can look at it can he know and love and transform it. God, in creating him the ruler of the earth, had to separate him and thrust him into aloneness. Man is also therefore able to be spoken to by God and by man. He can ask questions and give answers and make decisions. He has the freedom for good or evil. Only he who has an impenetrable centre in himself is free. Only he who is alone can claim to be a man. This is the greatness and this is the burden of man.

II

Our language has wisely sensed those two sides of man's being alone. It has created the word 'loneliness' to express the pain of being alone. And it has created the word 'solitude' to express the glory of being alone. Although, in daily life, we do not always distinguish between these words, we should do so consistently and thus deepen our understanding of our human predicament.

In the twenty-fifth Psalm we read: 'Turn thou to me and be gracious; for I am lonely and afflicted.' The psalmist feels the pain of loneliness. We do not know the character of his particular loneliness, but we know the many faces that loneliness can have. We have all experienced some of them.

Most widespread is our loneliness after those who helped us to forget that we are alone have left us, either through separation or death. I refer not only to those nearest to us, but also to those human beings who give us the feeling of communion, groups with which we have worked, with which we have had social contact, with which we have had spiritual communication. For many people such loneliness becomes a permanent state and a continuous source of profound melancholy. The sighing of innumerable lonely people, all around us and over the world, fills the ears that are opened by love.

But let us also consider those among us who are surrounded by friends and neighbours, by co-workers and countrymen, who live in family groups and enjoy the communion of the sexes – everything that those others do *not* have. And let us ask – are they without the pain of loneliness? Is their aloneness covered up by the crowd in which they move? If we can number ourselves among these people, we might answer the question as follows: I never felt so lonely as in that particular hour when I was surrounded by people but suddenly realized my ultimate isolation. I became silent and retired from the group in order to be alone with my loneliness. I wanted my external predicament to match my internal one. Let us not minimize such an experience by asserting that some people are simply not strong enough to obtain a significant place in the group, and that their withdrawal is nothing but an expression of weakness that may call for counselling or psychiatric help. Certainly, such people do exist in large numbers, and they need help. But I speak now of the strong ones, who have achieved their place in the crowd, and who nevertheless experience the terror of ultimate loneliness. They are aware, in a sudden break through the world around them, of man's real predicament. Let us also not minimize this experience by pointing out the fact that some people feel misunderstood despite their urgent desire to make themselves understandable, and therefore feel lonely in the crowd. No one can deny that there are such people and, further, that they even demonstrate a certain truth – for who is really understood, even by himself? The mystery of a person cannot be encompassed by a neat description of his character. Those, however, who always feel misunderstood confuse the mystery of each personality with imaginary treasures which they themselves believe they possess and which demand recognition from others. When such recognition is not forthcoming, they feel lonely and withdraw. They also need help. But again, there are those whose real treasures are great enough to find expression, to be understood and received, and yet who have this terrifying experience of ultimate loneliness. In such moments they break through the surface of their average life into the depth of man's predicament.

Many feel lonely because, in spite of their effort to love and be loved, their love is rejected. This loneliness is often self-created. These people may be claiming as a right what can only come to them as a gift. They withdraw into a self-chosen loneliness, taking revenge through bitterness and hostility towards those they feel have rejected them, actually enjoying the pain of their loneliness. There are many such persons, and they contribute heavily to the growth of neurotic loneliness in our time. They above all need help, for they easily become the prey of a demonic force that secludes them completely within themselves.

But there is also the genuine experience of rejected love. No special claim is made, but hope yearns towards another, and is disappointed. A community of love comes to an end or fails to exist at all. Such loneliness cuts our ties with the world. We are indeed ultimately alone, and not even love from other directions or the power of our own love can lift this burden from us. He who can endure the loneliness of disappointed love without bitterness experiences the depth of man's predicament radically and creatively.

There are, finally, two forms of loneliness that cannot either be covered or escaped : the loneliness of guilt and the loneliness of death. Nobody can remove from us what we have committed against our true being. We feel both our hidden guilt and our open guilt as *ours*, and ours alone. We cannot really make anybody else responsible for what we have done. We cannot run away from our guilt, and we cannot honestly cover it up. We are alone with it. And it is a loneliness that permeates all other forms of loneliness, transforming them into experiences of judgment.

Then, there is that ultimate loneliness of having to die. In the anticipation of our death we remain alone. No communication with others can remove it, as no other's presence in the actual hour of our dying can conceal the fact that it is *our* death, and our death alone. In the hour of death we are cut off from the whole universe and everything in it. We are deprived of all the things and beings that made us forget our being alone. Who can endure this loneliness?

III

Loneliness can be conquered only by those who can bear solitude. We have a natural desire for solitude because we are men. We want to feel what we are – namely, alone – not in pain and horror, but with joy and courage. There are many ways in which solitude can be sought and experienced. And each way can be called 'religious', if it is true, as one philosopher said, that 'religion is what a man does with his solitariness'.

One of these ways is the desire towards the silence of nature. We can speak without voice to the trees and the clouds and the waves of the sea. Without words they respond through the rustling of leaves and the moving of clouds and the murmuring of the sea. This solitude we can have, but only for a brief time. For we realize that the voices of nature cannot ultimately answer the questions in our mind. Our solitude in nature can easily become loneliness, and so we return to the world of man.

Solitude can also be found in the reading of poetry, in listening to music, in looking at pictures, and in sincere thoughtfulness. We are alone, perhaps in the midst of multitudes, but we are not lonely. Solitude protects us without isolating us. But life calls us back to its empty talk and the unavoidable demands of daily routine. It calls us back to its loneliness and the cover that it, in turn, spreads over our loneliness.

Without a doubt, this last describes not only man's general predicament, but also, and emphatically, our time. Today, more intensely than in preceding periods, man is so lonely that he cannot bear solitude. And he tries desperately to become a part of the crowd. Everything in our world supports him. It is a symptom of our disease that teachers and parents and the managers of public communication do everything possible to deprive us of the external conditions for solitude, the simplest aids to privacy. Even our houses, instead of protecting the solitude of each member of the family or group, are constructed to exclude privacy almost completely. The same holds true of the forms of communal life, the school, college, office and factory. An unceasing pressure attempts to destroy even our desire for solitude.

But sometimes God thrusts us out of the crowd into a solitude we did not desire, but which none the less takes hold of us. The prophet Jeremiah says: 'I sit alone, because thy hand was upon me.' God sometimes lays hands upon us. He wants us to ask the question of truth that may isolate us from most men, and that can be asked only in solitude. He wants us to ask the question of justice that may bring us suffering and death, and that can grow in us only in solitude. He wants us to break through the ordinary ways of men that may bring disrepute and hatred upon us, a breakthrough that can happen only in solitude. He wants us to penetrate to the boundaries of our being, where the mystery of life appears, and it can only appear in moments of solitude.

There may be some among you who long to become creative in some realm of life. But you cannot become or remain creative without solitude. One hour of conscious solitude will enrich your creativity far more than hours of trying to learn the creative process.

What happens in our solitude? Listen to Mark's words about Jesus' solitude in the desert: 'And he was in the wilderness forty days, tempted by Satan; and he was with the wild beasts, and the angels ministered to him.'

He is alone, facing the whole earth and sky, the wild beasts around him and within him, he himself the battlefield for divine and demonic forces. So, first, this is what happens in our solitude: we meet ourselves, not as ourselves, but as the battlefield for creation and destruction, for God and the demons. Solitude is not easy. Who can bear it? It was not easy even for Jesus. We read: 'He went up into the hills to pray. When evening came, he was there alone.' When evening comes, loneliness becomes more lonely. We feel this when a day, or a period, or all the days of our life come to an end. Jesus went up to pray. Is this the way to transform loneliness into solitude and to bear solitude? It is not a simple question to answer. Most prayers do not have this much power. Most prayers make God a partner in a conversation; we use him to escape the only true way to solitude. Such prayers flow easily from the mouths of both ministers and laymen. But they are not born out of a solitary encounter of God with men. They are certainly not the kind of prayer for which Jesus went up into the hills. Better that we remain silent and allow our soul, that is always longing for solitude, to sigh without words to God. This we can do, even in a crowded day and a crowded room, even under the most difficult external conditions. This can give us moments of solitude that no one can take from us.

In these moments of solitude something is done to us. The centre of our being, the innermost self that is the ground of our aloneness, is elevated to the divine centre and taken into it. Therein can we rest without losing ourselves.

Now perhaps we can answer a question you may have already asked – how can communion grow out of solitude? We have seen that we can never reach the innermost centre of another being. We are always alone, each for himself. But we can reach it in a movement that rises first to God and then returns from him to the other self. In this way man's aloneness is not removed, but taken into the community with that in which the centres of all beings rest, and so into community with all of them. Even love is reborn in solitude. For only in solitude are those who are alone able to reach those from whom they are separated. Only the presence of the eternal can break through the walls that isolate the temporal from the temporal. One hour of solitude may bring us closer to those we love than many hours of communication. We can take them with us to the hills of eternity.

And perhaps when we ask – what is the innermost nature of solitude? – we should answer: the presence of the eternal upon the crowded roads of the temporal. It is the experience of being alone but not lonely, in view of the eternal presence that shines through the face of the Christ, and that includes everybody and everything from which we are separated. In the poverty of solitude all riches are present. Let us dare to have solitude – to face the eternal, to find others, to see ourselves.

2. Forgetting and Being Forgotten

> One thing I do, forgetting what lies behind and straining forward to what lies ahead.
>
> PHILIPPIANS 3:13

These very personal words of Paul, which appear in one of his most personal letters, lead us to ask – what did he want to forget? What do we forget, and what do we remember? What is the function of forgetting in man's life and in the household of the universe? Above all, what *should* we remember and what *should* we forget?

But in raising these questions, another more disturbing one comes to mind: what does it mean for a thing, for a being, to *be* forgotten? What does it mean for us when we *are* forgotten, in parts of our being, or totally, for a period, or for life? What does the thought that we may be forgotten in eternity do to us? How can we endure the words of the Preacher when he says of the dead that 'the memory of them is dead', that they are forgotten 'with their love and their hate', and, according to the psalm, that their place knows them no more?

The simple word 'forget' can plunge us into the deepest riddles of life and death, of time and eternity. The Bible abounds in its use. For forgetting and remembering are two of the most astonishing qualities by which the divine image in man is made manifest. I ask you now to concentrate with me on the mystery of forgetting and remembering and of being forgotten, knowing in advance how limited our words and insights and courage must be in the face of such a mystery. Let us first consider forgetting and remembering, and then being forgotten and perhaps also being remembered.

I

Life could not continue without throwing the past into the past, liberating the present from its burden. Without this power life would be without a future; it would be enslaved by the past. Nothing new could happen; and even the old could not be, for what is now old was once something new, that might or might not have come into existence. Life, without pushing the past into the past, would be altogether impossible. But life has this power, as we are able to observe in the growth of every plant and of every animal. The earlier stages in the development of a living being are left behind in order to provide space for the future, for a new life. But not everything of the past is pushed into the past; something of the past remains alive in the present, so that there is ground from which to grow into the future. Every growth displays its conquered past, sometimes in the form of scars. Life uses its past and battles against it at the same time, in order to thrust forward towards its own renewal. In this pattern, man is united with all beings. It is the universal character of life, whether living beings are aware of it or not.

Only man can be fully aware of it. He saves the past by remembering it, and he pushes it back by forgetting it. This is the way that every child grows, both physically and in spirit. He preserves and he leaves behind. He remembers and he forgets. In healthy development, the balance between the two enables him to advance towards the new. But if too much is preserved, and too little forgotten, the way is barred: the past, with its infantile forces and memories, overpowers the future. We know that some of this occurs in the recesses of the inner life of all of us. We discover remnants of infancy that were never pushed into the past, where they belong. They constrict our freedom and narrow our path into the future. They may even produce a distortion of growth. Think of the preservation of infantile habits in our action and language: our adolescent withdrawal and aggression; the early images of ourselves and our world, far removed from reality; unfounded anxieties and foolish desires; a yet unshaken dependence on childhood authorities – father or mother; and our unquestioned prejudices that have no connection with our present stage of growth. There were occasions in the past when we lacked the strength to leave behind what belonged to the past; we forgot what belonged to oblivion. We forgot to forget, and now we may find it too late.

There have been nations that were unable to throw anything of their heritage into the past, and thus cut themselves off from new growth, until the weight of their past crushed their present and brought them to extinction. And sometimes we might ask if the Christian Church, as well as foreign religions, has not carried with it too much of its past, and left behind too little. Forgetting is probably more difficult for a religious tradition than any other human heritage. But God is not only the beginning from which we came; he is also the end to which we go. He is the creator of the *new* as well as the ancient of days. To all creatures he has given presence; and presence, although it rests on the past, drives into the future. Therefore, all life has received the gift of forgetting. A church that does not accept this gift denies its own creatureliness, and falls into the temptation of every church, which is to make itself God. Of course, no church or nation or person should ever forget its own identity. We are not asked to forget our name, the symbol of our inner self. And certainly, no church is required to forget its foundation. But if it is unable to leave behind much of what was built on this foundation, it will lose its future.

But all life, including man, not only leaves behind. It also preserves. It not only forgets. It also remembers. And the inability to remember is just as destructive as the inability to forget. An aged tree demonstrates that the life force of its original seed, which determined its final form, still exists. An animal would perish if it forgot the adjustments to life it learned from its first hour. The same is true of the human infant; and it is true of all his later growth in body and mind. Remembrance of the past preserves the identity of a human being with himself. Without it, he himself would be left behind by himself. This applies equally to all social groups. A formless rushing ahead, indiscriminate severing of the roots of the past, results in emptiness, a lack of presence, and thus, also, a lack of future. There are churches that, in their desire to forget, have lost the memory of their origins. There are nations that have cut themselves off from their traditions.

Perhaps one of the most conspicuous examples is our own nation, which has used a whole ocean as the drug of forgetfulness with respect to the sources of the civilization to which it belongs – Jerusalem and Athens. I do not speak of the scholarly knowledge of the past, of which there is no lack, but rather of the pushing forward of this nation into a future in which the creative forces of the past no longer exist. More than any other, our nation possesses the great power of forgetting. But this power is not balanced equally with the power of remembering, a fact that might become our undoing, spiritually and even politically. For if we lose our identity, we are lost.

II

We have considered forgetting a way in which life drives towards its own renewal. What and how do we forget? What did Paul forget, when he strained forward to what lay ahead? Obviously, he longed to forget his past as a Pharisee and a persecutor of Christianity. But every word of his letters proves that he never forgot.

There seem to be different kinds of forgetting. There is the natural forgetting of yesterday and most of the things that happened in it. If reminded, we might still remember some of them; but, slowly, even they tend to disappear. The whole day disappears, and only what was really significant in it is remembered. So most of the days of our lives vanish in forgetfulness. This natural process of forgetting operates without our co-operation, like the circulation of our blood.

But there is another aspect of forgetting that is familiar to us all. Something in us prevents us from remembering, when remembering proves to be too difficult or painful. We forget benefits, because the burden of gratitude is too heavy for us. We forget former loves, because the burden of obligations implied by them surpasses our strength. We forget former hates, because the task of nourishing them would disrupt our mind. We forget former pain, because it is still too painful. We forget former guilt, because we cannot endure its sting. Such forgetting is not the natural, daily form of forgetting. It demands our co-operation. We repress what we cannot stand. We forget it by entombing it within us. Ordinary forgetting liberates us from innumerable small things in a natural process. Forgetting by repression does not liberate us, but seems to cut us off from what makes us suffer. We are not entirely successful, however, because the memory is buried within us, and influences every moment of our growth. And sometimes it breaks through its prison and strikes at us directly and painfully.

Then there is a forgetting, to which Paul witnesses, that liberates us not from the memory of past guilt but from the pain it brings. The grand old name for this kind of forgetting is repentance. Today, repentance is associated with a half-painful, half-voluptuous emotional concentration on one's guilt, and not with a liberating forgetfulness. But originally it meant a 'turning around', leaving behind the wrong way and turning towards the right. It means pushing the consciousness and pain of guilt into the past, not by repressing it, but by acknowledging it, and receiving the word of acceptance in spite of it. If we are able to repent, we are able to forget, not because the forgotten act was unimportant, and not because we repress what we cannot endure, but because we have acknowledged our guilt and can now live with it. For it is *eternally* forgotten. This was how Paul forgot what lay behind him, although it always remained with him.

This kind of forgetting is decisive for our personal relationships. None of them is possible without a silent act of forgiving, repeated again and again. Forgiving presupposes remembering. And it creates a forgetting not in the natural way we forget yesterday's weather, but in the way of the great 'in spite of' that says: I forget although I remember. Without this kind of forgetting no human relationship could endure healthily. I don't refer to a solemn act of asking for and offering forgiveness. Such rituals as sometimes occur between parents and children, or friends, or man and wife, are often acts of moral arrogance on the one part and enforced humiliation on the other. But I speak of the lasting willingness to accept him who has hurt us. Such forgiveness is the highest form of forgetting, although it is not forgetfulness. The stumbling block of having violated another is pushed into the past, and there is the possibility of something new in the relationship.

Forgetting in spite of remembering is forgiveness. We can *live* only because our guilt is forgiven and thus *eternally* forgotten. And we can love only because we forgive and are forgiven.

III

Paul is straining to what lies ahead. What does lie ahead? When we ask this question, we are reminded of quite another kind of forgetting, forgetting that some day we shall be forgotten. Since we cannot endure the thought we repress it. The literature of mankind is full of stories in which kings as well as beggars are reminded of their having to die. Man cannot stand the anticipation of death, and so he represses it. But the repression does not remove his ever-present anxiety, and there are moments in the life of everyone when such repression is not even slightly effective. Then, we ask ourselves – will there be a time when I shall be forgotten, for ever? The meaning of the anxiety of having to die is the anxiety that one will be forgotten both now and in eternity. Every living being resists being pushed into the past without a new presence. A powerful symbol of this state of being forgotten is being buried. Burial means being removed from the realm of awareness, a removal from the surface of the earth. The meaning of Jesus' resurrection is intensified by the words in the Creed that he 'was buried'.

A rather superficial view of the anxiety of death states that this anxiety is the fear of the actual process of dying, which of course may be agonizing, but which can also be very easy. No, in the depth of the anxiety of having to die is the anxiety of being eternally forgotten.

Man was never able to bear this thought. An expression of his utter resistance is the way the Greeks spoke of glory as the conquest of being forgotten. Today, the same thing is called 'historical significance'. If one can, one builds memorial halls or creates memorial foundations. It is consoling to think that we might be remembered for a certain time beyond death not only by those who loved us or hated us or admired us, but also by those who never knew us except now by name. Some names are remembered for centuries. Hope is expressed in the poet's proud assertion that 'the traces of his earthly days cannot vanish in aeons'. But these traces, which unquestionably exist in the physical world, are not we ourselves, and they don't bear our name. They do not keep us from being forgotten.

Is there anything that can keep us from being forgotten? That we were known from eternity and will be remembered in eternity is the only certainty that can save us from the horror of being forgotten forever. We cannot be forgotten because we are known eternally, beyond past and future.

But, although we cannot be forgotten, we can forget ourselves — namely, our true being, that part of us that is eternally known and eternally remembered. And whether or not we forget or remember most of those things we experience every hour is not ultimately important. But it is infinitely important that we do not forget ourselves, this individual being, not to be repeated, unique, eternally precious, and delivered into our hands. Unfortunately, it may then be mistreated, overlooked, and imprisoned. Yet, if we remember it, and become aware of its infinite significance, we realize that we have been known in the past and that we will not be forgotten in the future. For the truth of our own being is rooted in the ground of being, from which it comes and to which it returns.

Nothing truly real is forgotten eternally, because everything real comes from eternity and goes to eternity. And I speak now of all individual men and not solely of man. Nothing in the universe is unknown, nothing real is ultimately forgotten. The atom that moves in an immeasurable path today and the atom that moved in an immeasurable path billions of years ago are rooted in the eternal ground. There is no absolute, no completely forgotten past, because the past, like the future, is rooted in the divine life. Nothing is completely pushed into the past. Nothing real is absolutely lost and forgotten. We are together with everything real in the divine life. Only the unreal, in us and around us, is pushed into the past forever. This is what 'last judgment' means – to separate in us, as in everything, what has true and final being from what is merely transitory and empty of true being. We are never forgotten, but much in us that we liked and for which we longed may be forgotten forever. Such judgment goes on in every moment of our lives, but the process is hidden in time and manifest only in eternity. Therefore, let us push into the past and forget what should be forgotten forever, and let us go forward to that which expresses our true being and cannot be lost in eternity.

3. The Riddle of Inequality

For to him who has will more be given; and from him who has not, even what he has will be taken away.

MARK 4:25

One day a learned colleague called me up and cried angrily, 'There is a saying in the New Testament which I consider to be one of the most immoral and unjust statements ever made!' And he began to quote our text – 'To him who has will more be given,' his anger increasing as he continued, 'and from him who has not, *even what he has will be taken away*'. I believe that most of us cannot but feel equally offended. And we cannot easily excuse the passage by suggesting what this colleague suggested – that the words may be due to a misunderstanding on the part of the disciples. No, they appear at least four times in the Gospels with great emphasis. And furthermore, it is clear that the writers of the Gospels feel exactly as we do. For them, the statement is a stumbling block, and they tried to interpret it in different ways. Probably none of the explanations satisfied them fully, for this particular saying of Jesus confronts us immediately with the greatest and perhaps most painful riddle of life – the inequality of all beings. We certainly cannot hope to solve it. Neither the Bible nor any of the great religions and philosophies was able to do so. But this we can do : we can explore the breadth and depth of the riddle of inequality; and we can try to find a way to live with it, unsolved as it may remain.

I

When we consider the words, 'to him who has will more be given', we ask ourselves – what *do* we have? And we may discover that much has been given us in terms of external goods, of friends, of intellectual gifts, and even of a comparatively high morality on which to base our action. So we can expect that even more will accrue to us, while at the same time, those who are lacking in all these attributes will lose the little they already have. Even further, according to Jesus' parable, the one poor talent they possess shall be handed over to those who have five or ten talents. We shall be richer because they will be poorer. And cry out as we may against such an injustice, we cannot deny that life abounds in it. We cannot deny it, but we might well ask – do we really *have* what we believe we have, so that it cannot be taken from us? It is a question full of anxiety, intensified by Luke's version of our text : 'From him who has not, even what he *thinks* that he has will be taken away.' Perhaps our having of those many things is not the kind of having that can be increased. Perhaps the having of a few things on the part of the poor is the kind of having that makes them grow. Jesus confirms this thought in the parable of the talents. The talents that are used, at the risk of their being lost, are the talents that we really have. Those that we try to preserve, without risking their use for growth, are those that we do not really have, and that will therefore be taken from us. They begin to disappear, until suddenly we feel that we have lost them, perhaps forever.

Let us apply the principle to our own life, be it long or short. In the memory of all of us, there are many things that we seemed to have, but that we really did *not* have, and that were therefore taken away from us. Some of them were lost because of the tragic limitations of life. They had to be sacrificed so that other things might grow. We were all given childish innocence, but innocence cannot be used and increased. The growth of our lives is made possible only by the sacrifice of the original gift of innocence. Sometimes, nevertheless, a melancholy longing arises in us for a purity that has been taken from us. We were all given youthful enthusiasm for many things and goals. But all this enthusiasm also cannot be used and increased. Most of the objects of our early enthusiasm must be sacrificed for a few, and those few approached soberly. No maturity is possible without this sacrifice. Yet often a deep yearning for the lost possibilities and that enthusiasm takes hold of us. Innocence and youthful enthusiasm: we had them, and we did not have them. Life itself demanded that they be taken from us.

But there are other things that we had and that were taken from us because we were guilty of taking them too much for granted. Some of us were deeply sensitive to the wonder of life as it is revealed in nature. Slowly, under the pressure of work and social life and the lure of cheap pleasures, we lost the wonder of our earlier years – the intense joy and sense of the mystery of life in the freshness of the young day or the glory of the dying afternoon, the splendour of the mountains and the infinity of the sea, or in the perfection of the movements of a young animal or of a flower breaking through the soil. We try perhaps to evoke such feelings again, but we find ourselves empty and do not succeed. We had that sensitivity and we did not have it, and it was taken from us.

Others of us have had the same experience with respect to music, poetry, great literature and the drama. We desired to devour all of these; we lived in them, and through them created for ourselves a life beyond our daily life. We had this experience and we did not have it. We did not allow it to grow. Our love for it was not strong enough, and so it was taken from us.

Many people remember a time when the desire to solve the riddles of the universe and to find *truth* was the driving force in their lives. They entered college and the university not in order to gain access to the upper middle classes or the preconditions for social and economic success, but because they felt driven by their thirst for knowledge. They had something to which, seemingly, more could be added. But their desire was not strong enough. They failed to nurture it, and so it was taken from them. Expediency and indifference towards truth took the place of genuine academic interest. Because their love for the truth was let go, they sometimes feel sick at heart; they realize that what they have lost may never be returned to them.

We all know that any deep relationship to another human being requires watchfulness and nourishment; otherwise, it is taken from us. And we cannot recapture it. This is a form of having and not having that is the root of innumerable human tragedies. We are all familiar with them.

And there is the most fundamental kind of having and not having – our having and losing God. Perhaps in our childhood, and even beyond it, our experience of God was rich. We may remember the moments in which we felt his presence intensely. We may remember our praying with an overflowing heart, our encounter with the holy in words and music and holy places. We communicated with God; but this communication was taken from us, because we had it and did not have it. We failed to let it grow, and therefore, it slowly disappeared, leaving only an empty space. We became unconcerned, cynical and indifferent, not because we doubted our religious traditions – such doubt belongs to a life rich in God – but because we turned away from what once concerned us infinitely.

Such thoughts mark the first step in approaching the riddle of inequality. Those who have receive more if they *really* have what they have, if they use it and cause it to grow. And those who have not lose what they seem to have, because they really do *not* have.

II

But the question of inequality has not yet been answered. For now we must ask – why do some of us receive more than others in the very beginning, before using or wasting our talents is even possible? Why does the one servant receive five talents, and the second, two, and the third, one? Why is one person born to desperate poverty, and another to affluence? To reply that much will be demanded of those to whom much is given, and little of those to whom little is given, is not adequate. For it is just this original inequality, internal and external, that gives rise to the question. Why is the power to gain so much more out of his being human given to one human being rather than to another? Why is so much given to one that much *can* be asked of him, while little can be asked of another, because little was given him? If we consider this problem in relation not only to individual men, but also to classes, races and nations, the question of political inequality also arises, and with it the many ways in which men have tried to abolish inequality. In every revolution and war, the will to solve the riddle of inequality is a driving force. But neither war nor revolution can answer it. And even though we may imagine that most social inequalities will be conquered in the future, there remain three realities: the inequality of talents in body and mind, the inequality created by freedom and destiny, and the inequality of justice deriving from the fact that all generations before the time of such equality would by nature be excluded from its blessings. This last would be the greatest inequality possible! No! In the face of one of the deepest and most tormenting problems of life, we cannot permit ourselves to be so shallow or foolish as to try to escape into a social dreamland. We have to live now. We have to live *this* life. We must face the riddle of inequality today.

Let us not confuse the riddle of inequality with the fact that each of us is a unique and incomparable self. Our being individual certainly belongs to our dignity as men. This being was given to us, and must be made use of and intensified, not drowned in the grey waters of conformity that threaten us so much today. One should defend every individuality and the uniqueness of every human self. But one should not be deluded into believing that this is a solution to the riddle of inequality. Unfortunately, there are social and political reactionaries who exploit this confusion in order to justify social injustice. They are at least as foolish as those who dream of the future abolition of inequality. He who has witnessed hospitals for the ill and insane, prisons, sweat shops, battlefields, people starving, family tragedies, or moral aberrations, should be cured of any confusion of the gift of individuality with the riddle of inequality. He should be cured of any sense of easy consolation.

III

And now we must take the third step in our attempt to penetrate the riddle of inequality by asking – why do some of us use and increase what was given to us, while others do not and thus lose what was given them? Why does God say to the prophet in the Old Testament that the ears and eyes of a nation are made insensitive to the divine message? Is it sufficient to answer – because some use their freedom responsibly and do what they ought to do, while others fail through their own guilt? This answer, which seems so obvious, *is* sufficient only when we apply it to ourselves. Each one of us must consider the increase or loss of what was given as a matter for his own responsibility. Our conscience tells us that we cannot blame anybody or anything other than ourselves for our losses.

But when we consider the plight of others, this answer is *not* sufficient. We cannot tell somebody who comes to us in great distress about himself – 'Make use of what was given you', for he may have come to us precisely because he is unable to do so! And we cannot tell those in despair because of what they are – 'Be something else', for the inability to get rid of oneself is the exact meaning of despair. We cannot tell those who failed to conquer the destructive influences of their surroundings and thence were driven into crime and misery – 'You should have been stronger', for it was just this strength of which they were deprived by heritage or environment. Certainly they are all men, and freedom is given to them all. But they are also all subject to destiny. It is not for us to condemn others because they *were* free, as it is also not for us to excuse them because of the burden of their destiny. We cannot judge them. And when we judge ourselves, we must keep in mind that even this judgment has no finality, because we, like them, stand under an ultimate judgment. In it the riddle of inequality is eternally answered. But the answer is not ours. It is our predicament that we must ask the question, and we ask with an uneasy conscience – why are they in such misery? Why not we? Thinking of those near to us, we ask – are we partly responsible? But even though we are, the riddle of inequality is not solved. The uneasy conscience asks also about those most distant from us – why they, why not we?

Why did my child, or any one of millions of children, die before he had the chance to grow out of infancy? Why was my child, or any child, born crippled in mind or body? Why has my friend or relative, or anyone's friend or relative, disintegrated in his mind, and thus lost both his freedom and his destiny? Why has my son or daughter, gifted as they were with many talents, wasted them and been deprived of them? Why do such things happen to any parent at all? And why have the creative powers of this boy or that girl been broken by a tyrannical father or a possessive mother?

None of these questions concern our own misery. At present, we are not asking – why did this happen to me? It is not Job's question that God answered by humiliating him and then elevating him into communion with him. It is not the old and urgent question – where is divine justice, where is divine love, for me? It is almost an opposite question – why did this *not* happen to me, while it did happen to another, to innumerable other ones, to whom not even Job's power to accept the divine answer was given? Why, Jesus asks also, are many called but few elected? He does not answer the question, but states simply that this is the human predicament. Shall we therefore cease to ask, and humbly accept a divine judgment that would hurl most human beings out of community with the divine and condemn them to despair and self-destruction? Can we accept the eternal victory of judgment over love? We can *not*, nor can any human being, though he may preach and threaten in such terms. As long as he is unable to visualize himself with absolute certainty as eternally rejected, his preaching and threats are self-deceptive. For who can see himself eternally rejected?

But if this is not the solution of the riddle of inequality at its deepest level, may we go outside the boundaries of Christian tradition to listen to those who would tell us that this life does not determine our eternal destiny? There will be other lives, they would say, predicated, like our present life, on previous ones and what we wasted or achieved in them. This is a serious doctrine and not completely strange to Christianity. But since we do not know and never shall know what each of us was in a previous existence, or will be in a future one, it is not really *our* destiny developing from life to life, but in each life, the destiny of someone *else*. Therefore, this doctrine also fails to solve the riddle of inequality.

Actually, there is no answer at all to our question concerning the temporal and eternal destiny of a single being separated from the destiny of the whole. Only in the unity of all beings in time and eternity can there be a humanly possible answer to the riddle of inequality. 'Humanly possible' does not mean an answer that removes the riddle of inequality, but one with which we can live.

There is an ultimate unity of all beings, rooted in the divine life from which they emerge and to which they return. All beings, non-human as well as human, participate in it. And therefore they all participate in each other. And we participate in each other's having and in each other's not having. When we become aware of this unity of all beings, something happens to us. The fact that others do *not* have, changes the character of our having: it undercuts our security and drives us beyond ourselves, to understand, to give, to share, to help. The fact that others fall into sin, crime and misery, alters the character of the grace that is given us: it makes us recognize our own hidden guilt; it shows us that those who suffer for their sin and crime suffer also for us, for we are guilty of their guilt and ought to suffer as they suffer. Our becoming aware of the fact that others who *could* have developed into full human beings did not change our state of full humanity. Their early death, their early or late disintegration, brings to our own personal life and health a continuous risk, a dying that is not yet death, a disintegration that is not yet destruction. In every death we encounter, something of us dies, and

in every disease, something of us tends towards disintegration.

Can we live with this answer? We can, to the degree
to which we are liberated from seclusion in ourselves.
But no one can be liberated from himself unless he is
grasped by that power which is present in everyone and
everything – the eternal, from which we come and to
which we go, and which gives us *to* ourselves and
liberates us *from* ourselves. It is the greatness and heart
of the Christian message that God, as manifest in the
Christ on the Cross, totally participates in the dying of a
child, in the condemnation of the criminal, in the disintegration of a mind, in starvation and famine, and even
in the human rejection of himself. There is no human
condition into which the divine presence does not penetrate. This is what the Cross, the most extreme of all
human conditions, tells us. The riddle of inequality cannot be solved on the level of our separation from each
other. It is eternally solved through the divine participation in the life of all of us and every being. The certainty of divine participation gives us the courage to endure the riddle of inequality, although our finite minds
cannot solve it.

4. The Good that I will, I do not

For I do not do the good I want, but the evil I do not
want is what I do. Now if I do what I do not want, it
is no longer I that do it, but sin which dwells within
me.

ROMANS 7:19-20

'I do not do the good I want, but the evil I do not want
is what I do.' Do these words of Paul correctly describe
our nature? Is the split between willing the good and
achieving it as radical as they would indicate? Or do

we resist the indictment by insisting that we often do the good that we want and avoid the evil that we do not want? Is not Paul perhaps grossly exaggerating the evil in man in order to emphasize the brightness of grace by depicting it against a very dark background? These are questions that every critic of Christianity asks. But are they not also the questions that *we* ask – we, who call ourselves Christians, or at least who desire to be what the Christian message wills us to be? Actually, none of us believes that he *always* does the evil he would like not to do. We know that we sometimes do achieve the good that we want – when, for example, we perform an act of love towards a person with whom we do not sympathize, or an act of self-discipline for the sake of our work, or an act of courageous non-conformity in a situation where it may endanger us. Our moral balance sheet is not as bad as it would be without these acts! And have we ever really known a preacher of what is called 'the total depravity of man' who did not show, in his own behaviour, reliance on a positive moral balance sheet? Perhaps even Paul did. At least, he tries to tell us so when he boasts about his sufferings and activities in a letter to the Corinthians. Certainly, he calls his boasting foolishness. But do not we also insist that our boasting is foolish? Yet we do not stop boasting. Are not perhaps those who believe, on the surface, that they have nothing to boast about, being sick, disintegrated, and without self-esteem? They may even be proud of the depth of despair in which they visualize themselves. For without a vestige of self-esteem no one can live, not even he who bases his self-esteem on despairing of himself.

But why then do we not simply dismiss Paul's words? Why do we react positively to his statement that 'I do not do the good that I want'? It is because we feel that it is not a matter of balance sheets between good and evil that the words express, but rather a matter of our whole being, of our situation as men, of our standing in the face of the eternal – the source, aim and judge of our being. It is our human predicament that a power takes hold of us, that does not come from us but is in us, a power that we hate and at the same time gladly accept. We are fascinated by it; we play with it; we obey it. But we know that it will destroy us if we are not grasped by another power that will resist and control it. We are fascinated by what can destroy us, and in moments even feel a hidden desire to be destroyed by it. This is how Paul saw himself, and how a great many of us see ourselves.

People who call themselves Christian – parents, teachers, preachers – tell us that we should be 'good' and obey the will of God. For many of them the will of God is not very different from the will of those socially correct beings whose conventions they ask us to accept. If we only willed such goodness, they say, we could achieve it, and would be rewarded in time and eternity – but first of all, in time.

One can thank God that such preaching has become more and more suspect, for it does not strike at the real human situation. The eyes of many serious people in our time have been opened to an awareness of their predicament as men. Every sentence in Paul's message is directed against the so-called 'men of good will'. They are the very ones he sees as driven by some power to act against their good will. And they are we. For who amongst us is not full of good will? But perhaps if we come to know ourselves better, we may begin to suspect that some of this good will is not so good after all, and that we are driven by forces of which we might not even be aware.

It is not necessary to describe those who embody good will and work towards just the opposite on a level hidden beneath their goodness. Psychologists and others have done this so fully that it needs no repetition. Despite what critics have to say of our time, one of the great things to have come out of it is the difficulty of anyone's being able to hide permanently from himself

(

and from others the motives for his actions. Whatever we may think about the methods employed to reach this insight, the insight itself is infinitely precious.

It has also become difficult for a man who works with dedication and success at his business or profession to feel assured about the goodness of what he is doing. He cannot hide from himself that his commitment to his work may also be a way of escaping genuine human commitments and, above all, a way of escaping himself.

And it has become difficult for a mother who loves her children passionately to be sure that she feels only love for them. She can no longer conceal from herself that her anxiety concerning their well-being may be an expression of her will to dominate them or a form of guilt for a heavily veiled hostility that desires to be rid of them.

And we cannot applaud every act of moral self-restraint, knowing that its cause may be cowardice preventing a revolution against inherited, though already questioned, rules of behaviour. Nor can we praise every act of daring non-conformism, knowing that its reason may be the inability of an individual to resist the persuasive irresponsibility of a group of non-conformists.

In these and countless other cases, we experience a power that dwells in us and directs our will against itself.

The name of this power is sin. Nothing is more precarious today than the mention of this word among Christians, as well as among non-Christians, for in everyone there is a tremendous resistance to it. It is a word that has fallen into disrepute. To some of us it sounds almost ridiculous and is apt to provoke laughter rather than serious consideration. To others, who take it more seriously, it implies an attack on their human dignity. And again, to others – those who have suffered from it – it means the threatening countenance of the disciplinarian, who forbids them to do what they would like and demands of them what they hate. Therefore, even

Christian teachers, including myself, shy away from the use of the word sin. We know how many distorted images it can produce. We try to avoid it, or to substitute another word for it. But it has a strange quality. It always returns. We cannot escape it. It is as insistent as it is ugly. And so it would be more honest – and this I say to myself – to face it and ask what it really is.

It is certainly not what men of good will would have us believe – failure to act in the right way, a failure to do the good one should and could have done. If this were sin, a less aggressive and less ugly term, such as human weakness, could be applied. But that is just what sin is *not*. And those of us who have experienced demonic powers within and around ourselves find such a description ludicrous. So we turn to Paul, and perhaps to Dostoevsky's Ivan Karamazov, or to the conversation between the devil and the hero in Thomas Mann's *Dr Faustus*. From them we learn what sin is. And perhaps we may learn it through Picasso's picture of that small Basque village, Guernica, which was destroyed in an unimaginably horrible way by the demonic powers of fascism and Nazism. And perhaps we learn it through the disrupting sounds in music that do not bring us restful emotions, but the feeling of being torn and split. Perhaps we learn the meaning of sin from the images of evil and guilt that fill our theatres, or through the revelations of unconscious motives so abundant in our novels. It is noteworthy that today, in order to know the meaning of sin, we have to look outside our churches and their average preaching to the artists and writers and ask *them*. But perhaps there is still another place where we can learn what sin is, and that is our own heart.

Paul seldom speaks of sins, but he often speaks of Sin – Sin in the singular with a capital 'S', Sin as a power that controls world and mind, persons and nations.

Have you ever thought of Sin in this image? It is the biblical image. But how many Christians or non-Christians have seen it? Most of us remember that at home, in school and at church, we were taught that there were many things that one would like to do that one should not. And if one did them, one committed a sin. We also remember that we were told of things we should do, although we disliked doing them. And if we did not do them, we committed a sin. We had lists of prohibitions and catalogues of commands; if we did not follow them, we committed sins. Naturally, we did commit one or more sins every day, although we tried to diminish their number seriously and with good will. This was, and perhaps still is, our image of sin – a poor, petty, distorted image, and the reason for the disrepute into which the word has fallen.

The first step to an understanding of the Christian message that is called 'good news' is to dispel the image of sin that implies a catalogue of sins. Those who are bound to this image are also those who find it most difficult to receive the message of acceptance of the unacceptable, the good news of Christianity. Their half-sinfulness and half-righteousness makes them insensitive to a message that states the presence of total sinfulness and total righteousness in the same man at the same moment. They never find the courage to make a total judgment against themselves, and therefore, they can never find the courage to believe in a total acceptance of themselves.

Those, however, who have experienced in their hearts that sin is more than the trespassing of a list of rules, know that all sins are manifestations of Sin, of the power of estrangement and inner conflict. Sin dwells in us, it controls us, and makes us do what we don't want to do. It produces a split in us that makes us lose identity with ourselves. Paul writes of this split twice: 'If I do what I do not want, it is no longer I that do it, but sin which dwells within me.' Those who have suffered this split know how unexpected and terrifying it can be. Thoughts entered our mind, words poured from our mouth, something was enacted by us suddenly and without warning. And if we look at what happened, we feel – 'It could not have been *I* who acted like this. I cannot find myself in it. Something came upon me, something I hardly noticed. But there it was and here am I. It is *I* who did it, but a strange I. It is not my real, my innermost self. It is as though I were possessed by a power I scarcely knew. But now I know that it not only can reach me, but that it dwells in me.'

Is this something we really know? Or do we, after a moment of shock, repress such knowledge? Do we still rely on our comparatively well-ordered life, avoiding situations of moral danger, determined by the rules of family, school and society? For those who are satisfied with such a life, the words of Paul are written in vain. They refuse to face their human predicament. But something further may happen to them: God himself may throw them into more sin in order to make them aware of what they really are. This is a bold way of speaking, but it is the way people of the profoundest religious experiences have spoken. By his throwing them into more sin, they have felt the awakening hand of God. And awakened, they have seen themselves in the mirror from which they had always turned away. No longer able to hide from themselves, they have asked the question, from the depth of their self-rejection, to which the Christian message is the answer – the power of acceptance that can overcome the despair of self-rejection. In this sense, *more* sin can be the divine way of making us aware of ourselves.

Then, we ask with Paul – what is it within us that makes a dwelling place for this power? He answers that it is our members in which sin hides. He also calls this place 'flesh', and sometimes he speaks of 'our body of death'. But there are also forces within us that resist the power – our innermost self, our mind, our spirit. With these words, Paul wrestles with the deep mystery of human nature just as we do today. And it is no easier to understand him than our present scholarly language about man. But one thing is certain: Paul, and with him the whole Bible, never made our body responsible for our estrangement from God, from our world and from our own self. Body, flesh, members – these are not the only sinful part of us, while the innermost self, mind and spirit, comprises the other, sinless part. Our whole being, every cell of our body, and every movement of our mind is both flesh and spirit, subjected to the power of sin and resisting its power. The fact that we accuse ourselves proves that we still have an awareness of what we truly are, and therefore ought to be. And the fact that we excuse ourselves shows that we cannot acknowledge our estrangement from our true nature. The fact that we are ashamed shows that we still know what we ought to be.

There is no part of man that is bad in itself, as there is no part of man that is good in itself. Any Christian teaching that has forgotten this has fallen short of the height of Christian insight. And here all Christian churches must share the grave guilt of destroying human beings by casting them into despair over their own guilt where there should be no guilt. In pulpits, schools and families, Christians have called the natural strivings of the living, growing and self-propagating body sinful. They concentrate in an inordinate and purely pagan way on the sexual differentiation of all life and its possible distortions. Certainly, these distortions are as real as the distortions of our spiritual life – as, for example, pride and indifference. But to see the power of sin in the sexual power of life as such is itself a distortion. Such preaching completely misses the image of sin as Paul depicts it. What is worse, it produces distorted feelings of guilt in countless personalities, that drive them from anxiety to despair, from despair to escape into mental disease, and thence the desire to destroy themselves altogether.

And still other consequences of this preaching about

sin become apparent. Paul points to the perversion of sexual desires as an extreme expression of sin's control of mankind. Have we as Christians ever asked ourselves whether or not, in our defamation of the natural as sin, or at least as a reason for shame, we have perhaps contributed most potently to this state of affairs? For all this results from that petty image of sin, that contradicts reality as much as it contradicts the biblical understanding of man's predicament.

It is dangerous to preach about sin, because it may induce us to brood over our sinfulness. Perhaps one should not preach about it at all. I myself have hesitated for many years. But sometimes it must be risked in order to remove the distortions which increase sin, if, by the persistence of wrong thoughts, wrong ways of living are inevitable.

I believe it possible to conquer the dangers implied in the concentration on sin, if we look at it *indirectly*, in the light of that which enables us to resist it – reunion overcoming estrangement. Sin is our act of turning away from participation in the divine Ground from which we come and to which we go. Sin is the turning towards ourselves, and making ourselves the centre of our world and of ourselves. Sin is the drive in every one, even those who exercise the most self-restraint, to draw as much as possible of the world into oneself. But we can be fully aware of this only if we have found a certain level of life above ourselves. Whoever has found himself after he has lost himself knows how deep his loss of self was. If we look at our estrangement from the point of reunion, we are no longer in danger of brooding over our estrangement. We can speak of Sin, because its power over us is broken.

It is certainly not broken by ourselves. The attempt to break the power of sin by the power of good will has been described by Paul as the attempt to fulfil the law, the law in our mind, in our innermost self that is the law of God. The result of this attempt is failure, guilt and despair. The law, with its commands and prohibitions, despite its function in revealing and restricting evil, provokes resistance against itself. In a language both poetic and profoundly psychological, Paul says that the sin that dwells in our members is asleep until the moment in which it is awakened by the 'thou shalt not'. Sin uses the commandments in order to become alive. Prohibition awakens sleeping desire. It arouses the power and consciousness of sin, but cannot break its power. Only if we accept with our whole being the message that it *is* broken, is it also broken in us.

This picture of sin is a picture full of ugliness, suffering and shame, and, at the same time, drama and passion. It is the picture of us as the battleground of powers greater than we. It does not divide men into categories of black and white, or good and evil. It does not appear as the threatening finger of an authority urging us – do not sin! But it is the vision of something infinitely important, that happens on this small planet, in our bodies and minds. It raises mankind to a level in the universe where decisive things happen in every moment, decisive for the ultimate meaning of all existence. In each of us such decisions occur, in us, and through us. This is our burden. This is our despair. This is our greatness.

5. *Heal the Sick; Cast out the Demons*

Address to graduating students at Union Theological Seminary, New York, 1955
Heal the sick; . . . cast out the demons.

MATTHEW 10:8

Members of the outgoing class! Friends!

The first difficulty you will experience when Jesus sends you ahead of him and gives you the power of healing is that many people will tell you that they do not need to be healed. And if you come to them with the claim that you will cast out the demons that rule their lives, they will laugh at you and assure you that *you* are possessed by a demon – just as they said to Jesus.

Therefore, the first task of a minister is to make men aware of their predicament. Many of those who have gone out from our seminary to various congregations and communities have despaired over this task. And they have either given up the ministry altogether, or they minister only to those who consider themselves healthy. They have forgotten that their task is to heal those who *are* sick, which includes those who are not aware that they are sick. There is no easy way to make them aware of their predicament. God, certainly, has his ways of doing so. He shakes the complacency of those who consider themselves healthy by hurling them, both externally and internally, into darkness and despair. He reveals to them what they are by splitting the foundations of their self-assurance. He reveals their blindness towards themselves. This *we* cannot achieve, not even for ourselves. But we can be open to the moment when it happens to us. And if it happens, we can become tools of the power that may heal others. To try this is the first task of the minister, and perhaps the hardest of them all. But you are not the only ones who are used as tools. Everyone is potentially a tool of healing for anyone else. And it often happens that healing power works outside the Church and the ministry. The fact that Jesus gave the disciples responsibility for healing and casting out demons does not constitute a special prerogative on the part of the minister. Every Christian receives this charge, and each of us should take it seriously in our relation to one another. Everyone should accept his priestly responsibility for everyone else. The minister has no magic power to heal. Even his administration of the liturgy and sacraments does not give him this power. But in his special vocation, he stands for the universal power given to the Church to heal and to cast out demons.

Why have these assertions, that were so central at the time the gospel was first preached, lost their significance in our own period? The reason, I believe, lies in the words 'healing' and 'casting out demons', that have been misunderstood as miracle-healing, based on magic power and magic self-suggestion. There is no doubt that such phenomena occur. They happen here, and everywhere else in the world. They happen and are used in the midst of Christianity. But the Church was right when it felt that this was not the task of the Church and its ministers. It is an abuse of the name of the Christ to use it as a magic formula. Nevertheless, the words of our text remain valid. They belong to the message of the Christ, and they tell us about something that belongs to the Christ as the Christ – the power to conquer the demonic forces that control our lives, mind and body. And I believe that, of all the different ways to communicate the message of the Christ to others, this way will prove to be the most adequate for the people of our time. It is something they can understand. For in every country of the world, including our own, there is an awareness of the power of evil that has not existed for centuries. If we look at our period as a whole, we realize that not only special groups fall under the judgment of Jesus' ironic words – 'Those who are well have no need of a physician, but those who are sick.' In spite of the many who resist this insight, we know that we are sick, that we are not whole. The central message for our contemporaries, including ourselves, the message awaited by many both within and outside our congregation is the good news of the healing power that is in the world and whose expression is the Christ.

The task of healing demands of you insight into the nature of life and the human situation. People often ask, in passionate despair, why the divine order of things includes sickness, if sickness is one of the things to be healed by divine order. This very natural question, which, for many of us, is *the* stumbling block of our faith, points to the riddle of evil in the world of God. You will have to deal with this question more often than with any other. And you must not avoid the question by retiring behind the term 'mystery'. Of course, there is mystery – divine mystery – and in contrast to it, the mystery of evil. But it belongs to the insights demanded of you that you put the mystery in its right place, and explain what can and must be explained. Evil in the divine order is not only mystery; it is also revelation. It reveals the greatness and danger of life. He who can become sick is greater than he who cannot, than that which is bound to remain what it is, unable to be split in itself. He alone who is free is able to surrender to the demonic forces that turn his freedom into bondage. The gift of freedom implies the danger of servitude; and the abundance of life implies the danger of sickness. Man's life is abundant life, infinitely complex, inexhaustible in its possibilities, even in the vitally poorest human beings. Men's life is most open to disease. For in man's life, more than in any other being, there are divergent trends that must continuously be kept in unity. Health is not the lack of divergent trends in our bodily or mental or spiritual life, but the power to keep them united. And healing is the act of reuniting them after the disruption of their unity. 'Heal the sick' means – help them to regain their lost unity without depriving them of their abundance, without throwing them into a poverty of life, perhaps by their own consent.

For there is a sick desire to escape sickness by cutting off what can produce sickness. I have known people who are sick only because of their fear of sickness. Sometimes it may be necessary to reduce the richness of life, and to establish a poorer life on a smaller basis. But this in itself is not health. It is the most widespread mental disease. It can be transformed into health only if what is lost on a lower level is regained on a higher level, perhaps on the highest level – that of our infinite concern, our life with God.

Reduction to poverty of life is not healing. But where there is abundance there is also the danger of conflict, of disease and demonic bondage. In the light of this insight, let us look at a most important example, most important certainly for you who are sent to heal and to cast out demons – the Church that sends you. It may well be that the disease of many churches, denominations and congregations is that they try to escape disease by cutting off what can produce disease, and what also can produce greatness of life. A church that has ceased to risk sickness and even demonic influences has little power to heal and to cast out demons. Every minister who is proud of a smooth-running or gradually growing church should ask himself whether or not such a church is able to make its members aware of their sickness, and to give them the courage to accept the fact that they are healed. He should ask himself why the great creativity in all realms of man's spiritual life keeps itself consistently outside the churches. In many expressions of our secular culture, especially in the present decades, the awareness of man's sickness is great. Is it only because of prejudice that these people, who powerfully express the demonic bondage of man, do not look to the Church or to you, the ministers, for healing and for casting out demons? Or is it because of the lack of healing power in the Church, sick in its fear of sickness?

When Jesus asks the disciples to heal and to cast out demons, he does not distinguish between bodily and mental or spiritual diseases. But every page of the Gospels demonstrates that he means all of them, and many stories show that he sees their inter-relationship, their unity. We see this unity today more clearly than many generations just behind us. This is a great gift, and you who have studied in the places you now are leaving have had much occasion to share in this gift. Above all, you have learned the truth of the good news – that laws and commands do not heal, but increase, the sickness of the sick. You have learned that the name of the healing power is grace, be it the grace of nature on which every physician depends, as even ancient medicine knew, or the grace in history that sustains the life of mankind by traditions and heritage and common symbols, or the grace of revelation that conquers the power of the demons by the message of forgiveness and of a new reality. And you have learned that disease that seems bodily may be mental at root, and that a disease that seems individual may be social at the same time, and that you cannot heal individuals without liberating them from the social demons that have contributed to their sickness. Beyond this, you may have become aware of the fact that both physical and mental, individual and social, illness is a consequence of the estrangement of man's spirit from the divine Spirit, and that no sickness can be healed nor any demon cast out without the re-union of the human spirit with the divine Spirit. For this reason you have become ministers of the message of healing. You are not supposed to be physicians; you are not supposed to be psychotherapists; you are not supposed to become political reformers. But you are supposed to pronounce and to represent the healing and demon-conquering power implied in the message of the Christ, the message of forgiveness and of a new reality. You must be conscious of the other ways of healing. You must co-operate with them, but you must not sub-stitute them for what you represent.

Can you represent the Christian message? This may be your anxious question in this solemn hour. Should you ask me – can we heal without being healed our-selves? – I would answer – you can! For neither the disciples nor you could ever say – we are healed, so let us heal others. He who would believe this of himself is least fit to heal others; for he would be separating himself from them. Show them whom you counsel that their predicament is also your predicament.

And should you ask me – can we cast out demons without being liberated from demonic power ourselves?

— I would answer — you can! Unless you are aware of the demonic possibility in yourselves, you cannot recognize the demon in others, and cannot do battle against it by knowing its name and thus depriving it of its power. And there will be no period in your life, so long as it remains creative and has healing power, in which demons will not split your souls and produce doubts about your faith, your vocation, your whole being. If they fail to succeed, they may accomplish something else — self-assurance and pride with respect to your power to heal and to cast out demons. Against this pride Jesus warns — 'Do not rejoice in this that the spirits are subject to you; but rejoice that your names are written in heaven.' And 'written in heaven' means written in spite of what is written against you in the records of your life.

Let me close with a word of reassurance. There is no greater vocation on earth than to be called to heal and to cast out demons. Be joyous in this vocation! Do not be depressed by its burden, nor even by the burden of having to deal with those who do not want to be healed. Rejoice in your calling. In spite of our own sickness, in spite of the demons working within you and your churches, you have a glimpse of what can heal ultimately, of him in whom God made manifest his power over demons and disease, of him who represents the healing power that is in the world, and sustains the world and lifts it up to God. Rejoice that you are his messengers. Take with you this joy when you leave this place!

6. Man and Earth

When I look at thy heavens, the work of thy fingers, the moon and the stars which thou hast established; what is man that thou art mindful of him, and the son of man that thou dost care for him? Yet thou hast made him little less than God, and dost crown him with glory and honour. Thou hast given him dominion over the works of thy hands; thou hast put all things under his feet.

PSALM 8:3-6

I

Some time ago representatives of the world of science demanded a new line of research. They called it 'science of survival'. They did not mean the survival of individuals or social groups, of nations or of races – that would not be new – but the survival of civilized mankind, or of mankind as a whole, or even of life altogether on the surface of this planet. Such a proposition is a sign that we have reached a stage of human history that has only one analogy in the past, the story of the 'Great Flood', found in the Old Testament and also among the myths and legends of many nations. The only difference between our situation and that of the Flood is that in these stories the gods or God bring about the destruction of life on earth because men have aroused divine anger. As the book of Genesis describes it: 'The Lord was sorry that he had made man on the earth and it grieved him to his heart. So the Lord said, I will blot out man, whom I have created, from the face of the ground, man and beast and creeping things and birds of the air, for I am sorry that I have made them.' In the next verse, the story answers the question of possible survival: 'But Noah found favour in the eyes of the Lord.' Through him, we read, not only man but also a pair of each species of animal was to make possible the survival of life upon the earth. Today, the destruction and survival of life have been given into the hands of man. Man who has dominion over all things, according to the psalm, has the power to save or destroy them, for he is little less than God.

How does man react to this new situation? How do *we* react? How *should* we react? 'The earth and we' has ceased to be merely a subject for human curiosity, artistic imagination, scientific study, or technical conquest. It has become a question of profound human concern and tormenting anxiety. We make desperate attempts to escape its seriousness. But when we look deep into the minds of our contemporaries, especially those of the younger generation, we discover a dread that permeates their whole being. This dread was absent a few decades ago and is hard to describe. It is the sense of living under a continuous threat; and although it may have many causes, the greatest of these is the imminent danger of a universal and total catastrophe. Their reaction to this feeling is marked either by a passionate longing for security in daily life, or an exaggerated show of boldness and confidence in man, based on his conquest of earthly and trans-earthly space. Most of us experience some of these contradictory reactions in ourselves. Our former naïve trust in the 'motherly' earth and her protective and preserving power has disappeared. It is possible that the earth may bear us no longer. We ourselves may prevent her from doing so. No heavenly sign, like the rainbow given to Noah as a promise that there would not be a second flood, has been given to us. We have no guarantee against man-made floods, that destroy not by water but by fire and air.

Such thoughts give rise to the question – what has the Christian message to say about this, our present predicament? What has it to say about life on this planet, its beginning and end, and man's place on it? What has it to say about the significance of the earth, the scene of human history, in view of the vastnesses of the universe? What about the short span of time allotted to this planet and the life upon it, as compared to the unimaginable length of the rhythms of the universe?

Such questions have been rarely asked in Christian teaching and preaching. For the central themes of Christianity have been the dramas of the creation and fall, of salvation and fulfilment. But sometimes peripheral questions move suddenly into the centre of a system of thought, not for any theoretical reason, but because such questions have become, for many, matters of life and death. This kind of movement has very often occurred in human history as well as in Christian history. And whenever it has occurred, it has changed man's view of himself in all respects, as it has changed the understanding of the Christian tradition on all levels. It may well be that we are living in such a moment, and that man's relation to the earth and the universe will, for a long time, become the point of primary concern for sensitive and thoughtful people. Should this be the case, Christianity certainly cannot withdraw into the deceptive security of its earlier questions and answers. It will be compelled forward into the more daring inroads of the human spirit, risking new and unanswered questions, like those we have just asked, but at the same time pointing in the direction of the eternal, the source and goal of man and his world.

Our predicament has been brought about chiefly by the scientific and technical development of our century. It is as foolish as it is futile to complain of this development. For there it lies before us – a realm created by man quite beyond the realm that was given him by nature when he first emerged from earlier forms of life. There it *is*, changing our lives and thoughts and feelings in all dimensions, consciously and, even more, unconsciously. Today's students are not what students of the preceding generation were. Today's hopes and anxieties are strange and often unintelligible to the older among us. And if we compare our two generations with any in earlier centuries, the distance separating us from them becomes really immense.

Since this sudden thrust forward has been brought about by science and its application, must not science itself have the last word about man, his earth and the universe? What can religion add? Indeed, has not religion, whenever it did try to explore these subjects, interfered with scientific development, and therefore been pushed aside? This certainly happened in the past, and is happening again today. But it is not religion in itself that interferes; it is the anxiety and fanaticism of religious people – laymen as well as theologians – marked by a flight from serious thought and an unwillingness to distinguish the figurative language of religion from the abstract concepts of scholarly research. In many sections of the Christian world, however, such distortion and misuse of religion have been overcome. Here one can speak freely of man and his earth in the name of religion, with no intention of adding anything to scientific and historical knowledge, or of prohibiting any scientific hypothesis, however bold.

What then has the Christian message to say about man's predicament in this world? The eighth Psalm, written hundreds of years before the beginning of the Christian era, raises the same question with full clarity and great beauty. It points, on the one hand, to the infinite smallness of man as compared to the universe of heavens and stars, and, on the other hand, to the astonishing greatness of man, his glory and honour, his power over all created things, and his likeness to God himself. Such thoughts are not frequent in the Bible. But when we come across them, they sound as though they had been written today. Ever since the opening of the universe by modern science, and the reduction of the great earth to a small planet in an ocean of heavenly bodies, man has felt real vertigo in relation to infinite space. He has felt as though he had been pushed out of the centre of the universe into an insignificant corner in it, and has asked anxiously – what about the high destiny claimed by man in past ages? What about the idea that the divine image is impressed in his nature? What about his history that Christianity always considered to be the point at which salvation for all beings took place? What about the Christ who, in the New Testament, is called the Lord of the universe? What about the end of history, described in biblical language as a cosmic catastrophe, in which the sun, the moon and the stars are perhaps soon to fall down upon the earth? What remains, in our present view of reality, of the importance of the earth and the glory of man? Further, since it seems possible that other beings exist on other heavenly bodies, in whom the divine image is also manifest, and of whom God is mindful, and also whom he has crowned with glory and honour, what is the meaning of the Christian view of human history and its centre, the appearance of the Christ?

These questions are not merely theoretical. They are crucial to every man's understanding of himself as a human being placed upon this star, in an unimaginably vast universe of stars. And they are disturbing not only to people who feel grasped by the Christian message, but also to those who reject it but who share with Christianity a belief in the meaning of history and the ultimate significance of human life.

Again, the eighth Psalm speaks as though it had been conceived today – 'Thou has made him little less than God; thou hast given him dominion over the works of thy hands.' It gives, as an example, man's dominion over the animals; but only since modern technology subjected all the spheres of nature to man's control has the phrase 'little less than God' revealed its full meaning. The conquest of time and space has loosened the ties that kept man in bondage to his finitude. What was once imagined as a prerogative of the gods has become a reality of daily life, accessible to human technical power. No wonder that we of today feel with the psalmist that man is little less than God, and that some of us feel even equal with God, and further that others would not hesitate to state publicly that mankind, as a collective mind, has replaced God.

We therefore have to deal with an astonishing fact: the same events that pushed man from his place in the centre of the world, and reduced him to insignificance, also elevated him to a God-like position both on earth and beyond!

Is there an answer to this contradiction? Listen to the psalmist: he does not say that man *has* dominion over all things or that man *is* little less than God; he says: '*Thou* hast given him dominion over the works of thy hands; *thou* hast made him little less than God.' This means that neither man's smallness nor his greatness emanates from himself, but that there is something above this contrast. Man, together with all things, comes from him who has put all things under man's feet. Man is rooted in the same Ground in which the universe with all its galaxies is rooted. It is this Ground that gives greatness to everything, however small it may be, to atoms as well as plants and animals; and it is this that makes all things small, however great – the stars as well as man. It gives significance to the apparently insignificant. It gives significance to each individual man, and to mankind as a whole. This answer quiets our anxiety about our smallness, and it quells the pride of our greatness. It is not a biblical answer only, nor Christian only, nor only religious. Its truth is felt by all of us, as we become conscious of our predicament – namely, that we are not of ourselves, that our presence upon the earth is not of our own doing. We are brought into existence and formed by the same power that bears up the universe and the earth and everything upon it, a power compared to which we are infinitely small, but also one which, because we are conscious of it, makes us great among creatures.

II

Now let us recall the words of God in the story of the Flood: 'I am sorry that I have made man.' They introduce a new element into our thinking about man and the earth – an element of judgment, frustration and tragedy. There is no theme in biblical literature, nor in any other, more persistently pursued than this one. The earth has been cursed by man innumerable times, because she produced him, together with all life and its misery, which includes the tragedy of human history. This accusation of the earth sounds through our whole contemporary culture, and understandably so. We accuse her in all our artistic expressions, in novels and drama, in painting and music, in philosophical thought and descriptions of human nature. But even more important is the silent accusation implied in our cynical denunciation of those who would say 'yes' to life, in our withdrawal from it into the refuges of mental disturbance and disease, in our forcing of life beyond itself or below itself by drugs and the various methods of intoxication, or in the social drugs of banality and conformity. In all these ways we accuse the destiny that placed us in this universe and upon this planet. 'Thou dost crown him with glory and honour,' says the psalmist. But many of us long to get rid of that glory and wish we had never possessed it. We yearn to return to the state of creatures, which are unaware of themselves and their world, limited to the satisfaction of their animal needs.

In the story of the Flood it is God who is sorry that he made man, and who decides to blot him from the face of the earth. Today it is man who has the power to blot himself out, and often he is so sorry that he has been made man that he desires to withdraw from his humanity altogether. Many more people than we are aware of in our daily experience feel this desire; and perhaps something in us responds to them. Can it be that the earth, fully conquered by man, will cease to be a place where man wants to live? Is our passionate thrust into outer space perhaps an unconscious expression of man's flight from the earth? There are no sure answers to these questions, which, nevertheless, must be asked, because they cut through false feelings of security about the relation of man to the earth. The old insight that 'man is but a pilgrim on earth' is echoed in these questions, and applicable today to mankind as a whole. Mankind itself is a pilgrim on earth, and there will be a moment when this pilgrimage comes to an end, at some indefinitely remote time, or perhaps soon, in the very near future. Christianity gives no indication of the length of man's history; the early Church expected the end at any moment, and when it did not come and the Christians were profoundly disappointed, the span was extended. In modern times, the span has been stretched to an unlimited extent. Scientists speak today of the millions of years that human history could continue. Millions of years, or thousands of years, or tomorrow — we do not know! But we ask — what is the meaning of this history, whenever it began, whenever it will end? And we ask at the moment not what it means for you and me, but rather, what it means for the universe and its ultimate goal.

In the old story, God repented of having created man. The implication is that God took a risk when he created man, and every risk carries with it the possibility of failure. God himself considered the creation of man a failure, and made a new effort. But nothing assures us that this new effort did not also result in failure. The first time, according to the story, nature executed the divine judgment on man. This time, man may himself be the executioner. Should this occur, the privileged position of the earth, of which the astronomers speak and in which man has always believed, would seem to prove to have been of no avail. It would seem as though its unique role had been given it in vain.

We should not crowd such thoughts away, for they deserve to be taken seriously. Indeed, it seems to me, it is impossible for thoughtful people today to crowd them away. What has the Christian message to say about them? I repeat — it tells us nothing about the duration of human history. It does not say that it will continue after tomorrow, nor how it will come to an end in scientific terms. None of this is its concern. What the Christian message does tell us is that the meaning of history lies above history, and that, therefore, its length is irrelevant to its ultimate meaning. But it is not irrelevant with respect to the innumerable opportunities time affords for creation of life and spirit, and it is for these that we must fight with all our strength. Furthermore, if history should end tomorrow, through mankind's self-annihilation, the appearance of this planet and of man upon it will *not* have been in vain. For a being will have at least appeared once, in the billions of years of the universe, towards whose creation all the forces of life on earth worked together, and in whom the image of the divine Ground of all life was present. At least once, a living being will have come into existence, in whom life achieved its highest possibility – spirit. This is the ultimate source of man's greatness, and those of us who openly or covertly accuse life should open ourselves to this truth: in the short span of our life, and the short span of human history and even of the existence of this planet, something of eternal significance *did* happen – the depth of all things became manifest in *one* being, and the name of that being is *man*, and you and I are men! If we cannot accept this, and insist that this could have been so but was not, and that mankind is evil, and that the earth is contaminated by man's guilt, and that the blood of the murdered in all periods cries for revenge to heaven so that even God was forced to repent of his creation, then let us contemplate these words: 'The man Noah found favour in the eyes of God.' This one man represents something in every man that makes him a mirror of the divine in spite of evil and distortion. And the Christian message continues: there is one man in whom God found his image undistorted, and who stands for all mankind – the one, who for this reason, is called the Son and the Christ. The earth, contaminated

by man, is purified and consecrated through man —
namely, through the divine power of healing and fulfilment, of love and blessedness, made manifest in the one
man and at work in all mankind, in all periods and in all
places. This is what justifies human history, as it also
justifies the earth that, for millions of years, prepared
for the advent of man, and justifies the universe that
produced the earth.

And yet, the universe is justified not only by the earth,
nor is creation justified by man alone. Other heavenly
bodies, other histories, other creatures in whom the
mystery of being is manifest may replace us. Our ignorance and our prejudice should not inhibit our thought
from transcending the earth and our history and even
our Christianity. Science and the poetic imagination have
made this leap, and Christianity should not hesitate to
join them. Further, it should not hesitate to show that
the Christian experience of divine power and glory implies an inexhaustible divine creativity, beyond the
limits of earth or man and any part or state of the universe.

This means that we cannot seek for a beginning or an
end of the universe within the past and future of meas-
urable time. 'Beginning' and 'end' are not behind and
awareness of the eternal presence. For only the eternal
everything comes and to it everything goes, in every
moment of life and history, in every moment of our
planet and the universe to which it belongs. Creation is
past *and* present. Fulfilment is future *and* present. It is in
the present that past and future meet, because they
come from, and go to, eternity.

The question of man and his earth, this question that
has plunged our time into such anxiety and conflict of
feeling and thought, cannot be answered without an
awareness of the eternal presence. For only the eternal
can deliver us from our sensation of being lost in the face
of the time and space of the universe. Only the eternal

can save us from the anxiety of being a meaningless bit of matter in a meaningless vortex of atoms and electrons. Only the eternal can give us the certainty that the earth, and with it, mankind, has not existed in vain, even should history come to an end tomorrow. For the last end is where the first beginning is, in him to whom 'a thousand years are but as yesterday'.

PART TWO

THE DIVINE REALITY

*

7. *Spiritual Presence*

Not that we are sufficient of ourselves to claim anything as coming from us; our sufficiency is from God,
who has qualified us to be ministers of a new covenant,
not in a written code but in the Spirit; for the written
code kills, but the Spirit gives life.

2 CORINTHIANS 3:5-6

I

'Not that we are sufficient' – writes Paul. Who are 'we'?
Obviously, 'we' are the apostle himself and those who
work with him. These include all those who are qualified to serve the 'new covenant', as he calls it – namely,
the new relationship between God and man, and through
it the 'new creation', the new state of things in man and
his world, of which Paul is a messenger. And everyone
who participates in it, however fragmentarily, is qualified to serve. But when we ask, who *does* participate in
the new creation, we soon find this to be an unanswer-
able question. For nobody can look into the innermost
centre of another being, nor even fully into his own
heart. Therefore, nobody can say with certainty that
anyone else shares in the new state of things, and he
can scarcely say it of himself. But even less can he say
of another, however distorted the man's life may be,
that he does not participate at all in the new reality, and
that he is not qualified to serve its cause. Certainly, nobody can say this of himself.

Perhaps it is more important in our time to emphasize
this last – namely, the qualification of ourselves and

those around us to serve the new creation, our ability to be priests in mutual help towards achieving it. Not long ago, many people, especially members of the Church, felt qualified to judge others and to tell them what to believe and how to act. Today we feel deeply the arrogance of this attitude. Instead, there is a general awareness of our lack of qualification, especially among the middle-aged and younger generations. We are inclined to disqualify ourselves, and to withdraw from the service of the new creation. We feel that we do not participate in it, and that we cannot bring others into such participation. We decline the honour and the burden of mutual priesthood. Often this is caused by unconcern for our highest human vocation. But it is equally caused by despair about ourselves, by doubt, guilt and emptiness. We feel infinitely removed from a new state of things, and totally unable to help others towards it.

But then the other words of our text must become effective, that our qualification is from God and not from ourselves, and the all-consoling word that God is greater than our heart. If we look beyond ourselves at that which is greater than we, then we can feel called to help others in just the moment when we ourselves need help most urgently – and astonishingly, we *can* help. A power works through us which is not of us. We may remember situations when words rose out of the depth of our being, perhaps in the midst of our own great anxiety, that struck another in the depth of *his* being and *his* great anxiety so strongly that they helped him to a new state of things. Perhaps we remember other situations when an action of a person, whose life we knew was disrupted, had a priestly awakening, and healing effect upon us. It did not come from him, but was in him, as it did not come from us, but was in us. Let us not assume the task of being mediators of the new creation to others arrogantly, be it in personal or ecclesiastical terms. Yet, let us not reject the task of being priest for each other because of despair about ourselves or unconcern about what should be our highest concern. Against both arrogance and despair stands the word that our qualification does not come from us, nor from any man or any institution, not even from the Church, but from God. And if it comes from God it is his spiritual presence in our spirit.

II

When we now hear the word 'Spirit', we are somehow prepared for it: the power in us, but not of us, qualifying us for the service of a new state of things is what Spirit means. This may sound strange to many both inside and outside the churches for whom the term Holy Spirit is the strangest of the strange terms that appear among Christian symbols. Rarely a subject of preaching, it is also neglected in religious teaching. Its festival, Pentecost, has almost disappeared in the popular consciousness of this country. Some groups that claim spiritual experiences of a particular character are considered unhealthy, and often rightly so. Liturgically, the use of the term 'Holy Ghost' produces an impression of great remoteness from our way of speaking and thinking. But spiritual experience is a reality for everyone, as actual as the experience of being loved or the breathing of air. Therefore, we should not shy away from the word 'Spirit'. We should become fully aware of the Spiritual Presence, around us and in us, even though we realize how limited our experience of 'God present to our spirit' may be. For this is what Divine Spirit means: God present to our spirit. Spirit is not a mysterious substance; it is not a part of God. It is God himself; but not God as the creative ground of all things and not God directing history and manifesting himself in its central event, but God as present in communities and personalities, grasping them, inspiring them, and transforming them.

For Spirit is first of all power, the power that drives the human spirit above itself towards what it cannot attain by itself, the love that is greater than all other gifts, the truth in which the depth of being opens itself to us, the holy that is the manifestation of the presence of the ultimate.

You may say again: 'I do not know this power. I have never had such an experience. I am not religious or, at least, not Christian and certainly not a bearer of the Spirit. What I hear from you sounds like ecstasy; and I want to stay sober. It sounds like mystery, and I try to illuminate what is dark. It sounds like self-sacrifice and I want to fulfil my human possibilities.' To this I answer – Certainly, the spiritual power can thrust some people into an ecstasy that most of us have never experienced. It can drive some towards a kind of self-sacrifice of which most of us are not capable. It can inspire some to insights into the depth of being that remain unapproachable to most of us. But this does not justify our denial that the Spirit is also working in us. Without doubt, wherever it works, there is an element, possibly very small, of self-surrender, and an element, however weak, of ecstasy, and an element, perhaps fleeting, of awareness of the mystery of existence. Yet these small effects of the spiritual power are enough to prove its presence.

But there are other conscious and noticeable manifestations of the Spiritual Presence. Let me enumerate some of them, while you ask yourselves whether and to what degree they are of your own experience. The Spirit can work in you with a soft but insistent voice, telling you that your life is empty and meaningless, but that there are chances of a new life waiting before the door of your inner self to fill its void and to conquer its dullness. The Spirit can work in you, awakening the desire to strive towards the sublime against the profanity of the average day. The Spirit can give you the courage that says 'yes' to life in spite of the destructiveness you have experienced around you and within you. The Spirit can reveal to you that you have hurt somebody deeply, but it also can give you the right word that reunites him with you. The Spirit can make you love, with the divine love, someone you profoundly dislike or in whom you have no interest. The Spirit can conquer your sloth towards what you know is the aim of your life, and it can transform your moods of aggression and depression into stability and serenity.

The Spirit can liberate you from hidden enmity against those whom you love and from open vengefulness against those by whom you feel violated. The Spirit can give you the strength to throw off false anxieties and to take upon yourself the anxiety which belongs to life itself. The Spirit can awaken you to sudden insight into the way you must take your world, and it can open your eyes to a view of it that makes everything new. The Spirit can give you joy in the midst of ordinary routine as well as in the depth of sorrow.

The Spirit can create warmth in the coldness you feel within you and around you, and it can give you wisdom and strength where your human love towards a loved one has failed. The Spirit can throw you into a hell of despair about yourself and then give you the certainty that life has accepted you just when you felt totally rejected, and when you rejected yourself totally. The Spirit can give you the power of prayer, that nobody has except through the Spiritual Presence. For every prayer – with or without words – that reaches its aim, namely the re-union with the divine Ground of our being, is a work of the Spirit speaking in us and through us. Prayer is the spiritual longing of a finite being to return to its origin.

These are works of the Spirit, signs of the Spiritual Presence with us and in us. In view of these manifestations, who can assert that he is without Spirit? Who can say that he is in no way a bearer of the Spirit? He may be in a small way. But is there anybody among us who could say more than that about himself?

One can compare the Spiritual Presence with the air we breathe, surrounding us, nearest to us, and working life within us. This comparison has a deep justification: in most languages, the word 'spirit' means breath or wind. Sometimes the wind becomes storm, grand and devastating. Mostly it is moving air, always present, not always noticed. In the same way the Spirit is always present, a moving power, sometimes in stormy ecstasies of individuals and groups, but mostly quiet, entering our human spirit and keeping it alive; sometimes manifest in great moments of history or a personal life, but mostly working hiddenly through the media of our daily encounters with men and world; sometimes using its creation, the religious communities and their spiritual means, and often making itself felt in spheres far removed from what is usually called religious. Like the wind the Spirit blows where it wills! It is not subject to rule or limited by method. Its ways with men are not dependent on what men are and do. You cannot force the Spirit upon yourself, upon an individual, upon a group, or even upon a Christian church. Although he who is the foundation of the Church was himself of the Spirit, and although the Spirit as it was present in him is the greatest manifestation of Spiritual Presence, the Spirit is not bound to the Christian Church or any one of them. The Spirit is free to work in the spirits of men in every human situation, and it urges men to let him do so; God as Spirit is always present to the spirit of man.

But why does the psalmist pray – 'Take not thy Spirit from me!'? And why do we speak today of the 'absent God', a term which plays a role in literature and art, and most of all in the personal experience of innumerable people? How can we unite the message of the Spiritual Presence with the experience of the absent God? Let me say something about the 'absent God', by asking – what is the cause of his absence? We may answer – our resistance, our indifference, our lack of seriousness, our honest or dishonest questioning, our genuine or cynical doubt. All these answers have some truth, but they are not final. The final answer to the question as to who makes

God absent is God himself!

It is the work of the Spirit that removes God from our sight, not only for some men, but sometimes for many in a particular period. We live in an era in which the God we know is the absent God. But in knowing God as the absent God, we *know* of him; we feel his absence as the empty space that is left by something or someone that once belonged to us and has now vanished from our view. God is always infinitely near and infinitely far. We are fully aware of him only if we experience both of these aspects. But sometimes, when our awareness of him has become shallow, habitual – not warm and not cold – when he has become too familiar to be exciting, too near to be felt in his infinite distance, then he becomes the absent God. The Spirit has not ceased to be present. The Spiritual Presence can never end. But the Spirit of God hides God from our sight. No resistance against the Spirit, no indifference, no doubt can drive the Spirit away. But the Spirit that always remains present to us can hide itself, and this means that it can hide God. Then the Spirit shows us nothing except the absent God, and the empty space within us which is *his* space. The Spirit has shown to our time and to innumerable people in our time the absent God and the empty space that cries in us to be filled by him. And then the absent one may return and take the space that belongs to him, and the Spiritual Presence may break again into our consciousness, awakening us to recognize what we are, shaking and transforming us. This may happen like the coming of a storm, the storm of the Spirit, stirring up the stagnant air of our spiritual life. The storm will then recede; a new stagnancy may take place; and the awareness of the present God may be replaced by the awareness of the empty space within us. Life in the Spirit is ebb and flow – and this means – whether we experience the present or the absent God – it is the work of the Spirit.

III

And now let me describe a symptom of the Spiritual
Presence within us, the greatest of all, most powerfully
expressed in Paul's words — 'Not in a written code, but
in the Spirit; for the written code kills but the Spirit
gives life.' The work of the Spiritual Presence in a man
reaches its height when it liberates him from the yoke
of the commandments to the freedom of the Spirit. This
is like a release from the sentence of death to a new
life. A tremendous experience lies behind such words,
an experience in which we all can share, but one that is
rare in its full depth, and is then a revolutionary power
that, through men like Paul and Augustine and Luther,
changes the spiritual world and, through it, the history
of mankind. Can we, you and I, share in such an experience?

First, have we not all felt the deadening power of the
written code, written not only in the ten commandments and their many interpretations in the Bible and
history, but also with the authoritative pen of parents
and society into the unconscious depths of our being, recognized by our conscience, judging us by what we do
and, above all, by what we are? Nobody can flee from
the voice of this written code, written internally as well
as externally. And if we try to silence it, to close our
ears against it, the Spirit itself frustrates these attempts,
opening our ears to the cries of our true being, of that
which we are and ought to be in the sight of eternity.
We cannot escape this judgment against us. The Spirit
itself, using the written code, makes this impossible. For
the Spirit does not give life without having led us
through the experience of death. And, certainly, the
written code in its threatening majesty has the power to
kill. It kills the joy of fulfilling our being by imposing
upon us something we feel as hostile. It kills the freedom
of answering creatively what we encounter in things
and men by making us look at a table of laws. It kills our

ability to listen to the calling of the moment, to the voiceless voice of others, and to the here and now. It kills our courage to act, through the scruples of our anxiety-driven conscience. And among those who take it most seriously, it kills faith and hope, and throws them into self-condemnation and despair.

There is no way out from the written code. The Spirit itself prevents us from becoming compromisers, half fulfilling, half defying the commandments. The Spirit itself calls us back when we try to escape into indifference, or lawlessness, or (most usually) average self-righteousness. But when the Spirit calls us back, it does so not in order to *hold* us within the written code, but in order to give us life.

How can we describe the life that the Spirit gives us? I could use many words, well known to everybody, spoken by Paul himself, and after him by the great preachers and teachers of the Church. I could say that the work of the Spirit, liberating us from the law, is freedom. Or I could say that its work is faith, or that its work is hope, and, above all, that the Spirit creates love, the love in which all laws are confirmed and fulfilled and at the same time overcome. But if I used such words, the shadow of the absent God would appear and make you and me aware that we cannot speak like this today. If we did, freedom would be distorted into wilfulness, faith into belief in the absurd, hope into unreal expectations, and love – the word I would like most to use for the creation of the Spirit – into sentimental feeling. The Spirit must give us new words, or revitalize old words to express true life. We must wait for them; we must pray for them; we cannot force them. But we know, in some moments of our lives, what life is. We know that it is great and holy, deep and abundant, ecstatic and sober, limited and distorted by time, fulfilled by eternity. And if the right words fail us in the absence of God, we may look without words at the image of him in whom the Spirit and the Life are manifest without limits.

8. The Divine Name

You shall not take the name of the Lord your God in
vain; for the Lord will not hold him guiltless who takes
his name in vain.

EXODUS 20:7

There must be something extraordinary about the name
if the second commandment tries to protect it as the
other commandments try to protect life, honour, property. Of course, God need not protect himself, but he
does protect his name, and so seriously that he adds to
this single commandment a special threat. This is done
because, within the name, that which bears the name is
present. In ancient times, one believed that one held in
one's power the being whose hidden name one knew.
One believed that the saviour-god conquered the demons
by discovering the mystery of the power embodied in
their names, just as we today try to find out the hidden
names of the powers that disrupt our unconscious depths
and drive us to mental disturbances. If we gain insight
into their hidden striving, we break their power. Men
have always tried to use the divine name in the same
way, not in order to break its power, but to harness its
power for their own uses. Calling on the name of God in
prayer, for instance, can mean attempting to make God
a tool for our purposes. A name is never an empty
sound; it is a bearer of power; it gives Spiritual Presence
to the unseen. This is the reason the divine name can
be taken in vain, and why one may destroy oneself by
taking it in vain. For the invocation of the holy does not
leave us unaffected. If it does not heal us, it may disintegrate us. This is the seriousness of the use of the divine
name. This is the danger of religion, and even of anti-
religion. For in both the name of God is used as well
as misused.

Let me speak to you today of the danger of the use of the word God, when it is both denied and affirmed, and of the sublime embarrassment that we feel when we say 'God'. We may distinguish three forms of such embarrassment: the embarrassment of tact, the embarrassment of doubt, and the embarrassment of awe.

I

Not long ago, an intellectual leader was reported as saying, 'I hope for the day when everyone can speak again of God without embarrassment.' These words, seriously meant, deserve thoughtful consideration, especially in view of the fact that the last fifteen years have brought to this country an immense increase in the willingness to use the name of God – an unquestionable and astonishing revival, if not of religion, certainly of religious awareness. Do we hope that this will lead us to a state in which the name of God will be used without sublime embarrassment, without the restriction imposed. by the fact that in the divine name there is more present than the name? Is an unembarrassed use of the divine name desirable? Is unembarrassed religion desirable? Certainly not! For the Presence of the Divine in the name demands a shy and trembling heart.

Everyone at one time or another finds himself in a situation where he must decide whether he shall use or avoid the name of God, whether he shall talk with personal involvement about religious matters, either for or against them. Making such a decision is often difficult. We feel that we should remain silent in certain groups of people because it might be tactless to introduce the name of God, or even to talk about religion. But our attitude is not unambiguous. We believe we are being tactful, when actually we may be cowardly. And then sometimes we accuse ourselves of cowardice, although it is really tact that prevents us from speaking out. This happens not only to those who would speak out *for* God, but also to those who would speak out *against* God.

Whether for or against him, his name is on our lips and we are embarrassed because we feel that more is at stake than social tact. So we keep silent, uncertain as to whether we are right or wrong. The situation itself is uncertain.

Perhaps we might isolate ourselves or seem ridiculous by even mentioning the divine name, affirming or denying it. But there might also be another present for whom the mention of the divine name would produce a first experience of the Spiritual Presence and a decisive moment in his life. And again, perhaps there may be someone for whom a tactless allusion to God would evoke a definite sense of repulsion against religion. He may now think that religion *as such* is an abuse of the name of God. No one can look into the hearts of others, even if he converses with them intimately. We must risk *now* to talk courageously and *now* to keep silent tactfully. But in no case should we be pushed into a direct affirmation or denial of God which lacks the tact that is born of awe. The sublime embarrassment about his real presence in and through his name should never leave us.

Many persons have felt the pain of this embarrassment when they have had to teach their children the divine name, and others have felt it perhaps when they tried to protect their children against a divine name that they considered an expression of dangerous superstition. It seems natural to teach children about most objects in nature and history without embarrassment, and there are parents who think it is equally natural to teach them divine things. But I believe that many of us as parents in this situation feel a sublime embarrassment. We know as Jesus knew that children are more open to the Divine Presence than adults. It may well be, however, that if we use the divine name easily, we may close this openness and leave our children insensitive to the depth and the mystery of what is present in the divine name. But if we try to withhold it from them, whether because we affirm or because we deny it, emptiness may take hold of their hearts, and they may accuse us later of having cut them off from the most important thing in life. A Spirit-inspired tact is necessary in order to find the right way between these dangers. No technical skill or psychological knowledge can replace the sublimely embarrassed mind of parents or teachers, and especially of teachers of religion.

There is a form of misuse of the name of God that offends those who hear it with a sensitive ear, just because it did not worry those who misused it without sensitivity. I speak now of a public use of the name of God which has little to do with God, but much to do with human purpose – good or bad. Those of us who are grasped by the mystery present in the name of God are often stung when this name is used in governmental and political speeches, in opening prayers for conferences and dinners, in secular and religious advertisements, and in international war propaganda. Often the frequent use of the name of God is praised, as this is an indication that we are a religious nation. And one boasts of this, comparing one's nation with others. Should this be condemned? It is hard *not* to do so, but neither is it easy. If the divine name is used publicly with full conviction, and therefore with embarrassment and spiritual tact, it may be used without offence, although this is hardly ever so. It is usually taken in vain when used for purposes that are not to the glory of his name.

II

There is another more basic cause for sublime embarrassment about using the divine name – the doubt about God himself. Such doubt is universally human, and God would not be God if we could possess him like any object of our familiar world, and verify his reality like any other reality under inquiry. Unless doubt is conquered, there is no faith. Faith must overcome something; it must leap over the ordinary processes that provide evidence, because its object lies above the whole realm

where scientific verification is possible. Faith is the courage that conquers doubt, not by removing it, but by
taking it as an element into itself. I am convinced that
the element of doubt, conquered in faith, is never completely lacking in any serious affirmation of God. It is
not always on the surface; but it always gnaws at the
depth of our being. We may know people intimately
who have a seemingly primitive unshaken faith, but it is
not difficult to discover the underswell of doubt that in
critical moments surges up to the surface. Religious
leaders tell us both directly and indirectly of the struggle
in their minds between faith and unfaith. From fanatics
of faith we hear beneath their unquestioning affirma-
tions of God the shrill sound of their repressed doubt.
It is repressed, but not annihilated.

On the other hand, listening to the cynical denials of
God that are an expression of the flight from a meaning
of life, we hear the voice of a carefully covered despair,
a despair that demonstrates not assurance but doubt
about their negation. And in our encounter with those
who assume scientific reasons to deny God, we find that
they are certain of their denial only so long as they
battle – and rightly so – against superstitious ideas of
God. When, however, they ask the question of God who
is really God – namely, the question of the meaning of
life as a whole and their own life, including their scientific work, their self-assurance tumbles, for neither he
who affirms nor he who denies God can be ultimately
certain about his affirmation or his denial.

Doubt, and not certitude, is our human situation,
whether we affirm or deny God. And perhaps the difference between them is not so great as one usually
thinks. They are probably very similar in their mixture
of faith and doubt. Therefore, the denial of God, if serious, should not shake us. What should trouble everyone
who takes life seriously is the existence of indifference.
For he who is indifferent, when hearing the name of God,
and feels, at the same time, that the meaning of his life

is being questioned, denies his true humanity.

It is doubt in the depth of faith that often produces sublime embarrassment. Such embarrassment can be an expression of conscious or unconscious honesty. Have we not felt how something in us sometimes makes us stop, perhaps only for one moment, when we want to say 'God'? This moment of hesitation may express a deep feeling for God. It says something about the power of the divine name, and it says something about him who hesitates to use it. Sometimes we hesitate to use the word 'God' even without words, when we are alone; we may hesitate to speak to God even privately and voicelessly, as in prayer. It may be that doubt prevents us from praying. And beyond this we may feel that the abyss between God and us makes the use of his name impossible for us; we do not dare to speak to him, because we feel him standing on the other side of the abyss from us. This can be a profound affirmation of him. The silent embarrassment of using the divine name can protect us against violating the divine mystery.

III

We have considered the silence of tact and the silence of honesty concerning the divine name. But behind them both lies something more fundamental, the silence of awe, that seems to prohibit the speaking of God altogether. But is this the last word demanded by the divine mystery? Must we spread silence around what concerns us more than anything else – the meaning of our existence? The answer is – no! For God himself has given mankind names for himself in those moments when he has broken into our finitude and made himself manifest. We can and must use these names. For silence has power only if it is the other side of speaking, and in this way becomes itself a kind of speaking. This necessity is both our justification and our being judged, when we gather together in the name of God. We are an assembly where we speak about God. We are a church. The church is the place where the mystery of the holy should be experienced with awe and sacred embarrassment. But is this our experience? Are our prayers, communal or personal, a use or a misuse of the divine name? Do we feel the sublime embarrassment that so many people outside the churches feel? Are we gripped by awe when, as ministers, we point to the Divine Presence in the sacraments? Or, as theological interpreters of the holy, are we too sure that we can really explain him to others? Is there enough sacred embarrassment in us when fluent biblical quotations or quick, mechanized words of prayer pour from our mouths? Do we preserve the respectful distance from the Holy-Itself, when we claim to have the truth about him, or to be at the place of his Presence or to be the administrators of his Power – the proprietors of the Christ? How much embarrassment, how much awe is alive in Sunday devotional services all over the world?

And now let me ask the Church and all its members, including you and myself, a bold question. Could it be that, in order to judge the misuse of his name within the Church, God reveals himself from time to time by creating silence about himself? Could it be that sometimes he prevents the use of his name in order to protect his name, that he withholds from a generation what was natural to previous generations – the use of the word God? Could it be that godlessness is not caused only by human resistance, but also by God's paradoxical action – using men and the forces by which they are driven to judge the assemblies that gather in his name and take his name in vain? Is the secular silence about God that we experience everywhere today perhaps God's way of forcing his Church back to a sacred embarrassment when speaking of him? It may be bold to ask such questions. Certainly there can be no answer, because we do not know the character of the divine providence. But even without an answer, the question itself should warn all those inside the Church to whom the use of his name comes too easily.

Let me close with a few words that are both personal and more than personal. While thinking about this sermon I tried to make it not only one about the divine name, but also about God himself. Such an attempt stands under the judgment of the very commandment I tried to interpret, for it was a refined way of taking the name of God in vain. We can speak only of the names through which he has made himself known to us. For he himself 'lives in unapproachable light, whom no man has ever seen nor can see'.

9. God's Pursuit of Man

Then all the disciples forsook him and fled.

MATTHEW 26:56

I

Listening one evening to Bach's 'Passion according to St Matthew', I was struck by the text and music of the line, 'Then all the disciples forsook him and fled.' It anticipates the words of Jesus on the Cross, 'My God, my God, why hast thou forsaken me?' He who is forsaken by all men feels forsaken by God. And, indeed, all men left him, and those who were nearest him fled farthest from him. Ordinarily, we are not aware of this fact. We are used to imagining the crucifixion in terms of those beautiful pictures where, along with his mother and other women, at least one disciple is present. The reality was different. They all fled, and some women dared to watch from afar. Only an unimaginable loneliness remained during the hours his life and his work were broken.

How shall we think about these disciples? Our first reaction is probably the question – how *could* they for-

sake him whom they had called the Messiah, the Christ,
the bringer of the new age, whom they had followed
after leaving behind everything for his sake? But this
time, when I heard the words and tones of the music, I
admired the disciples! For it is *they* to whom we owe
the words of our text. They did not hide their flight;
they simply stated it in one short sentence, a statement
that judges them for all time. The Gospel stories contain many judgments against the disciples. We read
that they misunderstood Jesus continuously, as did his
mother and brothers, and that, day by day, their misunderstanding intensified his suffering. We read that
some of the most important among them demanded a
place of exceptional glory and power in the world to
come. We read that Jesus reproached them because their
zeal made them fanatical against those who did not
follow him. And we read that Jesus had to call Peter
'Satan', because Peter tried to dissuade him from going
to Jerusalem to his death, and that Peter denied his discipleship in the hour of trial. These reports are astonishing. They show what Jesus did to the disciples. He
taught them to accept judgment, and not to present
themselves in a favourable light. Without the acceptance
of such judgment, they could not have been his disciples.
And if the disciples had suppressed the truth about their
own profound weakness, our Gospels would not be what
they are. The glory of the Christ and the misery of his
followers would not be so clearly manifest. And yet even
in the same records, man's desire to cover up his own
ugliness makes itself felt. Later traditions in the Gospels
try to smooth the hard and hurting edges of the original
picture. Apparently, it was unbearable to established
congregations that *all* the disciples fled, that none of
them witnessed the crucifixion and the death of the
master. They could not accept the fact that only far
away in Galilee was their flight arrested by the appearance of him whom they deserted in his hour of agony

and despair. So, it was stated that Jesus himself had told them to go to Galilee; their flight was not a real flight. And still later, it was said that they did not flee at all, but remained in Jerusalem. From earliest times, the Church could not stand this judgment against itself, its past and its present. It has tried to conceal what the disciples openly admitted – that we all forsook him and fled. But this is the truth about all men, including the followers of Jesus today.

II

The flight from God begins in the moment we feel his presence. This feeling is at work in the dark, half-conscious regions of our being, unrecognized, but effective; in the restlessness of the child's asking and seeking; of the adolescent's doubts and despairs; of the adult's desires and struggles. God is present, but not as God; he is present as the unknown force in us that makes us restless.

But in some moments he appears *as* God. The unknown force in us that caused our restlessness becomes manifest as the God in whose hands we are, who is our ultimate threat and our ultimate refuge. In such moments it is as though we were arrested in our hidden flight. But it is not an arrest by brute force, but one that has the character of a question. And we remain free to continue our flight. This is what happened to the disciples: they were powerfully arrested when Jesus first called them, but they remained free to flee again. And they did when the moment of trial arrived. And so it is with the Church and all its members. They are arrested in their hidden flight and brought into the conscious presence of God. But they remain free to flee again, not only as individual men, but also as bearers of the Church, carrying the Church itself on the road to Galilee, separating it as far away as possible from the point where the eternal breaks into the temporal. Man flees from God even in the Church, the place where we are supposed to be arrested by the presence of God. Even there we are in flight from him.

III

If the ultimate cuts into the life of a man, he tries to take cover in the preliminary. He runs for a safe place, fleeing from the attack of that which strikes him with unconditional seriousness. And there are many places that look as safe to us as Galilee looked to the fleeing disciples.

Perhaps the most effective refuge in our time from the threatening presence of God is the work we are doing. This was not always so. The attitude of ancient man towards work is well summed up in the curse God pronounced over Adam – 'In the sweat of your face you shall eat bread', and in the words of the ninetieth Psalm concerning the short years of our life – 'yet their span is but toil and trouble'. Later, physical labour with its toil and its drudgery was left to the slaves and serfs or uneducated classes. And it was distinguished from creative work that was based on leisure time and, hence, the privilege of the few. Medieval Christianity considered work a discipline, especially in the monastic life. But in our period of our history, work has become the dominating destiny of all men, if not in reality, at least by demand. It is everything – discipline, production, creation. The difference between labour and work is gone. The fact that it stands under a curse in the biblical view is forgotten. It has become a religion itself, the religion of modern industrial society. And it has all of us in its grip. Even if we were able to escape the punishment of starvation for not working, something within us would not permit an escape from the bondage to work. For most of us it is both a necessity and a compulsion. And as such, it has become the favoured way of the flight from God.

And nothing seems to be safer than this way. From it we get the satisfaction of having fulfilled our duty. We are praised by others and by ourselves for 'work well done!' We provide support for our family or care for its members. We overcome daily the dangers of leisure, boredom and disorder. We acquire a good conscience out of it and, as a cynical philosopher said, at the end of it, a good sleep. And if we do the kind of work that is called creative, an even higher satisfaction results – the joy of bringing something new into being. Should somebody protest that this is not his way of fleeing from God, we might ask him : have you not sometimes drawn a balance sheet of your whole being, and upon honestly discovering many points on the negative side, then balanced the sheet by your *work* on the other? The Pharisee of today would boast before God not so much of his obedience to the law and of his religious exercises as of his hard work and his disciplined, successful life. And he would also find sinners with whom he could compare himself favourably.

IV

There is another way to flee from God – the way that promises to lead us into the abundance of life, a promise that is kept to a certain extent. It is not necessarily the way of the prodigal son in the parable of Jesus. It can be the acceptance of the fullness of life, opened to us by a searching mind and the driving power of love towards the greatness and beauty of creation. Such longing for life does not need to close our eyes to the tragedy within pleasure, to the ugliness within beauty. More men and women should dare to experience the abundance of life. But this also can be a way of fleeing from God, like labour and work. In the ecstasy of living, the limits of the abundance of life are forgotten. I do not speak of the shallow methods of having a good time, of the desire for fun and entertainment. This is, in most cases, the other side of the flight from God under the cover of labour and work, called recreation; it is justified by everybody as a means for working more effectively. But I speak of the ecstasy of living that includes participation in the highest and lowest of life in one and the same experience. This demands courage and passion, but it also can be a flight from God. And whoever lives in this way should not be judged morally, but should be made aware of his restlessness, and his fear of encountering God. The man who is under the bondage of work should not boast of being superior to him. But neither should *he* boast to those who are in the bondage of work.

V

There are many in our time who have experienced the limits of both ways, for whom successful work has become as meaningless as plunging into the abundance of life. I am speaking of the sceptics and cynics, of those in anxiety and despair, of those who for a moment in their lives have been stopped in their flight from God and then continued it – though in a new form, in the form of consciously questioning or denying him. Their attitude is intensely described and analysed in our period by literature and the arts. And somehow they are justified. If they are serious sceptics, their seriousness, and the suffering following it, justifies them. If they are in despair, the hell of their serious despair makes them symbols through which we can better understand our own situation.

But they are also in flight from God. God has struck them; but they do not recognize him. Their need to deny him in thought and attitude shows that they have been arrested in their flight for a moment. If they were satisfied with the success of work or with the abundance of life, they would not have become 'accusers of being'. They accuse being, because they flee from the power that gives being to every being.

VI

This cannot be said of the last group of those who are

in flight from God. They do not flee away from the Cross as did the disciples. They flee towards it. They watch it and witness to it; they are edified by it. They are better than the disciples! But are they really? If the Cross becomes a tenet of our religious heritage, of parental and denominational tradition, does it remain the Cross of Christ, the decisive point where the eternal cuts into the temporal? But perhaps it is not paternal tradition that keeps us near the Cross. Perhaps it is a sudden emotional experience, a conversion under the impact of a powerful preacher or evangelist that has brought us, for the first time, face to face with the Cross! Even then, in the height of our emotion, we should ask ourselves – is not our bow to the Cross the safest form of our flight from the Cross?

VII

But whatever the way of our flight from God, we can be arrested. And if this happens, something cuts into the regular processes of our life. It is a difficult but also great experience! One may be thrown out of work and think now that the meaning of life is gone. One may feel suddenly the emptiness of what seemed to be an abundant life. One may become aware that one's cynicism is not serious despair but hidden arrogance. One may see in the midst of a devotional act that one has exchanged God for one's religious feelings. All this is as painful as being wounded by a knife. But it is also great, because it opens up in us a new dimension of life. God has arrested us and something new takes hold of us.

This new reality that appears in us does not remove the old realities, but transforms them by giving them a new dimension. We still work; and work remains hard and full of anxiety and, as before, takes the largest part of our day! But it does not give us the meaning of our life. The strength or the opportunity to work may be taken from us, but not the meaning of our life. We realize that work cannot provide it and that work cannot take it from us. For the meaning of work itself has become something else. In working, we help to make real the infinite possibilities that lie hidden in life. We co-operate with life's self-creating powers, in the smallest or the greatest form of work. Through us, as workers, something of the inexhaustible depth of life becomes manifest. This is what one may feel, at least in some moments, if one is arrested by God. Work points beyond itself. And because it does so, it becomes blessed, and we become blessed through it. For blessedness means fulfilment in the ultimate dimension of our being.

And if someone is arrested by experiencing the profound emptiness of the abundant life, the abundance itself is not taken from him; it may still give great moments of ecstasy and joy. But it does not give him the meaning of his life. The external opportunities or the inner readiness to experience the ecstasies of life may vanish, but not the meaning of his life. He realizes that abundance cannot give it, and that want cannot take it away. For the abundance of life becomes something new for him who is arrested by God. It becomes a manifestation of the creative love that reunites what it separates, that gives and takes, that elevates us above ourselves and shows us that we are finite and must receive everything, that makes us love life and penetrate everything that is to its eternal ground.

And if someone is arrested by God and made aware of the lack of seriousness of his doubt and his despair, the doubt is not taken away from him, and the despair does not cease to be a threat. But his doubt does not have to lead to despair. It does not have to deprive him of the meaning of his life. Doubt cannot give it to him, as he secretly believed in his cynical arrogance; and doubt cannot take it from him, as he felt in his despair. For doubt becomes something else for him who is arrested by God. It becomes a means of penetrating the depth of his being and into the depth of all being. Doubt ceases to be intellectual play or a method of research. It becomes a courageous undercutting of all the untested assumptions on which our lives are built. They break down one after the other, and we come deeper and nearer to the ground of our life. And then it happens that those who live in serious doubt about themselves and their world discover that dimension that leads to the ultimate by which they had been arrested. And they realize that hidden in the seriousness of their doubt was the truth.

And if someone is arrested by God and made aware of the ambiguous character of his religious life, religion is not taken away from him. But now he realizes that even this cannot give him the meaning of his life. He does not have to lose the meaning of his life if he loses his religion. Whoever is arrested by God stands beyond religion and non-religion. And if he holds fast to his religion, it becomes something else to him. It becomes a channel, not a law, another way in which the presence of the ultimate has arrested him, not the only way. Since he has reached freedom *from* religion, he also has reached freedom *for* religion. He is blessed in it and he is blessed outside of it. He has been opened to the ultimate dimension of being.

Therefore, don't flee! Let yourself be arrested and be blessed.

10. Salvation

Save us from the evil one.
MATTHEW 6:13

The easy petition in our Lord's Prayer is known to all of us in the form: 'Deliver us from evil'. This form is not wrong, but it does not reach the depth of the original words which say: 'Save us from the evil one'. Let us meditate about them and, above all, about the one word 'save'.

Christianity has rightly been called a religion of salvation, and the 'Christ' is another word for him who brings salvation: the 'Saviour'. Salvation, saving, and saviour are words used many times in both the Old and the New Testament, innumerable times in the Church, in the works of the great theologians, in the hymns of the Christian poets, in liturgies and sermons, in solemn statements of the faith of the Church, in catechisms and, most important, in personal prayers. They permeate Christian thought and life as do few other words. How then, is it possible to speak about them in the short space of a sermon?

Perhaps it is impossible! But, even so, let me say with great seriousness that it is necessary, for the words which are most used in religion are also those whose genuine meaning is almost completely lost and whose impact on the human mind is nearly negligible. Such words must be reborn, if possible; and thrown away if this is not possible, even if they are protected by a long tradition. But there is only one way to re-establish their original meaning and power, namely, to ask ourselves what these words mean for our lives; to ask whether or not they are able to communicate something infinitely important to us. This is true of all important terms of our religious language: God and the Christ, the Spirit and the Church, sin and forgiveness, faith, love, and hope, Eternal Life, and the kingdom of God. About each of them we must ask whether it is able to strike us in the depth of our being. If a word has lost this power for most of those in our time who are seriously concerned about things of ultimate significance, it should *not* be used again, or at least not as long as it is not reborn in its original power.

Perhaps it is still possible for the words salvation, saving, and saviour to be saved themselves. They are profound in their original meaning, but this has been covered by the dust of the centuries and emaciated by mechanical repetition. So let us try what may be impossible, and make 'salvation' the object of our thoughts in this hour.

The two translations of the seventh petition of our Lord's Prayer use two different images of what salvation is: 'saving' and 'delivering'. The word salvation is derived from the Latin word *salvus*, which means heal and whole. The saviour makes 'heal and whole' what is sick and disrupted. In Greece, the healing god, Asclepius, was called the saviour. Jesus calls himself the physician who has come to the sick and not to the healthy.

But saving also means delivering, liberating, setting free. This is another image: we are in bondage. It is the evil one – the symbol of the distorting and destroying powers in the world – that keeps us in servitude. The saviour, then, is the conqueror of the evil one and of his powers. No one has used this image more impressively than Paul in his great song of triumph in the eighth chapter of Romans, when he says that none of the demonic powers which govern this world can separate us from the love of God.

Saving is healing from sickness and saving is delivering from servitude; and the two are the same. Let me give you an example of their unity. We consider the neurotic or psychotic person who cannot face life as sick. But if we describe his disease, we find that he is under the power of compulsions from which he cannot extricate himself. He is, as the New Testament expresses it, demoniacally possessed. In him, disease and servitude are the same; and we ask whether, in some degree, this is not true of all of us. In which sense, we ask, do we need healing? In which sense liberation? What should salvation mean to us?

It is certainly not, what popular imagination has made of it, escaping from hell and being received in heaven, in what is badly called 'the life hereafter'. The New Testament speaks of eternal life, and eternal life is not continuation of life after death. Eternal life is beyond past, present, and future: we come from it, we live in its presence, we return to it. It is never absent – it is the divine life in which we are rooted and in which we are destined to participate in freedom – for God alone has eternity. Man should not boast of having an immortal soul as his possession for, as the letter to Timothy says: God 'alone has immortality'. We are mortal like every creature, mortal with our whole being – body and soul – but we are also kept in the eternal life *before* we lived on earth, *while* we are living in time, and *after* our time has come to an end.

If it is our destiny to participate in freedom in the divine life here and now, in and above time, we can say that the 'evil one' is he from whom we pray to be delivered: it is the enslaving power which prevents us from fulfilling our human destiny; it is the wall that separates us from the eternal life to which we belong; and it is the sickness of our being and that of our world caused by this separation. Salvation happens whenever the enslaving power is conquered, whenever the wall is broken through, whenever the sickness is healed. He who can do this is called the saviour. Nobody except God can do this. Those who are in chains cannot liberate themselves, and those who are sick cannot heal themselves. All liberating, all healing power comes from the other side of the wall which separates us from eternal life. Whenever it appears, it is a manifestation of eternal, divine life in our temporal and mortal existence. All liberators, all healers are sent by God; they liberate and heal through the power of the eternal given to them.

Who are these healers? Where are these saviours? The first answer is: 'they are *here*; they are *you*. Each of you has liberating and healing power over someone to whom you are a priest. We all are called to be priests to each other; and if priests, also physicians. And if physicians, also counsellors. And if counsellors, also liberators. There are innumerable degrees and kinds of saving grace. There are many people whom the evil one has enslaved so mightily that the saving power which may work through them has almost disappeared. On the other hand, there are the great saviour figures in whom large parts of mankind have experienced a lasting power of liberating and healing from generation to generation. Most of us are in between. And there is the one saviour in whom Christianity sees the saving grace without limits, the decisive victory over the demonic powers, the tearing down of the wall of guilt which separates us from the eternal, the healer who brings to light a new reality in man and his world. But if we call him the saviour we must remember that *God* is the saviour *through* him and that there are a host of liberators and healers, including ourselves, through whom the divine salvation works in all mankind. God does not leave the world at any place, in any time, without saviours – without healing power.

But now I must repeat a question asked before. What does all this mean for our own lives? When and where do we, ourselves, experience such saving power? When and where are we liberated, healed?

It is one of the most memorable facts in the biblical stories about Jesus that a large part of them are healing stories. There are three types: those in which people sick of body are forgiven and healed; and those in which people sick of mind are delivered from what was called demonic possession. It is regrettable that most preaching emphasizes the miraculous character of these stories, often using a poor, superstitious notion of miracles instead of showing the profound insight they betray into disease, health, and healing – the inseparable unity of body and mind. They are stories of salvation, performed by him who was called the Saviour. In them, it is visible that saving is healing. If the Church had shown more understanding of this part of its message, the regrettable split between religion and medicine might never have happened. In both, the power of saving is at work. If we look at the miracles of medical and mental healing today, we must say that here the wall between eternal and perishable life is pierced at *one* point; that liberation from the evil one has happened in *one* dimension of our life; that a physician or mental helper becomes a saviour for someone. He functions, as every saviour does, as an instrument of the healing power given to nature as well as to man by the divine presence in time and space.

But there are also limits to this kind of healing and liberating. The people healed by Jesus became sick again and died. Those who were liberated from demonic compulsion might, as Jesus himself warned, relapse into more serious states of mental disease. It was a breakthrough of eternal life in one moment of time, as all our medical healing is.

Also, there is a second limit of the healing of body and mind: the attitude of him who is to be healed may prevent healing. Without the desire for delivery from the evil one there is no liberation; without longing for the healing power, no healing! The wall which separates us from eternal life is broken through only when we desire it, and even then only when we trust in the bearers of healing power. Trust in saviours does not mean what is called today faith-healing, which is at best psychic sanctification of oneself or someone else. But it means openness to liberation from evil, whenever we encounter the possibility of such liberation.

This openness is not always present. We may prefer disease to health, enslavement to liberty. There are many reasons for the desire not to be healed, not to be liberated. He who is weak can exercise a power over his environment, over his family and friends, which can destroy trust and love but which gives satisfaction to him who exercises this power through weakness. Many amongst us should ask ourselves whether it is not this that we unconsciously do toward husband or wife; toward children or parents; toward friends or groups. There are others who do not want liberation because it forces them to encounter reality as it is and to take upon

themselves man's heaviest burden: that of making responsible decisions. This is especially true of those who
are in bondage to mental disturbances. Certainly they
suffer, as do those with bodily diseases, but the compensation of gaining power or escaping responsibility appears more important to them than the suffering. They
cut themselves off from the saving power in reality.
For them, this saving power would first of all mean
opening themselves up to the desire for salvation of body
or mind. But even Jesus could not do it with many –
perhaps most – of his listeners. One could perhaps say
that the first work of every healer and liberator is to
break through the love of disease and enslavement in
those whom he wants to save.

Now let us look at quite a different form of enslavement and liberation brought about by our finitude in
this world. In contrast to much of what has been said
and much of what I myself have said against technology, I want to speak *for* the saving power of the
technical control of nature. This is a bold statement to
make in a period when such control has reached a peak
and, at the same time, its injurious and destructive aspects have become more manifest than ever. Every technical invention elevates man above his animal stage,
liberating him from much drudgery, conquering the
narrow limits of his movements in time and space,
saving him from innumerable smaller and greater evils
to which he is subject as a part of nature; for instance,
unnecessary pain and unnecessary death. These technical innovations have a saving power, as countless
people have learned who have been broken in body and
mind by being suddenly deprived of them. We know the
destructive possibilities in technology; we know that
it can annihilate all life on earth and bring history to an
end. We also know that it can keep man's spirit away
from salvation in a deeper and more lasting sense. We
know that it can transform man himself into a thing and

a tool. Nevertheless, in the great feats of technical control we have a breakthrough of the eternal into the temporal; they cannot be ignored when we speak of saving power and salvation.

In the ancient world, great political leaders were called saviours. They liberated nations and groups within them from misery, enslavement, and war. This is another kind of healing, reminiscent of the words of the last book of the Bible, which says in poetic language that 'the leaves of the tree of life are for the healing of the nations'. How can nations be healed? One may say: they can be liberated from external conquerors or internal oppressors. But can they be healed? Can they be saved? The prophets give the answer: nations are saved if there is a small minority, a group of people, who represent what the nation is called to be. They may be defeated, but their spirit will be a power of resistance against the evil spirits who are detrimental to the nation. The question of saving power in the nation is the question of whether there is a minority, even a small one, which is willing to resist the anxiety produced by propaganda, the conformity enforced by threat, the hatred stimulated by ignorance. The future of this country and its spiritual values is not dependent as much on atomic defence as on the influence such groups will have on the spirit in which the nation will think and act.

And this is true of mankind as a whole. Its future will be dependent on a saving group, embodied in one nation or crossing through all nations. There is saving power in mankind, but there is also the hidden will to self-destruction. It depends on every one of us which side will prevail. There is no divine promise that humanity will survive this or the next year. But it may depend on the saving power effective in you or me, whether it will survive. (It may depend on the amount of healing and liberating grace which works through any of us with respect to social justice, racial equality, and political wisdom.) Unless many of us say to ourselves: through the saving power working in me, mankind may be saved or lost – it will be lost.

But in order to be the bearers of saving power, we must be saved ourselves; the wall separating us from eternal life must be broken through. And here is one thing which strengthens the wall and keeps us sick and enslaved. It is our estrangement and guilt which are the impediments which keep us from reaching eternal life here and now. The judgment against us which we confirm in our conscience is the sickness unto death, the despair of life, from which we must be halted in order to say *yes* to life. Healed life is new life, delivered from the bondage of the evil one. Here the last two petitions of our Lord's Prayer become one petition: forgive our trespasses, and deliver us from the evil one – this is one and the same thing. And if we call Jesus, the Christ, our saviour, then we mean that in him we see the power which heals us by accepting us and which liberates us by showing us in his being a new being – a being in which there is reconciliation with ourselves, with our world, and with the divine ground of our world and ourselves.

And now the last question: who shall be saved, liberated, healed? The Fourth Gospel says: The world! The reunion with the eternal from which we come, from which we are separated, to which we shall return, is promised to everything that is. We are saved not as individuals, but in unity with all others and with the universe. Our own liberation does not leave the enslaved ones alone, our own healing is a part of the great healing of the world. Therefore, two other petitions of our Lord's Prayer also ask the same: save us from the evil one, and thy kingdom come! This kingdom is his creation, liberated and healed. This is what we hope for when we look from time to eternity. Deliver us – heal us – that is the cry of everything that is; of each of us in unity with all mankind and in unity with the whole universe. The divine answer is: I shall return to me

what is separated from me because it belongs to me. I
am liberating you today as I did before and will do in
the future. Today, when you hear these words, 'I am
liberating you, I am healing you', do not resist!

11. *The Eternal Now*

I am the Alpha and the Omega, the beginning and the
end.

REVELATION 21:6

It is our destiny and the destiny of everything in our
world that we must come to an end. Every end that we
experience in nature and mankind speaks to us with a
loud voice: you also will come to an end! It may reveal
itself in the farewell to a place where we have lived for
a long time, the separation from the fellowship of intimate associates, the death of someone near to us. Or it
may become apparent to us in the failure of a work that
gave meaning to us, the end of a whole period of life,
the approach of old age, or even in the melancholy side
of nature visible in autumn. All this tells us: you will
also come to an end.

Whenever we are shaken by this voice reminding us
of our end, we ask anxiously — what does it mean that
we have a beginning and an end, that we come from the
darkness of the 'not yet' and rush ahead towards the
darkness of the 'no more'? When Augustine asked this
question, he began his attempt to answer it with a
prayer. And it is right to do so, because praying means
elevating oneself to the eternal. In fact, there is no other
way of judging time than to see it in the light of the
eternal. In order to judge something, one must be partly
within it, partly out of it. If we were totally within
time, we would not be able to elevate ourselves in
prayer, meditation and thought, to the eternal. We

would be children of time like all other creatures and could not ask the question of the meaning of time. But as men we are aware of the eternal to which we belong and from which we are estranged by the bondage of time.

I

We speak of time in three ways or modes – the past, present and future. Every child is aware of them, but no wise man has ever penetrated their mystery. We become aware of them when we hear a voice telling us: you also will come to an end. It is the future that awakens us to the mystery of time. Time runs from the beginning to the end, but our awareness of time goes in the opposite direction. It starts with the anxious anticipation of the end. In the light of the future we see the past and present. So let us first consider our going into the future and towards the end that is the last point that we can anticipate in our future.

The image of the future produces contrasting feelings in man. The expectation of the future gives one a feeling of joy. It is a great thing to have a future in which one can actualize one's possibilities, in which one can experience the abundance of life, in which one can create something new – be it new work, a new living being, a new way of life, or the regeneration of one's own being. Courageously one goes ahead towards the new, especially in the earlier part of one's life. But this feeling struggles with other ones: the anxiety about what is hidden in the future, the ambiguity of everything it will bring us, the shortness of its duration that decreases with every year of our life and becomes shorter the nearer we come to the unavoidable end. And finally the end itself, with its impenetrable darkness and the threat that one's whole existence in time will be judged as a failure.

How do men, how do you, react to this image of the future with its hope and threat and inescapable end? Probably most of us react by looking at the immediate future, anticipating it, working for it, hoping for it, being anxious about it, while cutting off from our awareness the future which is farther away, and above all, by cutting off from our consciousness the end, the last moment of our future. Perhaps we could not live without doing so most of our time. But perhaps we will not be able to die if we *always* do so. And if one is not able to die, is he really able to live?

How do we react if we become aware of the inescapable end contained in our future? Are we able to bear it, to take its anxiety into a courage that faces ultimate darkness? Or are we thrown into utter hopelessness? Do we hope against hope, or do we repress our awareness of the end because we cannot stand it? Repressing the consciousness of our end expresses itself in several ways.

Many try to do so by putting the expectation of a long life between now and the end. For them it is decisive that the end be delayed. Even old people who are near the end do this, for they cannot endure the fact that the end will not be delayed much longer.

Many people realize this deception and hope for a continuation of this life after death. They expect an endless future in which they may achieve or possess what has been denied them in this life. This is a prevalent attitude about the future, and also a very simple one. It denies that there *is* an end. It refuses to accept that we are creatures, that we come from the eternal ground of time and return to the eternal ground of time and have received a limited span of time as *our* time. It replaces eternity by endless future.

But endless future is without a final aim; it repeats itself and could well be described as an image of hell. This is not the Christian way of dealing with the end. The Christian message says that the eternal stands above past and future. 'I am the Alpha and the Omega, the beginning and the end.'

The Christian message acknowledges that time runs

towards an end, and that we move towards the end of
that time which is our time. Many people – but not the
Bible – speak loosely of the 'hereafter' or of the 'life
after death'. Even in our liturgies eternity is translated
by 'world without end'. But the world, by its very
nature, is that which comes to an end. If we want to
speak in truth without foolish, wishful thinking, we
should speak about the eternal that is neither timeless-
ness nor endless time. The mystery of the future is answered in the eternal of which we may speak in images
taken from time. But if we forget that the images are
images, we fall into absurdities and self-deceptions.
There is not time *after* time, but there is eternity *above*
time.

II

We go towards something that is not yet, and we come
from something that is no more. We are what we are
by what we came from. We have a beginning as we
have an end. There was a time that was not *our* time.
We hear of it from those who are older than we; we
read about it in history books; we try to envision the
unimaginable billions of years in which neither we nor
anyone was who could tell us of them. It is hard for us
to imagine our 'being-no-more'. It is equally difficult to
imagine our 'being-not-yet'. But we usually don't care
about our not yet being, about the indefinite time before
our birth in which we were not. We think: *now* we
are; this is *our* time – and we do not want to lose it. We
are not concerned about what lies before our beginning.
We ask about life after death, yet seldom do we ask
about our being before birth. But is it possible to do
one without the other? The Fourth Gospel does not
think so. When it speaks of the eternity of the Christ, it
does not only point to his return to eternity, but also
this coming *from* eternity. 'Truly, truly, I say to you,
before Abraham was, I *am*.' He comes from another
dimension than that in which the past lies. Those to

whom he speaks misunderstand him because they think of the historical past. They believe that he makes himself hundreds of years old and they rightly take offence at this absurdity. Yet he does not say, 'I *was*' before Abraham; but he says, 'I *am*' before Abraham was. He speaks of his beginning out of eternity. And this is the beginning of everything that is – not the uncounted billions of years but the eternal as the ultimate point in our past.

The mystery of the past from which we come is that it is and is not in every moment of our lives. It is, in so far as we are what the past has made of us. In every cell of our body, in every trait of our face, in every movement of our soul, our past is the present.

Few periods knew more about the continuous working of the past in the present than ours. We know about the influence of childhood experiences on our character. We know about the scars left by events in early years. We have rediscovered what the Greek tragedians and the Jewish prophets knew, that the past is present in us, both as a curse and as a blessing. For 'past' always means both a curse and a blessing, not only for individuals, but also for nations and even continents.

History lives from the past, from its heritage. The glory of the European nations is their long, inexhaustibly rich tradition. But the blessings of this tradition are mixed with curses resulting from early splits into separated nations whose bloody struggles have filled century after century and brought Europe again and again to the edge of self-destruction. Great are the blessings *this* nation has received in the course of its short history. But from earliest days, elements have been at work that have been and will remain a curse for many years to come. I could refer, for instance, to racial consciousness, not only within the nation itself, but also in its dealings with races and nations outside its own boundaries. 'The American way of life' is a blessing that comes from the past; but it is also a curse, threatening the future.

Is there a way of getting rid of such curses that threaten the life of nations and continents and, more and more, of mankind as a whole? Can we banish elements of our past into the past so that they lose their power over the present? In man's individual life this is certainly possible. One has rightly said that the strength of a character is dependent on the amount of things that he has thrown into the past. In spite of the power his past holds over him, a man can separate himself from it, throw it out of the present into the past in which it is condemned to remain ineffective – at least for a time. It may return and conquer the present and destroy the person, but this is not necessarily so. We are not inescapably victims of our past. We can make the past remain nothing but *past*. The act in which we do this has been called repentance. Genuine repentance is not feeling sorrow about wrong actions, but it is the act of the whole person in which he separates himself from elements of his being, discarding them into the past as something that no longer has any power over the present.

Can a nation do the same thing? Can a nation or any other social group have genuine repentance? Can it separate itself from curses of the past? On this possibility rests the hope of a nation. The history of Israel and the history of the Church show that it is possible and they also show that it is rare and extremely painful. Nobody knows whether it will happen to *this* nation. But we know that its future depends on the way it will deal with its past, and whether it can discard into the past elements which are a curse!

In each human life a struggle is going on about the past. Blessings battle with curses. Often we do not recognize what are blessings and what are curses. Today, in the light of the discovery of our unconscious strivings, we are more inclined to see curses than blessings in our past. The remembrance of our parents, which in the Old Testament is so inseparably connected with their blessings, is now much more connected with the curse they have unconsciously and against their will brought upon us. Many of those who suffer under mental afflic-tions see their past, especially their childhood, only as the source of curses. We know how often this is true. But we should not forget that we would not be able to live and to face the future if there were not blessings that support us and which come from the same source as the curses. A pathetic struggle over their past is going on almost without interruption in many men and women in our time. No medical healing can solve *this* conflict, because no medical healing can change the past. Only a blessing that lives above the conflict of blessing and curse can heal. It is the blessing that changes what seems to be unchangeable – the past. It cannot change the facts; what has happened has happened and remains so in all eternity! But the *meaning* of the facts can be changed by the eternal, and the name of this change is the experience of 'forgiveness'. If the meaning of the past is changed by forgiveness, its influence on the future is also changed. The character of curse is taken away from it. It becomes a blessing by the transforming power of forgiveness.

There are not always blessings and curses in the past. There is also emptiness in it. We remember experiences that, at the time, were seemingly filled with an abund-ant content. Now we remember them, and their abund-ance has vanished, their ecstasy is gone, their fullness has turned into a void. Pleasures, successes, vanities have this character. We do not feel them as curses; we do not feel them as blessings. They have been swallowed by the past. They did not contribute to the eternal. Let us ask ourselves how little in our lives escapes this judg-ment.

III

The mystery of the future and the mystery of the past are united in the mystery of the present. Our time, the time we have, is the time in which we have 'presence'. But how can we have 'presence'? Is not the present moment gone when we think of it? Is not the present the ever-moving boundary line between past and future? But a moving boundary is not a place to stand upon. If nothing were given to us except the 'no more' of the past and the 'not yet' of the future, we would not have anything. We could not speak of the time that is *our* time; we would not have 'presence'.

The mystery is that we *have* a present; and, even more, that we have *our* future also because we anticipate it in the present; and that we have *our* past also, because we remember it in the present. In the present our future and our past are *ours*. But there is no 'present' if we think of the never-ending flux of time. The riddle of the present is the deepest of all the riddles of time. Again, there is no answer except from that which comprises all time and lies beyond it – the eternal. Whenever we say 'now' or 'today', we stop the flux of time for us. We accept the present and do not care that it is gone in the moment that we accept it. We live in it and it is renewed for us in every new 'present'. This is possible because every moment of time reaches into the eternal. It is the eternal that stops the flux of time for us. It is the eternal 'now' which provides for us a temporal 'now'. We live so long as 'it is still today' – in the words of the letter to the Hebrews. Not everybody, and nobody all the time, is aware of this 'eternal now' in the temporal 'now'. But sometimes it breaks powerfully into our consciousness and gives us the certainty of the eternal, of a dimension of time which cuts into time and gives us our time.

People who are never aware of this dimension lose the possibility of resting in the present. As the letter to the Hebrews describes it, they never enter into the divine rest. They are held by the past and cannot separate themselves from it, or they escape towards the future, unable to rest in the present. They have not entered the eternal rest which stops the flux of time and gives us the blessing of the present. Perhaps this is the most conspicuous characteristic of our period, especially in the Western world and particularly in this country. It lacks the courage to accept 'presence' because it has lost the dimension of the eternal.

'I am the beginning and the end.' This is said to us who live in the bondage of time, who have to face the end, who cannot escape the past, who need a present to stand upon. Each of the modes of time has its peculiar mystery, each of them carries its peculiar anxiety. Each of them drives us to an ultimate question. There is *one* answer to these questions – the eternal. There is *one* power that surpasses the all-consuming power of time – the eternal: he who was and is and is to come, the beginning and the end. He gives us forgiveness for what has passed. He gives us courage for what is to come. He gives us rest in his eternal Presence.

PART THREE

THE CHALLENGE TO MAN

*

12. Do not be Conformed

Do not be conformed to this aeon, but be transformed
by the renewal of your mind.

ROMANS 12:2

'Do not be conformed.' This warning of Paul is significant for all periods of history. It is urgently needed in
our period. It applies to each of us, to our civilization, to
mankind as a whole. It has many facets because of the
many things to which one may be conformed. But there
is *one* all-embracing thing to which the apostle does not
want us to be conformed – this aeon. Instead of being
conformed to this aeon he wants us to be transformed by
the coming aeon, the state of renewal of our world and
of ourselves. Not conformity, but transformation – that
is what Paul says in the words of our text.

Our period has experienced many revolutionary transformations. The older ones amongst us remember them,
often because they have suffered under them in their
early lives. Today, both old and young are reacting
against revolutions and further transformations of the
world in which they have settled down. A mood of conservatism permeates large sections of mankind and certainly the people in our Western civilization. This is
natural and, as such, need not be a matter of concern.
But it must become a matter of concern and be chal-
lenged if conservatism becomes conformism, if the motto
of the new generation is – not transformation, but conformity. And this seems to be the case starting in school
days, when some teachers prevent individual friendships

because they threaten 'adjustments' (this fallacious principle of education), on through the years when the laws of the gang are more important for the youngster than all divine and human laws together; through the years in the institutes of higher learning where the standards imposed by older upon younger students allow the most extravagant behaviour; through the years of entrance into the world of adult competition and adaptation to the means of success; through the years of maturity and power and the fear of violating social, political and religious taboos and through the later years of one's life when religious propagandists use the fear of the approaching end to preach new forms of old religious conformisms. All these stages of our life are accompanied by incessant pressure from the communications media, one of whose functions is to produce conformity without letting people even become aware of it.

'Do not be conformed,' says the apostle, challenging, in these four words, the main trend of our whole present civilization. But he challenges more than this. He challenges you and me, whether we are caught by this civilization or not. We may be conformist not only if we agree but also if we disagree, and we may be nonconformist, not only if we disagree but also if we agree. They are words of warning for those of us who believe that their revolutionary thrust liberates us from the danger of conformism. For it does not. The revolutionary gang can be as conformist as the conservative group.

One can be conformed not only to a group, but also to oneself. The revolutionary can become used to himself as a revolutionary, so that he loses his freedom and becomes a conformist to revolution. In the same way one can be conformed to one's attitude of indifference or to cynicism or strictness or perfectionism, or one's own emptiness. One can be conformed to oneself and be prevented from transforming oneself by a renewal of the spirit. One can be non-conformist without love, unable to transform anything because one has not transformed oneself.

Why does Paul attack conformism? Why does he not call the Christian the perfectly adjusted man? Why does he not describe the Christian way as the way to a complete acceptance of the moral and religious standards of society? His thought is far from this, and certainly he could not have been called a good educator according to the criterion of 'adjustment'. But he knew why he rejected conformism. He knew that all conformism is a state of being conformed to *this* aeon. So let us try to understand the meaning of this strange assertion. This aeon means the state of things in which we are living, which is, according to Paul, a state of corruption. Being conformed to it, therefore, means to participate in its corruptedness. Where there is conformism there is acceptance of corruption, subjection to the present questionable state of things. In our English Bibles, the Greek word for aeon is translated 'world'. This is somehow misleading. When we speak of world we think of the universe. But the universe, including our earth and everything in it, is the product of incessant divine creativity here and now. It is good in its created form, and it is the place to which the kingdom of God shall come, as we pray in the Lord's Prayer. It is one of the most dangerous misunderstandings of the Christian message to deny this world and its created glory, and to direct our eyes to a superworld, unrelated to the original creation. The Bible speaks of a new heaven and a new earth in contrast to the old heaven and the old earth. And now we understand what Paul means when he speaks of conformity to this aeon: he means the untransformed old earth and the untransformed old heaven. He means the corrupted state of the universe, and especially of our universe – the universe of men – when he warns us not to become conformed to it. The attitude towards this aeon, towards ourselves, and towards our world that the apostle demands is threefold: judgment, resistance, and transformation.

But one may ask – must I judge, must I resist, must I transform everything I encounter? Ought we not to adjust to that which is born out of the wisdom of the ages, bestowed upon us by the generations before us through their experience and insights? Could one not say – be conformed to what has been proved to be good and noble and in conformity with the spirit of love? We must ask this question with great seriousness and self-criticism. But we must not forget that we are living in *this* aeon, under the control of its forms and ways, where the uncorrupted is mixed with corruption, and the acceptable with the unacceptable, and good with evil. This is what makes conformity so dangerous. If the corruption of this aeon were obvious, very few would be tempted to be conformed to it. Not many people, in reality or in literature, make a pact with the devil. But there are many who are lured by elements of goodness, indeed of real goodness, into a pact with this aeon, into the state of being conformed to it. And, certainly, there are strong arguments for accepting conformity. We all are conformed to the family into which we are born whether we want to be or not. Shall we try to be nonconformists in our family because conformism would mean adjustment to this aeon, to the corrupted state of things? Would that not bring much suffering to the other members of the family, and deprive us of the many blessings that an intimate and ordered family life can provide? How can the commandment to honour father and mother be combined with the warning of the apostle not to be conformed to this aeon? Jesus says: 'I have come to set a man against his father and a daughter against her mother and a daughter-in-law against her mother-in-law; and a man's foes will be those of his own household. He who loves father or mother more than me is not worthy of me; and he who loves son or daughter more than me is not worthy of me' (Matthew 10:35-37). These are the most radical statements of non-conformity. And even Paul's radicalism sounds conservative in comparison with them. It is astonishing that a faith based on words like these has been used throughout its history as a most successful instrument of conformity inside and outside family relations. How did this happen? Why is it the predominant attitude within Western culture even today, in spite of all the forces of disintegration? It is infinitely difficult to find the point where the state of being conformed contradicts love as it is manifest in the Christ. It would be easy to notice the point where separation becomes unavoidable, if our family, as often was the case in early Christianity, tried to make us reject the Christ and what he stands for. But this is not so today. Instead of it, the question of conforming or not conforming arises in innumerable small moments of our daily life. And in each moment, our answer is a risk, burdened with struggles within our own conscience. We do not know with certainty whether our non-conformity is based on a wrong conformity to ourselves or whether it is our awareness of corruption that drives us to non-conformity. And we do not know with certainty whether our non-resistance is based on a wrong surrender or whether it is an element of love and wisdom that keeps us conformed to the family group. We do not know these things with certainty, and we can act only at the risk of being wrong. But act we must. Most people try to avoid the risk by being conformed to the state of things into which they have been thrown by destiny. But those who have transformed our world risked wrong decisions. And the greater men they were, the more conscious were they of the risk. They did not cease to doubt in spite of the depth and the passion of their faith. For when they refused to be conformed to their families and traditions, they were not instead conformed to themselves, but were renewed in their own being and could thus renew other beings. And precisely for this reason they never became self-assured – they took upon themselves the risk of not being conformed and the anxiety and doubt and glory of this risk.

Paul demands this of every Christian. Every Christian must be strong enough to risk non-conformity, even in the radical sense that Jesus describes with respect to one's family. The situation in the family is an example, and more than an example. For all conformity is rooted in it. And resistance to conformity is first of all resistance to the family. But there are other larger groups in which we breathe the air of conformity day and night, and where resistance is sometimes easier, yet often more difficult, than in the family. I am thinking of educational, social, political, and religious groups. Let us look at each of them in the light of the apostolic word.

It seems that an educational group is least exposed to conformity. Those who are learning are usually more inclined to resist than to accept their teachers and what they are taught by them. And the teachers are chosen on the basis of the independence of their judgments and the freedom of their scholarly questioning. This seems to make the institutions of higher learning the representative places of non-conformity. I do not think that this is so, however. One only needs to ask the students two questions: don't you often build, out of your resistance to what you are taught, a new conformity of rebellion? And do you resist the group or gang to which you belong as strongly as you resist your teachers, or are you conquered by gang conformity and all the elements of this aeon, and the corruption implied in such conformity? How would you answer?

And one only needs to ask us teachers two questions: are we fully aware of our dependence on the intellectual fashion, especially when it receives social or political support? And have we perhaps become – and more so as we grow older – conformed to ourselves, to the fixed opinions on which we rest? I believe that all of us, both students and teachers, would fall silent if asked these questions. The institutions of higher learning have no monopoly of non-conformity. They need trans-

formation as much as any other group. They also belong
to *this* aeon.

Families and schools are part of those larger groups
that we call society and state. Much has been said and
written about the conformist influence that both of
them exercise on the way of life of each of us. I do not
need to repeat these often trenchant and distressing ob-
servations. I do not need to point to the pressures
exerted by suburban neighbourhoods, by the laws of
competition, by political threats, and by radio and TV,
filling our air waves twenty-four hours daily and im-
pressing our unconscious even as we try to resist them
in our conscious centre. Again, the difficulty in resisting
the conformist impact of all this is that it is not only evil
but also good. This mixture of good and evil in our
social and political forms makes every act of protest a
risk, not in the sense that we risk friendship, acknowledgment, or success – this we might be able to do – but
in the sense that we risk making the wrong decision and
losing ourselves in it. But even so, we must risk, as the
disciples to whom Jesus spoke had to risk. We must
risk 'being delivered up to councils, to stand before
governors and kings, to bear testimony before them, to
be put to death by friends and relatives, to be hated by
all'. This is certainly a picture of an extreme situation,
although it has happened in our century to many people.
Most of us will probably never have to face such grave
decisions. But in our daily life, in dealing with society
and state, we have to face social tribunals that accuse us
and may condemn us, because we are not conformed to
their way of life. The picture of extreme non-conformity
that Jesus paints includes all the small acts of non-
conformity that we must perform in our daily life. Do
not be conformed to the society group to which you
belong. Do not be conformed to those who have political
power over you, even if you obey them. But work for
their transformation.

Many churchmen would perhaps agree with this. But they would resist, if one applied the warning of the apostle to the Church itself. But we must do so. The conformism that threatened Jesus most effectively and brought him to death was the religious conformism of his time. And the situation was and is not different in the Church. For the Christian churches also belong to this aeon, although they witness to the coming aeon and represent the coming aeon in time and space. They share in the corruption of this aeon, its mixture of good and evil. And their history is a continuous witness to their corruption. Therefore, Paul's warning against being conformed is also valid for the Church. But is it possible, one may ask, to escape conformity if one belongs to a group that is united by a common creed, by rituals, by ethical standards, by old traditions and regular acts of common devotion? Can you adhere to a church and *not* be conformed? Indeed, there were non-conformist churches. But were they not non-conformist for only one historic moment, and then conformist themselves, like those from whom they separated? These are serious questions, especially for Protestants whose church came into existence through a protest against the conformity of the ruling church. I do not hesitate to state that one may have to resist being conformed even in the church community. Certainly, such an act also involves a risk. One may be in error. But it must be done. For it may represent the divine protest against everything human, even the highest forms of religion. A church in which this divine protest does not find a human voice through which it can speak has become conformed to this aeon. Here we see what non-conformity ultimately is – the resistance to idolatry, to making ultimates of ourselves and our world, our civilization and our church. And this resistance is the most difficult thing demanded of a man. It is so difficult that the prophets in the Old and New Testament, and the reformers, and the leaders of the struggle against idolatry in the history of religion as a whole, when called to fight the conformity to this aeon, tried to escape this task. It is almost too difficult for human beings. It is not too difficult to become a critic and rebel. But it is hard not to be conformed to anything, not even to oneself, and to pronounce the divine judgment against idolatry, not so much because the courageous act may lead to suffering and martyrdom, but because of the risk of failure. It is hard because something in our conscience, a feeling of guilt, tries to prevent us from becoming non-conformist.

But even this feeling of guilt we must take upon ourselves. He who risks and fails can be forgiven. He who never risks and never fails is a failure in his whole being. He is not forgiven because he does not feel that he needs forgiveness. Therefore, dare to be not conformed to this aeon, but transform courageously first in yourselves, then in your world – in the spirit and the power of love.

13. Be Strong

Be watchful, stand firm in your faith, be courageous, be strong. Let all that you do be done in love.

I CORINTHIANS 16:13-14

I

Out of this well-known passage, I chose two words on which I want you to centre your attention in this hour – be strong! They are surrounded in our text by other qualities that make strength possible – watchfulness, faith, courage, love. All together, they describe the strong Christian personality.

How can we attain strength? This is a question asked in all ages of man's life and in all periods of human history. It is a question asked with passion and despair in our time, and most impatiently by those who are no longer children and not yet adults.

In our text Paul uses the word 'be' several times: 'be strong', he says to the Corinthians. We easily slip over it. But it should arrest our attention as fully as, and perhaps, even more than, the main words of our text. For the word 'be' contains in its two letters the whole riddle of the relation of man to God.

Paul does not ask of the Christians in Corinth something that is strange to them. He asks them to be what they are, Christian personalities. All the imperatives he uses are descriptions of something that is, before they are demands for what ought to be. Be what you are — that is the only thing one can ask of any being. One cannot ask of a being to be something it was not before. It is as if life in all its forms desires to be asked, to receive demands. But no life can receive demands for something which it is not. It wants to be asked to become what it is and nothing else. This seems surprising, but a little thought shows us that it is true.

We know that one cannot ask fruits from thorns, or grain from weeds, or water from a dry fountain, or love from a cold heart, or courage from a cowardly mind, or strength from a weak life. If we ask such things from beings who do not have them, we are foolish; and either they will laugh at us or condemn us as unjust and hostile towards them. We can ask of anything or anyone only to bring forth what he has, to become what he is. Out of what is given to us, we can act. Receiving precedes acting.

'Be strong,' says Paul. He says it to those who have received strength as he himself received strength when the power of a new reality grasped him. Now some of us will ask — 'what about us who feel that we have *not* received, and that we do not have faith and courage and strength and love? We are wanting in all these, so the commanding "be" of Paul is not said to us. Or if it is said to us we remain unconcerned or become hostile towards him who says it. We are not strong, so nobody should ask us to be strong! We are weak. Shall we re-

main weak? Shall we fall into resignation, and become
cynical about your demands? They may be for others.
They are not for us.' I hear many people, more than we
imagine, saying this. I hear whole classes of young
people speaking thus. I hear many individuals in older
generations repeating these words.

And I do not find any consolation in the Bible. There
is the parable of the different soils on which the seed of
the divine message falls and of which only *one* brings
fruit. There is the word of the many who are called and
few who are elected. There is the terrifying, realistic
statement of Jesus that those to whom much is given
will receive more, and that from those to whom little is
given, even this will be taken away. There is the contrast
between those who are born of light and have become its
children and those who are born out of darkness and
have become its children. There is a parable of the man
as clay which cannot revolt against God the potter, no
matter what the potter does to the clay. *We* would like
to revolt, when we hear this. But if we look around us
into the lives of men we are forced to say – 'So it is, the
Bible is right!' We would like to say in good democratic
phrasing – 'Everyone has a God-given chance to reach
fulfilment, but not everybody uses it. Some do, some do
not. Both have their ultimate destiny in their own
hands.' We would like that to be so. But we cannot
escape the truth that it *is not* so. The chances are *not*
even. There is only a limited number of human beings
to whom we can say – 'Be strong', because they are
strong already. And the only honest thing I could say
to the others, to whom many of us may belong, is –
'Accept that you are weak. Do not pretend that you are
strong. And perhaps if you dare to be what you are,
your weakness will become your strength. Accept that
you are weak' – that is what we should say to those who
are weak. 'Accept that you are a coward' – that is what
we should say to those who are cowardly. 'Accept that
you are wavering in the faith' – that is what we should

say to those who are not firm in it. And to those who do not love, we should say – 'Accept that you are not able to love.'

This sounds strange! But everyone who knows the human soul, and knows his own soul above all, will understand what is meant. He will understand that the first step in becoming strong is to acknowledge and accept his weakness. He who does so will cease to deceive himself by saying to himself – 'I have at least something of what the apostle demands. He can demand it from me, for somehow I have it.' There are people who could rightly speak so to themselves. Yet there are others for whom such a judgment would be a self-deception. To them we must say – 'Accept that you are weak; be honest towards yourselves.'

Let me say to those who are responsible for others, as parents, teachers, ministers, counsellors, friends : do not say the demanding 'be' to anybody without fear and hesitation. If you use it, you approach the mystery of the divine election and you may destroy a life by demanding something of a person that he is not!

II

All these insights lie behind the first thing Paul asks of the Christians – namely, that they be watchful. The strong being is strong only if he watches his strength, aware of the fact that there is weakness in his strength. There is a non-Christian in every Christian. There is a weak being in every strong one. There is cowardice in every courage, and unbelief in every faith, and hostility in every love. Watchfulness means that the Christian never can rest on his being a Christian, that he who is strong can never rely on his strength.

One can be strong by subjecting oneself to a strong discipline. By suppressing much in oneself one may become powerful in relation to others. It is often this type that is called a strong personality. And, certainly, strength without the ability to direct oneself is not

strength. But those who have this ability and are admired as strong personalities should be watchful: they
should watch whether their strength has weakness at its
basis, whether it excludes elements of life that constitute the richness and the glory of life. If they do not
watch their hidden weakness, it may flow forth as hatred
for those who affirm the abundance of life. This abundance they cannot endure, because it reveals the weakness on which their strength is built. In order to reassure
themselves, they force upon others the same restrictions
they have imposed on their own life. Their domineering
strength creates weakness in others. There is a profound
ambiguity about the strong Christian personality: Christianity could not live, society could not go on, without
them. But many other Christians, many persons, who
perhaps could have become strong themselves, are destroyed or reduced to mental weakness and often illness
by them. They are the bearers of Christianity and
society; but their victims among Christians and non-
Christians, beginning with their children, their wives or
their husbands, are numerous. Be watchful when you are
considered, or consider yourselves, strong. Be watchful,
and do not demand of those around you to be what you
are, and what they are not. You will destroy them by
your strength.

Those who are considered strong usually have a strong
conviction. They seem to do what Paul asks them to –
namely, to 'stand in the faith'. Everybody needs a place
to stand upon. Without a foundation no strength is possible. In the physical universe it is a place on the well-
grounded earth, as the Greeks said; no experience seems
more disturbing, even for the strongest minds, than the
shaking of the ground in an earthquake. In the social
universe it is the home – the home town and the home
country on which we stand; and from earliest times
those who lost their homeland were considered weakest
and most unprotected. What about the spiritual universe? Language is the place we stand on in the spiritual

universe. For out of the word by which we grasp our world and our own being all other spiritual creations grow : knowledge and the arts, social traditions and philosophical beliefs. The word gives man the strength to build a world above the given world. It makes him the ruler of nature, as in the paradise story : he becomes the ruler over other living beings by giving them names. He who is strong in the spiritual universe is strong in the power of the word. A profound insight into human strength and human weakness is expressed in the story of the tower of Babel. Mankind was strong as long as it was united in one language. Its strength impelled it to enter the heavenly sphere. But when God wanted to destroy man's self-elevation and reveal his weakness, he confused the *one* language so that people no longer understood each other. We are in a similar situation today. Our period is weak, because we can no longer speak to each other. Each one has his own language, and the word has lost its power. It has become shallow and confused. We have experienced earthquake and exile in the spiritual world.

Paul asks the Corinthians to stand on something that is deeper than the physical and social and spiritual universe, something that cannot be shaken, because all levels of the universe rest upon it, their divine ground. To stand on this ground is, in Paul's words, to stand in the faith. He, of course, thinks of the faith in the form in which he has brought it to the Corinthians. But in this faith, faith itself is present – namely, the standing on the ultimate ground below any shaking and changing ground. Breaking the way to this ground is the meaning of the appearance of the Christ. 'Stand firm in your faith' means – do not give up that faith that alone can make you ultimately strong, because it gives you the ultimate ground on which to stand. Standing firm in one's faith does not mean adhering to a set of beliefs; it does not require us to suppress doubts about Christian or other doctrines, but points to something which lies beyond doubt in the depth in which man's being and all being is rooted. To be aware of this ground, to live in it and out of it is ultimate strength. 'Be strong' and 'stand in the faith' are one and the same command. But remembering now the word 'be', some may reply – 'Then the demand to be strong is not for us, because we do not stand in any faith. Doubt or unbelief is our destiny, not faith. We know you are right, there is no strength where there is no faith. But we have neither. And if there is some strength in us, it is the strength of honesty, the unwillingness to submit to a faith that is not ours, either for conventional reasons, or because of our longing for strength, or because of being taken in by our contemporary emotion-arousing evangelists. Our strength is to resist and to reject strength that is born of dishonesty.' Some of the best minds of our time would speak thus. To them I answer: 'Your honesty proves your faith and therefore your honesty is your strength! You may not believe in anything that can be stated in doctrines or symbols. But you stand on the ultimate ground, you stand firm in your faith as long as you stand in honesty and take your doubt and your belief seriously without restriction. Become aware of the faith that you *have*, and you will find words for it, perhaps even Christian words. But with or without words, be strong; for you *are* strong.'

Strength, according to Paul's words, includes courage. For human strength is built on human anxiety. Insecurity takes many forms. One of the most dangerous is the experience of being split within ourselves. He who is united with himself is invincibly strong. But who is? We are all dominated by forces that conquer parts of our being and split our personality. We have not merely lost the power of the word; we also have lost the strength that is given with a united, centred personality. We are disrupted by compulsions, known formerly as demonic powers. And who can command a split personality – 'Be strong!' To which side of the personality can such a command be addressed? Yet, there is the possibility of something else. Healing power, coming ultimately from the ground on which we stand in the faith, can enter the personality and unite it in an act of courage. It is the courage that takes upon itself the anxiety of our disruptions. This courage is the innermost centre of faith. It dares to affirm our being, while simultaneously rejecting it. Out of this courage the greatest strength emerges. It is the strength that overcomes the powers splitting world and soul. Be courageous! Say Yes to yourselves in spite of the anxiety of the No.

So Paul finishes his description of the strong personality: a courageous, watchful hero, firm in faith, worthy of great praise. But that is just what Paul does not do. Instead, he says: 'Let all that you do be done in love.' The strength of the personality whom Paul has in mind is based on something beyond courage and faith and watchfulness. It is not the strength of a hero. It is the strength of him who surrenders the praise he could receive as a hero to the humility of love. We are all familiar with strong personalities, perhaps in our families, among friends, or in public life, whom we admire, but in whom we feel something is wanting. This something is love. They may be friendly and be willing to help. This they demand of themselves. But everything they demand of themselves they also demand of others. They use the word 'be' without hesitation. They become tyrants through personal strength. Without love he who is strong becomes a law for the weak. And the law makes those who are weak even weaker. It drives them into despair, or rebellion, or indifference. Strength without love destroys, first others, then itself. For love is not something that may or may not be added to strength in its fullest sense; it is an element of strength. One cannot be strong without love. For love is not an irrelevant emotion; it is the blood of life, the power of reunion of the separated. Strength without love leads to separation, to judgment, to control of the weak. Love reunites what is separated; it accepts what is judged; it participates in what is weak, as God participates in our weakness and gives us strength by his participation.

14. In Thinking be Mature

Brethren, do not be children in your thinking; be babes in evil, but in thinking be mature.

I CORINTHIANS 14:20

In thinking be mature! Such an admonition one would hardly expect in the context of apostolic writing. But here it is, appearing in the same letter of Paul in which he contrasts sharply the wisdom of the world with that foolishness of God that is wiser than the wisdom of men. And he points to the fact that not many wise men belong to the ranks of the congregation, but that God has chosen what is foolish in the world. Maturity on the basis of divine foolishness – this is hard to understand – not only for the first readers of the letter to the Corinthians, but for all generations of Christians and non-Christians in the history of Christianity. In some way, the whole problem of the possibility of Christian existence is implied in this combination of divine foolishness and human maturity. But perhaps it is not only the problem of the possibility of human existence as such – how to unite divine foolishness with human maturity. Certainly, it is as valid for everyone outside the Church as for those inside, when Paul says: 'Whoever of you imagines that he is wise with this world's wisdom must become a fool if he is really to be wise' (3:18).

It is not this foolishness that conflicts with maturity, but the state of spiritual infancy, the state of being a babe in thinking, unable to receive solid food, milk-fed only. Paul complains that even now the Corinthians are not ready for solid food, that they are still immature, as shown in their theological jealousies and quarrels, that they are still far away from the divine foolishness, which is what makes them immature.

What does it mean to be mature in thinking? We speak of maturity in scholarly education, tested by examinations and scientific work. In some countries the basic examination for higher education is called 'examination of maturity'. But are those who have passed and become students in a professional school really mature in thinking? Are their teachers mature in thinking? If maturity means having mastered one's professional field and being able to work creatively in it, the great scholar, the good teacher, and his best pupils, are mature. And most of us, then, who are gathered here today should be able to call ourselves mature. We should not need the admonition – be mature in thinking!

But we do need it, both those who live within the Christian tradition and those who are outside it. We are *not* mature in thinking, not even those among us who are called outstanding scholars within and beyond the Christian horizon. Our immaturity is our lack of divine foolishness.

It might be well first to consider those who feel at home within the churches. It seems that faithful and active members often feel more certain of their own maturity than do those who stand aside in criticism and doubt. But their belief witnesses to their immaturity. This sense of certainty is understandable, however, when one realizes that it stems from an institution that has matured through centuries in life and thought, and whose foundation is the picture of the most mature personal life, that of Jesus as the Christ, in whom, at the same time, divine foolishness is manifest in every moment. Belonging to this community gives the members a feeling of being mature themselves. But they are not and, as Protestants, we must add that not even their churches are. For who is mature?

A mature man is one who has reached his natural power in life and thought and is able to use it freely. Maturity in thinking does not mean reaching the end of one's thinking, but rather the state in which the human power of thought is at one's disposal. This is the state we are asked to attain, but this is where we always fall short – first, the Christians, and then those who question Christianity. The Christian churches and individuals often bury their power of thinking, because they believe that radical thought conflicts with the divine foolishness that underlies all wisdom. But this is not true, certainly not for biblical thinking. Radical thought conflicts with human foolishness, with spiritual infancy, with ignorance, superstition and intellectual dishonesty. It is the temptation of the churches in all generations to justify their human foolishness by calling it divine foolishness. This is their defence against becoming mature in thinking. But although Christianity is based on the message of the divine foolishness, it knows that, out of the acceptance of this message, mature thinking can grow courageously and abundantly. What prevents it from growing is that the guardians of the message, churches and individual Christians, imprison the divine foolishness in vessels and forms that are produced by a wisdom that is mixed with foolishness, as is all human wisdom. And if these forms and vessels are declared indestructible and unchangeable, the way to maturity in thinking is barred. For the decisive step to maturity is risking the break away from spiritual infancy with its protective traditions and guiding authorities. Without 'no' to authority, there is no maturity. This 'no' need not be rebellious, arrogant, or destructive. As long as it is so, it indicates immaturity by this very attitude.

The 'no' that leads to maturity can be, and basically always is, experienced in anxiety, in discouragement, in guilt feelings, and despairing inner struggles. For the infant spiritual state with its traditions and authorities is invested with the holiness of man's ultimate concern and gives spiritual security and primitive strength. It is hard to break away from it. And, certainly, the way to maturity in thinking is a difficult path. Much must be left behind : early dreams, poetic imaginations, cherished legends, favoured doctrines, accustomed laws and ritual traditions. Some of them must be restored on a deeper level, some must be given up. Despite this price, maturity can be gained – a manly, self-critical, convincing faith, not *produced* by reasoning, but *reasonable*, and at the same time rooted in the message of the divine foolishness, the ultimate source of wisdom. A Church that is able to show this way to its members, and to follow the path itself, has certainly reached maturity.

And now I want to turn to those who consider themselves to be outside the Church and feel indifferent towards it, or perhaps even critical, hostile or fanatical in their negation. For them, too, the word of the apostle is as valid as it is for the Church – be mature in thinking ! It is not difficult, nor worthwhile, to deal with the petty immaturities of the secular mind. It is challenging and worthwhile, however, to penetrate to the source of its basic immaturity and to apply Paul's admonition to those who believe that they are mature just *because* they consider themselves to be outside the Church. No representative of the Church should criticize them carelessly, as if speaking with the possession of maturity to those who are immature. Nor should a Church representative criticize the secular world before having subjected the Church to the same serious scrutiny. And if he cannot do this in both directions with love, he should refrain from doing it altogether.

It is for this reason that I prefer not to refute the attacks of the secular mind on the Church. The self-criticism of the Church, as shown before, goes deeper than could any such attack. Also, I do not want to criticize any of the creative activities of the secular mind, the sciences, the arts, social relations, technical activities, and politics. These disciplines have their own criteria and their leaders apply these criteria with severity, honesty and self-criticism. In all this the secular mind is mature and religion should never interfere with it, as mature science would never interfere with religious symbols, since they lie in another dimension of experience and reality. To discuss the existence or non-existence of God as a being alongside other beings betrays the utter immaturity on both sides. It betrays complete ignorance about the meaning and power of the divine.

The secular mind, however, encounters a basic impediment to reaching maturity in thinking. It turns away from the divine foolishness found in the ground of its wisdom, and this makes its wisdom, however successful in conquering the world, humanly foolish. 'Be mature in thinking' is said to the great scholar as urgently as to the ordinary member of a congregation. For possessing a perfect brain does not ensure maturity, nor does having a creative mind mean that one is mature. There is no maturity where the awareness of the divine foolishness is lacking. So then, what is meant by this apparent paradox?

It is born out of an experience that cuts through all other experiences, shaking them, turning them to a new direction, and raising them beyond themselves. It is the experience of something ultimate, inexhaustible in meaning, unapproachable in being, unconquerable in power. We may call it the holy, the eternal, the divine. It is beyond every name because it is present in everything that has a name, in you and in me. If we try to utter it, we speak of the unspeakable; yet we *must* speak of it. For it is nearer to us than our own self, and yet it is more removed from us than the farthest galaxies. Such experience is the most human of all experiences. One can cover it up, one can repress it, but never totally. It is effective in the restlessness of the heart, in the anxious question of one's own value, in the fear of losing the meaning of one's life, in the anxiety of emptiness, guilt, and of having to die. Myth, poetry, and the philosophy of mankind everywhere express this experience. They witness to things that are deeply buried in the human heart and in the depth of our world. But sometimes they break through the surface with eruptive power. No artist, philosopher, or scientist is mature who has never questioned himself and his experience as an artist, as a philosopher, or as a scientist. No mature scholar is humanly mature who has not asked the question of the meaning of his existence. A scholar who rightly takes nothing for granted in his scholarly work, but who takes his being as a scholar and his being as a man for granted is immature.

But if he is pressed hard by the question of his existence so that he cannot push it aside, he is ready to be grasped by divine foolishness. Even more, he is already grasped by it. He is driven out of the safe reasonableness of his daily life. He must face a depth in himself of which he was not aware before, a depth of dangers and promises, of darkness and expectations. And what he finds in himself he sees reflected in his world, a depth that was hidden to him before he found it in himself. Now he has become aware of it in others, in everything alive, in the whole universe. And if he receives answers to the questions awakened in him, he can listen to them, even if their grammar and their style sound ecstatic and paradoxical, measured by the language of daily life. Such answers, received, are what faith means. They sound like sacred foolishness, but are armed with the power of truth. If, however, they are brought to the level of ordinary reasonableness and attacked or defended on this level, they sound untrue, meaningless, absurd, whether accepted or rejected. The name of the language of divine foolishness and of the life that is created by it, is love. Love is life under the power of divine foolishness. It is ecstatic and paradoxical. It cuts through the ordinary ways of life, elevating them to a higher level. But if love is brought down to the level of moral reasonableness, and is attacked or defended on this basis, it becomes sentimental, utopian, and unreal.

The divine foolishness of thought and the divine foolishness of life are united in the symbol of Christmas: God *in* the infant, God *as* infant, anticipating and preparing the symbol of Good Friday – God *in* the condemned slave, God *as* the condemned slave. This certainly is ecstatic and paradoxical, and it should not be brought down to the level of a divine-human chemistry. But it should be understood and experienced as an expression of the divine foolishness that is the source of wisdom and the power of maturity. Be mature in thinking. Be mature in love!

15. On Wisdom

The fear of the Lord is the beginning of wisdom. And the awareness of the Holy is insight.

PROVERBS 9:10

I

It was a grave loss when the term 'wisdom' almost disappeared from Christian preaching and teaching. Of course, it is still used sometimes in both popular and philosophical language. But its original significance and power have vanished. It has been called 'the virtue of old age', which is of no concern to youth. It has almost become as ridiculous as the ancient word 'virtue' itself.

One speaks of experience, insight, knowledge; and indeed those are related to wisdom and often part of it. But none of them is wisdom itself. Wisdom is greater than these. It is one of the great things that profoundly concern every human being in every period of his conscious life. Wisdom is not bound to old age. It is found equally in the young. And there are fools at all ages of life. It is my hope in this hour to communicate the meaning and the greatness of wisdom, particularly to those who are young and who must make wise decisions about their lives.

To understand the meaning of wisdom we must see it in the breadth and depth in which it was seen by the man whose words are our lesson. There are many more words about the glory of wisdom, both in the Old and the New Testament. And there is praise of wisdom and passionate seeking for it in many religions. Wisdom is universally human. It is present in the spiritual life of all mankind. And it is present not only in all mankind, but in the universe itself. For the universe is created by the divine power in the presence of Wisdom. This is the vision of the author of the book of Proverbs and of the poet who wrote the book of Job. Wisdom was beside God before creation of the world. 'When he marked out the foundations of the earth, then I was beside him,' Wisdom says. 'When he gave to the wind its weight and meted out the waters by measure; when he made a decree for the rain and a way for the lightning of the thunder, he saw Wisdom then and studied her.' The meaning of these words is that God explores Wisdom, which is like an independent power beside him, and according to what he finds in her he forms the world. The universe in all its parts is the embodiment of wisdom.

This vision was confirmed for me a few weeks ago when I met some well-known astronomers, physicists and biologists, who passionately expressed their conviction that they increased the awareness of the eternal wisdom in the structure of the universe by increasing the knowledge of our world. They rejected a science that gives knowledge without wisdom and a theology that neglects the divine wisdom shining through man's knowledge of nature.

At the height of the Middle Ages in the thirteenth century, when methods of scientific research were first in-

troduced, a keen observer made the prophetic remark:
'Under the new method science will increase but wisdom will decrease.' Wisdom was for him the understanding of the principles which determine life and world. He
was right: science conquered wisdom; knowledge replaced insight. From century to century it has become
more and more evident that knowledge without wisdom produces external and internal self-destruction.

The health of the younger generation is demonstrated
by the fact that it has experienced and violently expressed the emptiness of knowledge without wisdom.
Those who feel dissatisfied with learning facts without
an understanding of their meaning, and those who feel
the emptiness of the possession of knowledge without
wisdom are most important in our academic and
national society. May they never cease to express this
feeling! May they force us, the older ones, to listen!
But we shall *only* listen, if contempt of knowledge and
scholarship does not colour their complaints; then we
shall try with all that is given to us to become their
helpers on the road to wisdom.

II

Wisdom is not easy to find. It remains a divine mystery
in spite of its presence in all parts of the universe.
Wherever wisdom has been praised in literature, its
mystery has been recognized. The book of Job asks:
'Where shall wisdom be and where is the place of understanding? Man does not know the way to it and it is not
found in the land of the living. The deep says: Not in
me and the sea says: not in me. It is hidden from the
eyes of all living and concealed from the birds of the
air; only abyss and death say: we have heard a rumour
of it with our ears.' This means that wisdom is not a
human possibility. The praise of wisdom is not a praise
of man and his power. Only abyss and death – the boundary line of human existence – point to wisdom, but
even they cannot give it. They have heard about it only

from a distance, the poet says. Wisdom is not a matter of intellectual power; rationality is not wisdom. Death says more about wisdom than life; but death does not have the answer.

Why is wisdom so hidden, although manifest in everything that is? It is because in everything that lives there are two forces at battle with each other – a creative force and a destructive one, both of which emanate from the same divine ground. As the book of Job says: 'With God is wisdom and might; he has counsel and understanding. If *he* tears down, none can rebuild, if *he* shuts a man in, none can open. Power and providence belong to him, he is behind deceiver and deceived; he strips statesmen of their wits and makes a fool of councillors . . . he will extend a nation to destroy it, he will enlarge a nation to enslave it . . . Should not his majesty cause you to shudder?' No one can doubt that this is the way life is, but our poet knows that behind all this is the mystery of divine wisdom. Wisdom is in both creation and destruction. This is the deepest insight the Old Testament reached. Without it the men of the New Testament would not have been able to endure the Cross of him whom they called the Christ. Without it Paul could not have broken into the words – 'O the depth of the riches and wisdom and knowledge of God', just after he had spoken with an aching heart of the rejection of his nation for the sake of the Gentiles. Wisdom and mystery do not exclude each other. It is wisdom to see wisdom in the mystery and the conflicts of life.

III

But now we ask – how can we possess such wisdom? In the book of Proverbs, Wisdom says – 'I was . . . rejoicing before him always, rejoicing in his inhabited world and delighting in the sons of men . . . and now, my sons, listen to me . . . he who finds me, finds life . . . but all who hate me love death.' To aspire to wisdom, or to despise it, is a matter of life and death. This could never be said of knowledge in the ordinary sense of the word. Those who know much do not have life because of their knowledge. And those who know little, and do not try to learn much, do not prove that they love death. Wisdom is a matter of life and death because it is more than knowledge. It can be united with knowledge, but it can also stand alone. It belongs to a dimension which cannot be reached by scholarly endeavour. It is insight into the meaning of one's life, into its conflicts and dangers, into its creative and destructive powers, and into the ground out of which it comes and to which it must return.

Therefore, the preachers of wisdom tell us that the first step in acquiring it is the fear of God and the awareness of the holy. Such words can easily be misunderstood. They do not command subjection to a god who arouses fear. Nor do they advise us to accept doctrines about him. Such a command and such advice would lead us straight away from wisdom and not towards it. But our text says that there cannot be wisdom without an encounter with the holy, with that which creates awe, and shakes the ordinary way of life and thought. Without the experience of awe in face of the mystery of life, there is no wisdom. Most removed from wisdom are not those who are driven by desire for pleasure or power, but those brilliant minds who have never encountered the holy, who are without awe and know nothing sacred, but who are able to conceal their ultimate emptiness by the brilliant performances of their intellect. No wisdom shines through the knowledge of many men who play a great role in our academic and non-academic society. The wisdom at which God looks in the creation of the world, the eternal wisdom, calls them fools.

He who has encountered the mystery of life has reached the source of wisdom. In encountering it with awe and longing, he experiences the infinite distance of his being from that which is the ground of his being. He experiences the limits of his being, his finitude in face of the infinite. He learns that acceptance of one's limits is the decisive step towards wisdom. The fool rebels against the limits set by his finitude. He wants to be unlimited in power and knowledge. He who is wise accepts his finitude. He knows that he is not God.

To this all mankind's literature about wisdom is a witness. Wisdom is the acknowledgment of limits; it is the awareness of the right measure in all relations of life. But in saying this, one must protect wisdom against a dangerous distortion of its meaning – the confusion of wisdom with a philistine avoidance of radical decisions, with clever compromises and shrewd calculations of usefulness, all of which is far removed from the wisdom that comes upon us in the awe-inspiring encounter with the holy. We need only look at the great figures in whom men of all periods and cultures recognized wisdom, the men who gave new laws to their nations, the teachers of new ways of life for continents, the men who withdrew to the deserts of nature and the deserts of the soul to return with abundance. None of them kept to the middle of the road; they had to find new roads in the wilderness. You cannot find wisdom in those who always avoid radical decisions and adjust themselves to the given situation, the conformists who have decided to accept the accepted opinions of society. Wisdom loves the children of men, but she prefers those who come through foolishness to wisdom, and dislikes those who keep themselves equally distant from foolishness and from wisdom. They are the real fools, she would say, because they were never shaken by an encounter with the mystery of life, and therefore never able to see the unity of creation and destruction in the working of the divine wisdom. In those, however, who have recognized this working of wisdom, and become wise by it, artificial limits are broken down, often with great pain, and the real limits, the true measures, are found. That is what happens when wisdom comes to men.

Therefore, wisdom comes to all men, and not only to those who are learned. You can find quiet and often great wisdom among very simple people. There may be wise ones among those with whom you live, and those with whom you work, and those whom you encounter as strangers in crowded streets. There is wisdom in mothers and lonely women, in children and adolescents, in shepherds and cab-drivers; and sometimes there is wisdom also in those who have much learning. They all prove their wisdom by creatively accepting their limits and their finitude.

But who can accept his finitude? Who can accept that he is threatened by the vicissitudes of life, by sickness, by death? Who can take into himself the deep anxiety of being alive without covering it up with pleasure and activity? In the book of Job, which powerfully expresses the mystery of life, the question is asked and an answer given that is not an answer in the ordinary sense of the word. Only in the confrontation with eternal wisdom in all its darkness and inexhaustible depth can man accept the misery of his finitude, even if it is as extreme as Job's. In our encounter with the holy, facing with awe the ultimate mystery of life, we experience a dimension of life that gives us the courage and the strength to accept our limits and to become wise through this acceptance.

IV

In the literature about wisdom many special rules for our daily life are given. The Bible is full of them. But they are all connected with each other in that they all are ruled by the encounter with the holy. In all of them wisdom appears as the acceptance of one's finitude. In the light of this insight, let us look at expressions of wisdom in our daily life. Wisdom is present in parents who know the limits of their authority and so do not become idols first and crushed idols later. Wisdom is present in children who recognize the limits of their independence and do not despise the heritage they have received and on which they live, even in rebelling against their parents. Wisdom is present in teachers who are aware of their limits in dealing both with truth and with their pupils, and who ask themselves again and again whether wisdom shines through the knowledge they communicate. Wisdom is present in students who question the principles behind whatever they are studying and its meaning for their lives; wise are they who realize both the necessity and the limits of all learning and the superiority of love over knowledge. Wise are those men who are aware of their emotional and intellectual limitations as men in their encounter with women. Wise are those women who acknowledge their finitude by accepting the man as the other pole of a common humanity. And both show wisdom if they accept each other without anxiety, without hostility, without abuse, without dishonesty, but in the power of a love which is rooted in the awareness of the eternal.

The greatest wisdom is needed where it is most painful to accept our finitude – in our failures, errors, and the guilt acquired by our foolishness. It is hard for us to accept failure, perhaps total failure, in our work. It is difficult to acknowledge error, perhaps in our judgment of those we love in friendship or marriage. It is humanly impossible to confess guilt to oneself or to others without looking at that which is greater than our heart, the eternal. He who possesses this wisdom, this painfully acquired wisdom, knows that nothing can separate him from the eternal wisdom which is with God, neither failure nor error nor guilt.

Our final wisdom is to accept our foolishness and to look at the place in history in which wisdom itself appeared in the garb of utter foolishness, the Cross of the Christ. Here the wisdom that is eternally with God, that is present in the universe, and that loves the children of man, appears in fullness. And in those who look at it and receive it, faith and wisdom become one.

16. In Everything Give Thanks

Rejoice always, pray without ceasing, in everything
give thanks.

I THESSALONIANS 5:16-18

I

'In everything give thanks.' These are the words that we
want to make the centre of our meditation. Do we need
this admonition? Is not 'thank you' one of the most frequently employed phrases in our language? We use it
constantly for the smallest services performed, for a
friendly word, for every word praising ourselves and our
acts. We use it whether we are grateful or not. Saying
thanks has become a form that is employed with or without feeling. We must therefore say it with great emphasis and in strong words when we really mean it. Anyone who observes the behaviour of religious groups –
ministers as well as laymen – is familiar with their inclination to say 'thank you' to God almost as often as to
their neighbours. It seems important, therefore, to ask
the reason for this behaviour towards men and God.
Why do we thank? What does it mean to give thanks
and to receive thanks? Can this event of our daily life,
and of daily religious life, be understood in its depth and
elevated above automatic superficiality? If this proves
possible, we might discover that the simple 'thank you'
can tell us much about what we are within ourselves
and our world. We might find that one of the most used
and abused words of our language can become a revelation of the deeper levels of our being.

Saying thanks is not always merely a form of social
intercourse. Often we are driven by real emotion; we
are almost compelled to thank someone, whether he

expects it or not. And sometimes our emotion over-powers us and we say thanks in words much too strong for the gift we have received. This is not dishonest. It is honestly felt in the moment. But soon afterwards we feel somehow empty, somehow ashamed – not much perhaps, but a little! Occasionally, it also happens that for one moment we feel abundantly grateful. But since, for external reasons, we have no immediate opportunity to express our thanks, we forget it and it never reaches the one to whom we are grateful. Of the ten lepers who were healed by Jesus probably none was without abun-dant gratefulness to Jesus, but only one returned from the priests to whom they had shown themselves to thank Jesus. And Jesus was astonished and disappointed.

Not only are we driven by a deep emotion to give thanks, but we also have a profound need to receive thanks when we have given ourselves in either a large or small way. When thanks is not forthcoming, we feel a kind of emptiness, a vacuum in that place of our inner being which the words or acts of thanks should fill. But just as we feel ashamed when we use too strong an expression of gratitude, we feel uneasy when we receive exaggerated thanks. There is no place in us to receive it and we refuse to accept it, whether we say so or not. It is always difficult to receive thanks without some resistance. The American reply, 'you are wel-come', or the German reply, 'please', expresses the re-fusal to accept thanks without hesitation. 'Don't men-tion it' is the simplest expression of this resistance to accept thanks, which, however, we *do* accept at the same time.

These uncertainties in the simple act of giving or re-ceiving thanks teach us something about our relation-ship to others, and our predicament. In every act of giving or receiving thanks, we accept or reject someone, and we are accepted or rejected by someone. Such ac-ceptance or rejection is not always noticed, either by ourselves or by the other. If we are sensitive, we often feel it and react with joy or sorrow, with shame or pride, and mostly with mixtures of these emotions. A simple 'thank you' can be an attack or a withdrawal. It can be the expression of giving someone a place within us, or a successful way of protecting ourselves from someone's attempt to find a place within us. A word of thanks can be a complete rejection of him whom we thank, or it can be the unlocking of his and our heart. But probably in most cases, it is a polite form of stating that he whom we thank does not really concern us very much.

The fiftieth Psalm says: 'Offer to God a sacrifice of thanksgiving,' and 'He who brings thanksgiving as his sacrifice honours me.' Here the original meaning of thanks shines through. Giving thanks is a sacrifice. Here the literal meaning of 'thanksgiving' is felt. Thanks is expressed through sacrificial acts. Valuable objects are removed from their ordinary use and given to the gods. It is an acknowledgment of the fact that man did not create himself, that nothing belongs to him, that naked he was thrown into the world and naked he will be thrust out of it. What he has is given to him. In the act of sacrifice he expresses his awareness of this destiny. He gives a part of what is given to him, but something that is ultimately not his own. In sacrificing thanks he witnesses to his finitude, to his transitoriness. Every serious giving of thanks implies a sacrifice, an acknowledgment of one's finitude. A man who is able to thank seriously accepts that he is creature and, in acceptance, he is religious even though he denies religion. And a man who is able to accept honest thanks without embarrassment is mature. He knows his own finitude as well as that of the other, and he knows that the mutual sacrifice of thanks confirms that he and the other are creatures.

II

In all expressions of gratitude towards others, the object

of our thanks is usually visible. We know at least *whom* to thank, and what for, although we often do not know *how* to thank. But there is also gratefulness that is, so to speak, without a definite object towards which to turn. This is so not because we do not know the object, but because there is no object. We are simply grateful. Thankfulness has taken hold of us, not because something special has happened to us, but just because we *are*, because we participate in the glory and power of being. It is a mood of joy, but more than a mood, more than a transitory emotion. It is a state of being. And it is more than joy. It is a joy that includes the feeling that it is given, that we cannot accept it without bringing some sacrifice – namely, the sacrifice of thanks. But there is no one to whom we can bring it. And so it remains within us, a state of silent gratefulness.

You may ask – why is not God the object of such gratefulness? But that would not describe what happens in many men – Christians as well as non-Christians, believers and unbelievers. They are grateful. But they do not turn to God with direct words of prayer. It is just gratefulness in itself which fills them. If they were told to turn to *God* in a prayer of thanks, they would feel that such a command would destroy their spontaneous experience of gratefulness. How shall we judge this state of mind that many of us may have experienced at some time? Shall we say it is thanks without God, and therefore not real thanks? Shall we say that in this state we are like the pagans of whom Paul says that 'although they knew God, they did not honour him as God or give thanks to him'? Certainly not. The abundance of a grateful heart gives honour to God even if it does not turn to him in words. An unbeliever who is filled with thanks for his very being has ceased to be an unbeliever. His rejoicing is a spontaneous obedience to the exhortation of our text – 'Rejoice always!'

It is then possible to understand our text when it says – 'Rejoice *always*, pray *without ceasing*, give thanks in

everything!' It certainly does not mean – 'never feel
sorrow, day and night use words of prayer and thanks!'
Jesus characterizes this way of imposing oneself on God
as a perversion of religion. Then what do these ex-
hortations mean? They mean just what we called the
state of silent gratefulness, that may or may not express itself in prayers. We are not to tell God without
ceasing what we wish him to do for us or what he has
done for us. We are asked to rise to God always and in
all things. He shall never be absent from our awareness. Certainly, he is creatively present in everyone in
every moment whether we are aware of it or not. But
when we are in the state of silent gratefulness, we *are*
aware of his presence. We experience an elevation of
life that we cannot attain by profuse words of thanks,
but that can happen to us if we are open to it. A man
was once asked if he prayed. He answered, 'always and
never'. He meant that he was aware of the divine presence, but only rarely did he use words of prayer and
thanks to express this awareness. He did not belong to
those who do not thank because they are never aware
of the presence of the divine, and he did not belong to
those who believe that being aware of God means
addressing him continuously. He thought that words
directed towards God must come out of a state of elevation, of silent gratefulness. Another man was asked
whether he believed in God, and he answered, 'I don't
know, but if something very good happens to me, I need
someone to whom I can give thanks.' He experienced
the state of grateful elevation, like the first, but he was
driven to express his feelings in direct words of thanks.
He had need of another to whom to sacrifice. Both men
describe the fact that thanking God is a state of elevation
without words and also a desire to sacrifice in words
directed to God.

In these two ways of thanking, two kinds of relationship to God are manifest: he is the other to whom I
speak in words of thanks; and he is above myself and

every other, the one to whom I cannot speak, but who can make himself manifest to me through a state of silent gratefulness.

One of the great and liberating experiences of the Protestant reformers was their realization that our relation to God is not dependent on the continuous repetition of words of prayer and thanks directed to God, on sacrifices and other rituals but rather on the serenity and joy that is the answer to the good news that we are accepted by God because of his seeking us, and not because of anything we can do or say in and outside the church.

III

For what do we give thanks? Are there limits to giving thanks? Our text says – 'In *everything* give thanks!' This does not mean – give thanks for everything, but give thanks in every situation! There are no limits to situations in which to thank, but there are limits to things for which thanks can be expressed. This is again a question the answer to which might lead us into a new understanding of the human predicament.

In the letter to 1 Timothy 4:4 we read – 'For everything created by God is good and nothing is to be rejected if it is received with thanksgiving; for then it is consecrated by the word of God and prayer.' In these words, thanksgiving receives a new function. It consecrates everything created by God. Thanksgiving is consecration; it transfers something that belongs to the secular world into the sphere of the holy. It is not transformed, as superstition in and outside Christian beliefs would transform it, but it is elevated to represent the divine. It has become a bearer of grace. Therefore, we say 'grace' when we give thanks for our daily food, and thus consecrate it. Every created thing can be a bearer of holiness, an object of thanks, of consecration. There are no limits to thanksgiving in this respect. We can give thanks for our bodily and our mental powers, for the darkness of our unconscious as well as for the light of our consciousness, for the abundance of nature and the creations of history, for everything that is and manifests its power of being. We can give thanks for all these despite their rejection by those who, through world-hating asceticism and fanatical puritanism, blaspheme the God of creation. Everything for which we can give thanks with a good conscience is consecrated by our thanks. This is not merely a profound theological insight; it is also a practical standard in situations where we are uncertain about accepting or rejecting something. If, after having accepted it, we can give thanks for it, we witness to its goodness as created. In giving thanks seriously, we consecrate it to the holy source of being from which it comes. And we even take the risk that Protestant Christians must take – that their conscience may fall into error and consecrate something which should be rejected.

There are no limits to giving thanks in the whole of creation. But are there not limits in our life? Can we honestly give thanks for the frustrations, accidents, and diseases that strike us? We *cannot* in the moment when they take hold of us. Here is one of the many situations where piety can degenerate into dishonesty. For we rightly resist such evils. We want to remove them; we are often angry against our destiny and its divine ground. And there are depths of suffering, bodily and mental, in which even the question of thanking or not thanking does not appear. Out of the depths the psalmist *cries* to God; he does *not* thank him. This is honest, realistic – a realism born out of the awareness of the divine presence. And I believe that at some time in our lives all of us have had experiences that were nothing but evil when they happened, but that became good later and the object of honest thanks.

And we also cannot give thanks for our own acts that make us guilty or for those that make us good. We cannot give thanks for that which makes us guilty; and

sometimes things for which we have given thanks become evil by our own guilt. Nor should we give thanks
for that in us which makes us good. The thanks of the
Pharisee for his good works is an outstanding example
of thanks which should *not* be given. In reality, he does
not thank *God* when he is thankful for his own goodness, but thanks himself. How many of us thank ourselves when we give thanks to God! But one *cannot*
thank oneself, because the sacrifice of thanking, if given
to oneself, ceases to be a sacrifice. Thanks to oneself is
not thanks, even when prayers of thanks to God are
hidden ways of thanking oneself, as after work well
done or success achieved by great toil.

It is a surprising experience to read the Bible, and
especially the last third of the book of Psalms, with the
question of thanks in one's mind. One discovers that the
praise of God fills page after page in which the misery of
all men, including the writers of these books, is also most
drastically described. Reading them, we feel as though
we walk in another realm. We cannot reproduce in ourselves what is happening to these men. (*We* are not in
the mood of praising, hardly in the mood of thanking.)
We look into the depth of our predicament and do not
see much reason for praise and thanks. And if we think
that it is our duty to God to thank him, or if we participate in church services that include praise and thanks,
we do not feel that we have truly expressed our state
of mind. Although this experience is not invariable, it is
a predominant trait of our religious situation. It expresses itself in the messages of the best of our present
preachers and theologians. It is a dominating theme of
our great poets and philosophers. We are not called to
pass judgment on these men. We have a part in them.
They express *us* as they express themselves. And we
should thank those who do it seriously, and often out of
deep spiritual suffering.

The difference between our situation and that of
former periods becomes visible when we read about the

passion and intensity with which the members of the early Church gave thanks for the gift of the Christian message in a world of pagan glory, disintegration and despair. Is the same passion and intensity in us when we give thanks for the gift of God which is the Christ and his Church? Who can honestly answer 'yes'?

And do we not sense the same differences when we read how the fighters of the Reformation thanked God for the rediscovery of the good news of the divine acceptance of those who are sinners? Is the same infinite concern in us as was in them? Who can honestly answer 'yes'? We must therefore be grateful to those who express our present situation honestly.

But there is one consolation: we are not separated from the ever active presence of God, and we can become aware of it in every moment. Our hearts can become filled with praise and thanks without the use of words; and sometimes we may also find these words of praise and thanks. But this is not the first step, and often not even the last. Let us not follow those who use what is called 'the present religious revival' to force us back into forms of prayer and thanks that we cannot honestly accept, or that produce joy and thanks through self-suggestion. But let us keep ourselves open to the power that carries our life in every moment, that is here and now, that comes to us through nature and through the message of Jesus as the Christ. May we keep open to it, so that we may be filled with silent gratefulness for the power of being which is in us. And then perhaps words of thanks, words of sacrifice and consecration, may come to our tongues, so that we again may give thanks in truth and honesty.

PRAYER

Almighty God! We raise our hearts to thee in praise and thanks. For we are not by ourselves and nothing is ours except what thou hast given us. We are finite; we did not bring anything into our world; we shall not take anything out of our world. Thou hast given us the life which is ours so long as it is thy will. We thank thee that we have being, that we share in the inexhaustible riches of life, in the smallest and in the largest part of it. We praise thee when we feel strength in body and soul. We give thanks to thee when joy fills our hearts. We are gratefully aware of thy presence, be it in silence, or in words.

Awaken us to such awareness when our daily life hides thy presence from us, when we forget how near thou art to us in every place and in every moment, nearer than any other being is to us, nearer than we are to ourselves. Let us not turn away from thy giving and creating presence to the things thou hast given us. Let us not forget the creator behind the creation. Keep us always ready for the sacrifice of giving thanks to thee.

Thine is what we are and have. We consecrate it to thee. Receive our thanks when we say grace, consecrating our food and with it all that we receive in our daily life. Prevent us from using empty words and forms when we give thanks to thee. Save us from routine and mere convention when we dare to speak to thee.

We thank thee when we look back at our life, be it long or short, for all that we have met in it. And we thank thee not only for what we have loved and for what gave us pleasure, but also for what brought us disappointment, pain and suffering, because we now know that it helped us to fulfil that for which we were born. And if new disappointments and new suffering takes hold of us and words of thanks die on our tongues, remind us that a day may come when we will be ready to give thanks for the dark road on which thou hast led us.

Our words of thanks are poor and often we cannot find words at all. There are days and months and years in which we were or are still unable to speak to thee. Give us the power, at such times, to keep our hearts open to the abundance of life, and in silent gratefulness, to experience thy unchanging, eternal presence. Take the silent sacrifice of a heart when words of thanks become rare in us. Accept our silent gratefulness and keep our hearts and our minds open to thee always!

We thank thee for what thou hast given to this nation far beyond the gifts to any other nation! Let us remain thankful for it, so that we may overcome the dangers of shallowness of life and emptiness of heart that threaten our people. Prevent us from turning thy gifts into causes of injury and self-destruction. Let a grateful mind protect us against national and personal disintegration. Turn us to thee, the source of our being, eternal God! *Amen.*

THE NEW BEING

PART ONE

THE NEW BEING AS LOVE

*

1. 'To Whom Much Is Forgiven...'

One of the Pharisees asked him to eat with him, and
he went into the Pharisee's house, and sat at table.
And behold, a woman of the city, who was a sinner,
when she learned that he was sitting at table in the
Pharisee's house, brought an alabaster flask of ointment, and standing behind him at his feet, weeping,
she began to wet his feet with her tears, and wiped
them with the hair of her head, and kissed his feet,
and anointed them with the ointment. Now when the
Pharisee who had invited him saw it, he said to himself, 'If this man were a prophet, he would have
known who and what sort of woman this is who is
touching him, for she is a sinner.' And Jesus answering
said to him, 'Simon, I have something to say to you.'
And he answered, 'What is it, Teacher?' 'A certain
creditor had two debtors; one owed five hundred
denarii, and the other fifty. When they could not pay,
he forgave them both. Now which of them will love
him more?' Simon answered, 'The one, I suppose, to
whom he forgave more.' And he said to him, 'You
have judged rightly.' Then turning toward the woman
he said to Simon, 'Do you see this woman? I entered
your house, you gave me no water for my feet, but
she has wet my feet with her tears and wiped them
with her hair. You gave me no kiss, but from the time
I came in she has not ceased to kiss my feet. You did
not anoint my head with oil, but she has anointed my
feet with ointment. Therefore, I tell you, her sins,
which are many, are forgiven, for she loved much;
but he who is forgiven little, loves little.'

LUKE 7:36-47

The story we have read, like the parable of the Prodigal Son, is peculiar to the Gospel of Luke. In this story, as in the parable, someone who is considered to be a great sinner, by others as well as by herself, is contrasted with people who are considered to be genuinely righteous. In both cases Jesus is on the side of the sinner, and therefore he is criticized, indirectly in the parable by the righteous elder son, and directly in our story by the righteous Pharisee.

We should not diminish the significance of this attitude of Jesus by asserting that, after all, the sinners were not as sinful, nor the righteous as righteous as they were judged to be by themselves and by others. Nothing like this is indicated in the story or in the parable. The sinners, one a whore and the other the companion of whores, are not excused by ethical arguments which would remove the seriousness of the moral demand. They are not excused by sociological explanations which would remove their personal responsibility; nor by an analysis of their unconscious motives which would remove the significance of their conscious decisions; nor by man's universal predicament which would remove their personal guilt. They are called sinners, simply and without restriction. This does not mean that Jesus and the New Testament writers are unaware of the psychological and sociological factors which determine human existence. They are keenly aware of the universal and inescapable dominion of sin over this world, of the demonic splits in the souls of people, which produce insanity and bodily destruction; of the economic and spiritual misery of the masses. But their awareness of these factors, which have become so decisive for *our* description of man's predicament, does not prevent them from calling the sinners sinners. Understanding does not replace judging. We understand more and better than many generations before us. But our immensely increased insight into the conditions of human existence should not undercut our courage to call wrong wrong. In story and parable the sinners are seriously called sinners.

And in the same way the righteous ones are seriously called righteous. We would miss the spirit of our story if we tried to show that the righteous ones are not truly righteous. The elder son in the parable did what he was supposed to do. He does not feel that he has done anything wrong nor does his father tell him so. His righteousness is not questioned – nor is the righteousness of Simon, the Pharisee. His lack of love toward Jesus is not reproached as a lack of righteousness, but it is derived from the fact that little is forgiven to him.

Such righteousness is not easy to attain. Much self-control, hard discipline, and continuous self-observation are needed. Therefore, we should not despise the righteous ones. In the traditional Christian view, the Pharisees have become representatives of everything evil, but in their time they were the pious and morally zealous ones. Their conflict with Jesus was not simply a conflict between right and wrong; it was, above all, the conflict between an old and sacred tradition and a new reality which was breaking into it and depriving it of ultimate significance. It was not only a moral conflict – it was also a tragic one, foreshadowing the tragic conflict between Christianity and Judaism in all succeeding generations, including our own. The Pharisees – and this we should not forget – were the guardians of the law of God in their time.

The Pharisees can be compared with other groups of righteous ones. We can compare them, for example, with a group that has played a tremendous role in the history of this country – the Puritans. The name itself, like the name Pharisee, indicates separation from the impurities of the world. The Puritans would certainly have judged the attitude of Jesus to the whore as Simon the Pharisee did. And we should not condemn them for this judgment nor distort their picture in our loose talk about them. Like the Pharisees, they were the guardians of the law of God in their time.

And what about our time? It has been said, and not without justification, that the Protestant churches have become middle-class churches because of the way in which their members interpret Christianity, practically as well as theoretically. Such criticism points to their active adherence to their churches, to their well-established morality, to their charitable works. They are righteous – they would have been called so by Jesus. And certainly they would have joined Simon the Pharisee and the Puritans in criticizing the attitude of Jesus towards the woman in our story. And again I say, we should not condemn them for this. They take their religious and moral obligations seriously. They, like the Pharisees and the Puritans, are guardians of the law of God in our time.

The sinners are seriously called sinners and the righteous ones are seriously called righteous. Only if this is clearly seen can the depth and the revolutionary power of Jesus' attitude be understood. He takes the side of the sinner against the righteous although he does not doubt the validity of the law, the guardians of which the righteous are. Here we approach a mystery which is the mystery of the Christian message itself, in its paradoxical depth and in its shaking and liberating power. And we can hope only to catch a glimpse of it in attempting to interpret our story.

Simon the Pharisee is shocked by the attitude of Jesus to the whore. He receives the answer that the sinners have greater love than the righteous ones because more is forgiven them. It is *not* the love of the woman that brings her forgiveness, but it is the forgiveness she has received that creates her love. By her love she shows that much has been forgiven her, while the lack of love in the Pharisee shows that little has been forgiven him.

Jesus does not forgive the woman, but he declares that she *is* forgiven. Her state of mind, her ecstasy of love, show that something has happened to her. And nothing greater can happen to a human being than that he is forgiven. For forgiveness means reconciliation in spite of estrangement; it means reunion in spite of hostility; it means acceptance of those who are unacceptable, and it means reception of those who are rejected.

Forgiveness is unconditional or it is not forgiveness at all. Forgiveness has the character of 'in spite of', but the righteous ones give it the character of 'because'. The sinners, however, cannot do this. They cannot transform the divine 'in spite of' into a human 'because'. They cannot show facts, because of which they must be forgiven. God's forgiveness is unconditional. There is no condition whatsoever in man which would make him worthy of forgiveness. If forgiveness were conditional, conditioned by man, no one could be accepted and no one could accept himself. We know that this is our situation, but we loathe to face it. It is too great as a gift and too humiliating as a judgment. We want to contribute something, and if we have learned that we cannot contribute anything positive, then we try at least to contribute something negative: the pain of self-accusation and self-rejection. And then we read our story and the parable of the Prodigal Son as if they said: these sinners were forgiven *because* they humiliated themselves and confessed that they were unacceptable; because they suffered about their sinful predicament they were made worthy of forgiveness. But this reading of the story is a misreading, and a dangerous one. If that were the way to our reconciliation with God, we should have to produce within ourselves the feeling of unworthiness, the pain of self-rejection, the anxiety and despair of guilt. There are many Christians who try this in order to show God and themselves that they deserve acceptance. They perform an emotional work of self-punishment after they have realized that their other good works do not help them. But emotional works do not help either. God's forgiveness is independent of anything we do, even of self-accusation and self-humiliation. If this were not so, how could we ever be certain that our self-rejection is serious enough to deserve forgiveness? Forgiveness creates repentance – this is declared in our story and this is the experience of those who have been forgiven.

The woman in Simon's house comes to Jesus because she *was* forgiven. We do not know exactly what drove her to Jesus. And if we knew, we should certainly find that it was a mixture of motives – spiritual desire as well as natural attraction, the power of the prophet as well as the impression of the human personality. Our story does not psychoanalyse the woman, but neither does it deny human motives which could be psychoanalysed. Human motives are always ambiguous. The divine forgiveness cuts into these ambiguities, but it does not demand that they become unambiguous before forgiveness can be given. If this were demanded, then forgiveness would never occur. The description of the woman's behaviour shows clearly the ambiguities of her motives. Nevertheless, she *is* accepted.

There is no condition for forgiveness. But forgiveness could not come to us if we were not asking for it and receiving it. Forgiveness is an answer, the divine answer, to the question implied in our existence. An answer is answer only for him who has asked, who is aware of the question. This awareness cannot be fabricated. It may be in a hidden place in our souls, covered by many strata of righteousness. It may reach our consciousness in certain moments. Or, day by day, it may fill our conscious life as well as its unconscious depths and drive us to the question to which forgiveness is the answer.

In the minds of many people the word 'forgiveness' has connotations which completely contradict the way Jesus deals with the woman in our story. Many of us think of solemn acts of pardon, of release from punishment, in other words, of another act of righteousness by the righteous ones. But genuine forgiveness is participation, reunion overcoming the powers of estrangement. And only because this is so, does forgiveness make love possible. We cannot love unless we have accepted forgiveness, and the deeper our experience of forgiveness is, the greater is our love. We cannot love where we feel rejected, even if the rejection is done in righteousness. We are hostile towards that to which we belong and by which we feel judged, even if the judgment is not expressed in words.

As long as we feel rejected by him, we cannot love God. He appears to us as an oppressive power, as he who gives laws according to his pleasure, who judges according to his commandments, who condemns according to his wrath. But if we have received and accepted the message that he *is* reconciled, everything changes. Like a fiery stream his healing power enters into us; we can affirm him and with him our own being and the others from whom we were estranged, and life as a whole. Then we realize that his love is the law of our own being, and that it is the law of reuniting love. And we understand that what we have experienced as oppression and judgment and wrath is in reality the working of love, which tries to destroy within us everything which is against love. To love this love is to love God. Theologians have questioned whether man is able to have love towards God; they have replaced love by obedience. But they are refuted by our story. They teach a theology for the righteous ones but not a theology for the sinners. He who is forgiven knows what it means to love God.

And he who loves God is also able to accept life and to love it. This is not the same as to love God. For many pious people in all generations the love of God is the other side of the hatred for life. And there is much hostility towards life in all of us, even in those who have completely surrendered to life. Our hostility towards life is manifested in cynicism and disgust, in bitterness and continuous accusations against life. We feel rejected by life, not so much because of its objective darkness and threats and horrors, but because of our estrangement from its power and meaning. He who is reunited with God, the creative Ground of life, the power of life in everything that lives, is reunited with life. He feels accepted by it and he can love it. He understands that the greater love is, the greater the estrangement which is conquered by it. In metaphorical language I should like to say to those who feel deeply their hostility towards life: life accepts you; life loves you as a separated part of itself; life wants to reunite you with itself, even when it seems to destroy you.

There is a section of life which is nearer to us than any other and often the most estranged from us: other human beings. We all know about the regions of the human soul in which things look quite different from the way they look on its benevolent surface. In these regions we can find hidden hostilities against those with whom we are in love. We can find envy and torturing doubt about whether we are really accepted by them. And this hostility and anxiety about being rejected by those who are nearest to us can hide itself under the various forms of love: friendship, sensual love, conjugal and family love. But if we have experienced ultimate acceptance this anxiety is conquered, though not removed. We can love without being sure of the answering love of the other one. For we know that he himself is longing for our acceptance as we are longing for his, and that in the light of ultimate acceptance we are united.

He who is accepted ultimately can also accept himself. Being forgiven and being able to accept oneself are one and the same thing. No one can accept himself who does not feel that he is accepted by the power of acceptance which is greater than he, greater than his friends and counsellors and psychological helpers. They may point to the power of acceptance, and it is the function of the minister to do so. But he and the others also need the power of acceptance which is greater than they. The woman in our story could never have overcome her disgust at her own being without finding this power working through Jesus, who told her with authority, 'You *are* forgiven.' Thus, she experienced, at least in *one* ecstatic moment of her life, the power which reunited her with herself and gave her the possibility of loving even her own destiny.

This happened to her in one great moment. And in this she is no exception. Decisive spiritual experiences have the character of a breakthrough. In the midst of our futile attempts to make ourselves worthy, in our despair about the inescapable failure of these attempts, we are suddenly grasped by the certainty that we are forgiven, and the fire of love begins to burn. That is the greatest experience anyone can have. It may not happen often, but when it does happen, it decides and transforms everything.

And now let us look once more at those whom we have described as the righteous ones. They are really righteous, but since little is forgiven them, they love little. And this is their unrighteousness. It does not lie on the moral level, just as the unrighteousness of Job did not lie on the moral level where his friends sought for it in vain. It lies on the level of the encounter with ultimate reality; with the God who vindicates Job's righteousness against the attacks of his friends, with the God who defends himself against the attacks of Job and his ultimate unrighteousness. The righteousness of the righteous ones is hard and self-assured. They, too, want forgiveness, but they believe that they do not need much of it. And so their righteous actions are warmed by very little love. They could not have helped the woman in our story, and they cannot help us, even if we admire them. Why do children turn from their righteous parents and husbands from their righteous wives, and vice versa? Why do Christians turn away from their righteous pastors? Why do people turn away from righteous neighbourhoods? Why do many turn away from righteous Christianity and from the Jesus it paints and the God it proclaims?

Why do they turn to those who are not considered to be the righteous ones? Often, certainly, it is because they want to escape judgment. But more often it is because they seek a love which is rooted in forgiveness, and this the righteous ones cannot give. Many of those to whom they turn cannot give it either. Jesus gave it to the woman who was utterly unacceptable. The Church would be more the Church of Christ than it is now if it did the same, if it joined Jesus and not Simon in its encounter with those who are rightly judged unacceptable. Each of us who strives for righteousness would be more Christian if more were forgiven him, if he loved more and if he could better resist the temptation to present himself as acceptable to God by his own righteousness.

2. *The New Being*

For neither circumcision counts for anything nor uncircumcision, but a new creation.

GALATIANS 6:15

If I were asked to sum up the Christian message for our time in two words, I would say with Paul: It is the message of a 'new creation'. We have read something of the new creation in Paul's second letter to the Corinthians. Let me repeat one of his sentences in the words of an exact translation: 'If anyone is in union with Christ he is a new being; the old state of things has passed away; there is a new state of things.' Christianity is the message of the new creation, the New Being, the new reality which has appeared with the appearance of Jesus who for this reason, and just for this reason, is called the Christ. For the Christ, the Messiah, the selected and anointed one is he who brings the new state of things.

We all live in the old state of things, and the question

asked of us by our text is whether we *also* participate in
the new state of things. We belong to the old creation,
and the demand made upon us by Christianity is that
we *also* participate in the new creation. We have known
ourselves in our old being, and we shall ask ourselves
in this hour whether we also have experienced something of a New Being in ourselves.

What is this New Being? Paul answers first by saying
what it is *not*. It is neither circumcision, nor uncircumcision he says. For Paul and for the readers of his letter
this meant something very definite. It meant that neither
to be a Jew nor to be a pagan is ultimately important;
that only one thing counts, namely, the union with him
in whom the new reality is present. Circumcision or uncircumcision – what does that mean for *us*? It can also
mean something very definite, but at the same time
something very universal. It means that no religion as
such produces the New Being. Circumcision is a religious
rite, observed by the Jews; sacrifices are religious rites,
observed by the pagans; baptism is a religious rite, observed by the Christians. All these rites do not matter –
only a new creation. And since these rites stand, in the
words of Paul, for the whole religion to which they belong, we can say: no religion matters – only a new state
of things. Let us think about this striking assertion of
Paul. What it says first is that Christianity is more than
a religion; it is the message of a new creation. Christianity as a religion is not important – it is like circumcision or like uncircumcision: no more, no less! Are we
able even to imagine the consequences of the apostolic
pronouncement for our situation? Christianity in the
present world encounters several forms of circumcision
and uncircumcision. Circumcision can stand today for
everything called religion, uncircumcision for everything called secular, but making half-religious claims.
There are the great religions beside Christianity, Hin-
duism, Buddhism, Islam and the remnants of classical
Judaism; they have their myths and their rites – so to

speak their 'circumcision' – which gives each of them their distinction. There are the secular movements: fascism and communism, secular humanism, and ethical idealism. They try to avoid myths and rites; they represent, so to speak, uncircumcision. Nevertheless, they also claim ultimate truth and demand complete devotion. How shall Christianity face them? Shall Christianity tell them: come to us, we are a better religion, our kind of circumcision or uncircumcision is higher than yours? Shall we praise Christianity, our way of life, the religious as well as the secular? Shall we make of the Christian message a success story, and tell them, like advertisers: try it with us, and you will see how important Christianity is for everybody? Some missionaries and some ministers and some Christian laymen use these methods. They show a total misunderstanding of Christianity. The apostle who was a missionary and a minister and a layman all at once says something different. He says: no particular religion matters, neither ours nor yours. But I want to tell you that something has happened that matters, something that judges you and me, your religion and my religion. A new creation has occurred, a New Being has appeared; and we are all asked to participate in it. And so we should say to the pagans and Jews wherever we meet them: don't compare your religion and our religion, your rites and our rites, your prophets and our prophets, your priests and our priests, the pious amongst you, and the pious amongst us. All this is of no avail! And above all don't think that we want to convert you to English or American Christianity, to the religion of the Western world. We do not want to convert you to us, not even to the best of us. This would be of no avail. We want only to show you something we have seen and to tell you something we have heard: that in the midst of the old creation there is a new creation and that this new creation is manifest in Jesus who is called the Christ.

And when we meet fascists and communists, scientific humanists and ethical idealists, we should say to them: don't boast too much that you have no rites and myths, that you are free from superstitions, that you are perfectly reasonable, uncircumcised in every sense. In the first place, you also have your rites and myths, your bit of circumcision; they are even very important to you. But if you were completely free from them you would have no reason to point to your uncircumcision. It is of no avail. Don't think that we want to convert you away from your secular state to a religious state, that we want to make you religious and members of a very high religion, the Christian, and of a very great denomination within it, namely, our own. This would be of no avail. We want only to communicate to you an experience we have had that here and there in the world and now and then in ourselves is a new creation, usually hidden, but sometimes manifest, and certainly manifest in Jesus who is called the Christ.

This is the way we should speak to all those outside the Christian realm, whether they are religious or secular. And we should not be too worried about the Christian religion, about the state of the churches, about membership and doctrines, about institutions and ministers, about sermons and sacraments. This is circumcision; and the lack of it, the secularization which today is spreading all over the world is uncircumcision. Both are nothing, of no importance, if the ultimate question is asked, the question of a new reality. *This* question, however, is of infinite importance. We should worry more about it than about anything else between heaven and earth. The new creation – this is our ultimate concern; this should be our infinite passion – the infinite passion of every human being. This matters; this alone matters ultimately. In comparison with it everything else, even religion or non-religion, even Christianity or non-Christianity, matters very little – and ultimately nothing.

And now let me boast for a moment about the fact that we are Christians and let us become fools by boasting, as Paul called himself when he started boasting. It is the greatness of Christianity that it can see how small it is. The importance of being a Christian is that we can stand the insight that it is of no importance. It is the spiritual power of religion that he who is religious can fearlessly look at the vanity of religion. It is the maturest fruit of Christian understanding to understand that Christianity, as such, is of no avail. This is boasting, not personal boasting, but boasting about Christianity. As boasting it is foolishness. But as boasting about the fact that there is nothing to boast about, it is wisdom and maturity. Having as having not – this is the right attitude toward everything great and wonderful in life, even religion and Christianity. But it is not the right attitude toward the new creation. Toward it the right attitude is passionate and infinite longing.

And now we ask again: what is this New Being? The New Being is not something that simply takes the place of the Old Being. But it is a renewal of the Old which has been corrupted, distorted, split and almost destroyed. But not wholly destroyed. Salvation does not destroy creation; but it transforms the old creation into a new one. Therefore we can speak of the New in terms of a re-newal: the threefold 're', namely, re-conciliation, re-union, re-surrection.

In his letter, Paul combines new creation with reconciliation. The message of reconciliation is: be reconciled to God. Cease to be hostile to him, for he is never hostile to you. The message of reconciliation is not that God needs to be reconciled. How could he be? Since he is the source and power of reconciliation, who could reconcile him? Pagans and Jews and Christians – all of us have tried and are trying to reconcile him by rites and sacraments, by prayers and services, by moral behaviour and works of charity. But if we try this, if we try to give something to him, to show good deeds which may appease him, we fail. It is never enough; we never can satisfy him because there is an infinite demand upon us. And since we cannot appease him, we grow hostile toward him. Have you ever noticed how much hostility against God dwells in the depths of the good and honest people, in those who excel in works of charity, in piety and religious zeal? This cannot be otherwise; for one is hostile, consciously or unconsciously, toward those by whom one feels rejected. Everybody is in this predicament, whether he calls that which rejects him 'God', or 'nature', or 'destiny', or 'social conditions'. Everybody carries a hostility toward the existence into which he has been thrown, toward the hidden powers which determine his life and that of the universe, toward that which makes him guilty and which threatens him with destruction because he has become guilty. We all feel rejected and hostile toward what has rejected us. We all try to appease it and in failing, we become more hostile. This happens often unnoticed by ourselves. But there are two symptoms which we hardly can avoid noticing: the hostility against ourselves and the hostility against others. One speaks so often of pride and arrogance and self-certainty and complacency in people. But this is, in most cases, the superficial level of their being. Below this, in a deeper level, there is self-rejection, disgust, and even hatred of one's self. Be reconciled to God; that means at the same time, be reconciled to ourselves. But we are not; we try to appease ourselves. We try to make ourselves more acceptable to our own judgment and, when we fail, we grow more hostile toward ourselves. And he who feels rejected by God and who rejects himself feels also rejected by the others. As he grows hostile toward destiny and hostile toward himself, he also grows hostile toward other men. If we are often horrified by the unconscious or conscious hostility people betray toward us or about our own hostility toward people whom we believe we love, let us not forget: they feel rejected by us; we feel rejected by them. They tried hard to make themselves acceptable to us, and they failed. We tried hard to make ourselves acceptable to them, and we failed. And their and our hostility grew. Be reconciled with God – that means, at the same time, be reconciled with the others! But it does *not* mean to try to reconcile the others, as it does not mean try to reconcile yourselves. Try to reconcile God. You will fail. This is the message: a new reality has appeared in which you *are* reconciled. To enter the New Being we do not need to show anything. We must only be open to be grasped by it, although we have nothing to show.

Being reconciled – that is the first mark of the new reality. And being reunited is its second mark. Reconciliation makes reunion possible. The new creation is the reality in which the separated is reunited. The New Being is manifest in the Christ because in him the separation never overcame the unity between him and God, between him and mankind, between him and himself. This gives his picture in the Gospels its overwhelming and inexhaustible power. In him we look at a human life that maintained the union in spite of everything that drove him into separation. He represents and mediates the power of the New Being because he represents and mediates the power of an undisrupted union. Where the new reality appears one feels united with God, the ground and meaning of one's existence. One has what has been called the love of one's destiny, and what, today, we might call the courage to take upon ourselves our own anxiety. Then one has the astonishing experience of feeling reunited with one's self, not in pride and false self-satisfaction, but in a deep self-acceptance. One accepts one's self as something which is eternally important, eternally loved, eternally accepted. The disgust at one's self, the hatred of one's self has disappeared. There is a centre, a direction, a meaning for life. All healing – bodily and mental – creates this reunion of one's self with one's self. Where there is real healing, *there* is the New Being, the new creation. But real healing is not where only a part of body or mind is reunited with the whole, but where the whole itself, our whole being, our whole personality is united with itself. The new creation is healing creation because it creates reunion with oneself. And it creates reunion with the others. Nothing is more distinctive of the Old Being than the separation of man from man. Nothing is more passionately demanded than social healing, than the New Being within history and human relationships. Religion and Christianity are under strong accusation that they have not brought reunion, into human history. Who could deny the truth of this challenge? Nevertheless, mankind still lives; and it could not live any more if the power of separation had not been permanently conquered by the power of reunion, of healing, of the new creation. Where one is grasped by a human face as human, although one has to overcome personal distaste, or racial strangeness, or national conflicts, or the differences of sex, of age, of beauty, of strength, of knowledge, and all the other innumerable causes of separation – there new creation happens! Mankind lives because this happens again and again. And if the Church which is the assembly of God has an ultimate significance, this is its significance: that here the reunion of man to man is pronounced and confessed and realized, even if in fragments and weaknesses and distortions. The Church is the place where the reunion of man with man is an actual event, though the Church of God is permanently betrayed by the Christian churches. But, although betrayed and expelled, the new creation saves and preserves that by which it is betrayed and expelled: churches, mankind and history.

The Church, like all its members, relapses from the New into the Old Being. Therefore, the third mark of the new creation is re-surrection. The word 'resurrection' has for many people the connotation of dead bodies leaving their graves or other fanciful images. But resurrection means the victory of the new state of things, the New Being born out of the death of the Old. Resurrection is not an event that might happen in some remote future, but it is the power of the New Being to create life out of death, here and now, today and tomorrow. Where there is a New Being, *there* is resurrection, namely, the creation into eternity out of every moment of time. The Old Being has the mark of disintegration and death. The New Being puts a new mark over the old one. Out of disintegration and death something is born of eternal significance. That which is immersed in dissolution emerges in a new creation. Resurrection happens *now*, or it does not happen at all. It happens in us and around us, in soul and history, in nature and universe.

Reconciliation, reunion, resurrection – this is the new creation, the New Being, the new state of things. Do we participate in it? The message of Christianity is not Christianity, but a new reality. A new state of things has appeared, it still appears; it is hidden and visible, it is there and it is here. Accept it, enter into it, let it grasp you.

3. The Power of Love

When the Son of man comes in his glory, and all the angels with him, then he will sit on his glorious throne. Before him will be gathered all the nations, and he will separate them from one another as a shepherd separates the sheep from the goats, and he will place the sheep on his right hand, but the goats at the left. Then the King will say to those at his right hand, 'Come, O blessed of my Father, inherit the kingdom prepared for you from the foundation of the world; for I was hungry and you gave me food, I was thirsty and you gave me drink, I was a stranger and you welcomed me, I was naked, and you clothed me, I was sick and you visited me, I was in prison and you came to me.' Then the righteous will answer him, 'Lord, when did we see thee hungry and feed thee, or thirsty and give thee

drink? And when did we see thee a stranger and wel-
come thee, or naked and clothe thee? And when
did we see thee sick or in prison and visit thee?' And
the King will answer them. 'Truly. I say to you, as
you did it to one of these my brethren, you did it to
me.'

MATTHEW 25:31-40

So we know and believe the love God has for us. God is
love, and he who abides in love abides in God, and God
abides in him.

I JOHN 4:16

A new commandment I give to you, that you love one
another; even as I have loved you, that you also love
one another. By this all men will know that you are
my disciples, if you have love for one another.

JOHN 13:34-35

After two thousand years are we still able to realize
what it means to say, 'God *is* love'? The writer of the
First Epistle of John certainly knew what he wrote, for
he drew the consequences: 'He who abides in love
abides in God, and God abides in him.' God's abiding in
us, making us his dwelling place, is the same thing as our
abiding in love, as our having love as the sphere of our
habitation. God and love are not two realities; they are
one. God's Being is the being of love and God's infinite
power of Being is the infinite power of love. Therefore,
he who professes devotion to God *may* abide in God if he
abides in love, or he may not abide in God if he does not
abide in love. And he who does not speak of God may
abide in him if he is abiding in love. And since the manifestation of God as love is his manifestation in Jesus the
Christ, Jesus can say that many of those who do not
know him, belong to him, and that many of those who
confess their allegiance to him do not belong to him.
The criterion, the only ultimate criterion, is love. For
God is love, and the divine love is triumphantly manifest

in Christ the Crucified.

Let me tell you the story of a woman who died a few years ago and whose life was spent abiding in love, although she rarely, if ever, used the name of God, and though she would have been surprised had someone told her that she belonged to him who judges all men, because he is love and love is the only criterion of his judgment.

Her name was Elsa Brandström, the daughter of a former Swedish ambassador to Russia. But her name in the mouths and hearts of hundreds of thousands of prisoners of war during World War I was the Angel of Siberia. She was an irrefutable, living witness to the truth that love is the ultimate power of Being, even in a century which belongs to the darkest, most destructive and cruel of all centuries since the dawn of mankind.

At the beginning of World War I, when Elsa Brandström was twenty-four-years old, she looked out of the window of the Swedish Embassy in what was then St Petersburg and saw the German prisoners of war being driven through the streets on their way to Siberia. From that moment on she could no longer endure the splendour of the diplomatic life of which, up to then, she had been a beautiful and vigorous centre. She became a nurse and began visiting the prison camps. There she saw unspeakable horrors and she, a girl of twenty-four, began, almost alone, the fight of love against cruelty, and she prevailed. She had to fight against the resistance and suspicion of the authorities and she prevailed. She had to fight against the brutality and lawlessness of the prison guards and she prevailed. She had to fight against cold, hunger, dirt and illness, against the conditions of an undeveloped country and a destructive war, and she prevailed. Love gave her wisdom with innocence, and daring with foresight. And whenever she appeared despair was conquered and sorrow healed. She visited the hungry and gave them food. She saw the thirsty and gave them to drink. She welcomed the strangers, clothed the naked and strengthened the sick. She herself fell ill and was imprisoned, but God was abiding in her. The irresistible power of love was with her.

And she never ceased to be driven by this power. After the war she initiated a great work for the orphans of German and Russian prisoners of war. The sight of her among these children whose sole ever-shining sun she was, must have been a decisive religious impression for many people. With the coming of the Nazis, she and her husband were forced to leave Germany and come to this country. Here she became the helper of innumerable European refugees, and for ten years I was able personally to observe the creative genius of her love. We never had a theological conversation. It was unnecessary. She made God transparent in every moment. For God, who is love, was abiding in her and she in him. She aroused the love of millions towards herself and towards that for which she was transparent – the God who is love. On her deathbed she received a delegate from the king and people of Sweden, representing innumerable people all over Europe, assuring her that she would never be forgotten by those to whom she had given back the meaning of their lives.

It is a rare gift to meet a human being in whom love – and this means God – is so overwhelmingly manifest. It undercuts theological arrogance as well as pious isolation. It is more than justice and it is greater than faith and hope. It is the presence of God himself. For God is love. And in every moment of genuine love we are dwelling in God and God in us.

4. The Golden Rule

God is love, and he who abides in love abides in God and God abides in him. No man has ever seen God. If

we love one another, God abides in us and his love is
perfected in us . . .

                                    I JOHN 4:16, 12

So whatever you wish that men would do to you, do so
to them; for this is the law and the prophets.

                                    MATTHEW 7:12

Recently I have had to think about the relation of love
to justice. And it occurred to me that among the words
of Jesus there is a statement of what is called the 'Golden
Rule'. The Golden Rule was well known to Jews and
Greeks, although mostly in a negative form: what you
do NOT want that men should do to you, do NOT so to
them. Certainly, the positive form is richer in meaning
and nearer to love, but it is not love. It is calculating
justice. How, then, is it related to love? How does it fit
the message of the kingdom of God and the justice of
the kingdom as expressed in the Sermon on the Mount
where the Golden Rule appears?

Let us think of an ordinary day in our life and of
occasions for the application of the Golden Rule. We
meet each other in the morning, we expect a friendly
face or word and we are ready to give it although our
minds are full of anxious anticipation of the burdens
of the day. Somebody wants a part of our limited time,
we give it, having asked somebody else to give us a part
of his time. We need help and we give it if we are asked,
although it includes sacrifice. We are frank with others,
expecting that they will be frank with us even if it
hurts. We are fair to those who fight against us, expecting fairness from them. We participate in the sorrows
of our neighbours, certain that they will participate in
ours. All this can happen in one day. All this is the
Golden Rule. And if somebody has violated this rule,
consciously or unconsciously, we are willing to forgive
as we hope to be forgiven. It is not astonishing that for
many people the Golden Rule is considered as the real
content of Christianity. It is not surprising that in the

name of the Golden Rule criticism is suppressed, independent action discouraged, serious problems avoided.
It is even understandable that statesmen ask other
nations to behave towards their own nation according
to the Golden Rule. And does not Jesus himself say that
the Golden Rule is the law and the prophets?

But we know that this is not the answer of the New
Testament. The great commandment as Jesus repeats it
and the descriptions of love in Paul and John's tremendous assertion that God *is* love, infinitely transcend the
Golden Rule. It must be transcended, for it does not tell
us what we *should* wish that men would do to us. We
wish to have freedom from heavy duties. We are ready
to give the same freedom to others. But someone who
loves us refuses to give it to us, and he himself refuses
to ask us for it. And if he did, we should refuse to give
it to him because it would reduce our growth and violate
the law of love. We wish to receive a fortune which
makes us secure and independent. We would be ready
to give a fortune to a friend who asks us for it, if we
had it. But in both cases love would be violated. For the
gift would ruin us and him. We want to be forgiven and
we are ready to do the same. But perhaps it is in both
cases an escape from the seriousness of a personal problem, and therefore against love.

The measure of what we shall do to men cannot be
our wishes about what they shall do to us. For our
wishes express not only our right but also our wrong,
and our foolishness more than our wisdom. This is the
limit of the Golden Rule. This is the limit of calculating
justice. Only for him who knows what he *should* wish
and who actually wishes it, is the Golden Rule ultimately
valid. Only love can transform calculating justice into
creative justice. Love makes justice just. Justice without
love is always injustice because it does not do justice to
the other one, nor to oneself, nor to the situation in
which we meet. For the other one and I and we together in this moment in this place are a unique, un-

repeatable occasion, calling for a unique unrepeatable act of uniting love. If this call is not heard by listening love, if it is not obeyed by the creative genius of love, injustice is done. And this is true even of oneself. He who loves listens to the call of his own innermost centre and obeys this call and does justice to his own being.

For love does not remove, it establishes justice. It does not add something to what justice does but it shows justice what to do. It makes the Golden Rule possible. For we do not speak for a love which swallows justice. This would result in chaos and extinction. But we speak for a love in which justice is the form and structure of love. We speak for a love which respects the claim of the other one to be acknowledged as what he is, and the claim of ourselves to be acknowledged as what we are, above all as persons. Only distorted love, which is a cover for hostility or self-disgust, denies that which love unites. Love makes justice just. The divine love is justifying love accepting and fulfilling him who, according to calculating justice, must be rejected. The justification of him who is unjust is the fulfilment of God's creative justice, and of his reuniting love.

5. On Healing (I)

And he called to him his twelve disciples and gave them authority over unclean spirits, to cast them out, and to heal every disease and every infirmity.

MATTHEW 10:1

Recently I spent three months in Germany and what I saw was a sick people, sick as a whole and sick as individuals. Their faces are shaped by burdens too heavy to be carried, by sorrows too deep to be forgotten. And what their faces expressed, their words confirmed: tales of horror, stories of pain and despair, anxieties dwelling in their blood, confusions and self-contradictions disturbing their minds. And if you look deeper into them you find guilt-feeling, sometimes expressed, mostly repressed. For it hides itself under passionate denials of guilt, under self-excuse and accusations of others, under a mixture of hostility and humility, of self-pity and self-hate. The nation is split externally by the split between East and West which divides all mankind politically and spiritually. And the nation is split internally. Old hostilities are smouldering, new hostilities are growing, and there is no peace. A sick nation.

But within this nation I found people who were healthy, not because the sickness was not written in their faces also. But something else was in them, a healing power, making them whole in spite of their disruption, making them serene in spite of their sorrow, making them examples for all of us, examples of what could and should happen to us!

To us? But are we not a healthy nation? That certainly is what you believe when you return from Germany and Europe to this country! The faces of most people are shaped by smiles and not by tears. There is benevolence towards each other and even towards enemies. People here are willing to admit their shortcomings such as discrimination, exploitation, destructive competition. They are used to acting spontaneously and not under compulsions imposed on them by tyrants or conquerors, or what is even more difficult, imposed on them by newspapers, radios and public opinion polls, these tyrants of modern democracy. A healthy nation!

But we read that in this nation almost 40 per cent of all those young men who are rejected by the Armed Services are unacceptable because of mental disturbances and maladjustments. And we hear that of all illnesses mental illness is by far the most widespread in this country. What does this mean? It is a symptom of serious danger for our health. There may be something in the structure of our institutions which produces illness in more and more people. It may, for instance, be that the unlimited, ruthless competition which deprives everybody of a feeling of security, makes many in our healthy nation sick; not only those who are unsuccessful in competition, but also those who are most successful. And so something surprising occurs: we have fought victoriously against many forms of bodily sickness. We have discovered drugs with an almost miraculous power. The average length of our lives has been stretched beyond any former expectation. But many in our nation cannot stand this health. They want sickness as a refuge into which they can escape from the harshness of an insecure life. And since the medical care has made it more difficult to escape into bodily illness, they choose *mental* illness. But does not everybody dislike sickness, the pain, the discomfort and the danger connected with it? Of course, we dislike our sickness with some parts of our souls; but we like it with some other parts, mostly unconsciously, sometimes even consciously. But nobody can be healed especially of mental disorders and diseases who does not want it with his whole heart. And this is why they have become almost an epidemic in this country. People are fleeing into a situation where others must take care of them, where they exercise power through weakness or where they create an imaginary world in which it is nice to live as long as real life does not touch them. Don't underestimate this temptation. The basic insecurity of human existence and the driving anxiety connected with it are felt everywhere and by everyone. It is human heritage and it is increased immensely by our present world, even in this country full of vigour and health.

As in ours, so in the period of Jesus much talk was going on of sickness and healing. Jews and Greeks wrote about it. People felt that they lived in a sick period; they called it 'this world-period' and they described it in a way which is very similar to the way in which we describe it today. They saw not only the bodily infirmity of all of us, the innumerable bodily diseases in the masses of the people, they also saw the destructive powers possessing the minds of many. They called the mentally ill the possessed or the demoniacs and they tried to expel the evil spirits. They also knew that nations can be sick and that the diseases of social classes infect every individual in it. They looked even beyond the boundary lines of mankind into nature and spoke in visionary ecstasy about this earth becoming old and sick just as we did when we were under the first shock of the atomic power of self-destruction. Out of this knowledge of a sick period the question of a new period, a reality of health and wholeness was asked. Salvation and a saviour were expected. But salvation is healing. And the saviour is the healer. Therefore, Jesus answers the anxious question of the Baptist about whether he is the Saviour, by pointing to his healing power. This is what he says: 'If I am able to heal the deaf and the blind, if I am able to liberate the mentally sick, then a new reality has come upon you!' There are many healing stories in the Gospels, a stumbling block for scholars and preachers and teachers, because they take them as miracle stories of the past instead of taking them as healing stories of the present. For this they are. They show the human situation, the relation between bodily and mental disease, between sickness and guilt, between the desire of being healed and the fear of being healed. It is astonishing how many of our profoundest modern insights into human nature are anticipated in these stories: they know that becoming healthy means becoming whole, reunited, in one's bodily and psychic functions. They know that the mentally sick are afraid of the process of healing, because it throws them out of the limited but safe house of their neurotic self-seclusion, they know that the process of mental healing is a difficult and painful one, accompanied by convulsions of body and soul. They tell of the relation of guilt and disease, of the way in which unsolved conflicts of our conscience drive us to those cleavages of body and soul which we call sickness. We are told how Jesus, knowing this, pronounces to the paralytic first the forgiveness of his sins and then his regained health. The man lived in an inner struggle with himself, with his feeling of guilt. Out of this conflict his illness had grown; and now when Jesus forgives him, he feels reconciled with himself and the world; he becomes whole and healthy. There is little in our recent psychology of depth that surpasses these insights in truth and depth. These stories also describe the attitude which makes healing possible. They call it faith. Faith here, of course, does not mean the belief in assertions for which there is no evidence. It never meant that in genuine religion, and it never should be abused in this sense. But faith means being grasped by a power that is greater than we are, a power that shakes us and turns us, and transforms us and heals us. Surrender to this power is faith. The people whom Jesus could heal and can heal are those who did and do this self-surrender to the healing power in him. They surrendered their persons, split, contradicting themselves, disgusted and despairing about themselves, hateful of themselves and therefore hostile towards everybody else; afraid of life, burdened with guilt feelings, accusing and excusing themselves, fleeing from others into loneliness, fleeing from themselves to others, trying finally to escape from the threats of existence into the painful and deceptive safety of mental and bodily disease. As such beings they surrendered to Jesus and this surrender is what we call faith. But he did not keep them, as a good helper should never do. He gave them back to themselves, as new creatures, healed and whole. And when he died he left a group of people who, in spite of much anxiety and discord and weakness and guilt, had the certitude that they were healed, and that the healing power amongst them was great enough to conquer individuals and nations all over the world. We belong to these people, if we are grasped by the new reality which has appeared in him.

We *have* his healing power ourselves.

Jesus was called a physician, and it is the physician for whom we ask first when we are looking for health. And this is good. For, as all generations knew, there is healing power in nature. And much healing is possible if this power is wisely used and skilfully aided. Those who despise this aid and rely on the power of their will ignore both the destructive might and the constructive friendliness of nature. They do not know that our body contains not only forces of discord between its elements but also forces of concord. The great physician is he who does not easily cut off parts and does not easily suppress the one function in favour of the other, but he who strengthens the whole so that within the unity of the body the struggling elements can be reconciled. And this is possible even if deep traces of former struggles in our body remain as long as we live.

The physician can help, he can keep us alive, but can he make us whole? Can he give us salvation? Certainly not, if discord, cleavage, restlessness rule our mental life, if there is no unity and therefore no freedom in our soul, if we are possessed by compulsions and fantasies, by disordered anxiety and disordered aggression, if mental disorder or disease are threatening or have conquered us. Then if we want to be healed, we ask for the help of friends or counsellors or analysts or psychiatrists. And they, if they know what to do, try to aid the healing powers of our soul. They do not appeal to our will power; they do not ask for removal or suppression of any trend, but they work for reconciliation, reconciliation of the struggling forces of our soul. They accept us as we are and make it possible for us to look at ourselves honestly and with clarity, to realize the strange mechanisms under which we are suffering and to dissolve them, reconciling the genuine forces of our soul with each other and making us free for thought and action.

The counsellor and psychiatrist can *help*; he can liberate us, but can he make us whole? Can he give us sal-

vation? Certainly not if we are not able to use our freedom and if we are conquered by the tragic conflicts of
our existence. None of us is isolated. We belong to our
past, to our families, classes, groups, nations, cultures.
And in all of them health and illness are fighting with
each other. How can we be whole if the culture is split
within itself, if every value is denied by another one, if
every truth is questioned, if every decision is good and
bad at the same time? How can we be whole if the institutions in which we live create temptations, conflicts,
catastrophes too heavy for each of us? How can we be
whole if we are connected, often intimately connected,
with people who are in discord with themselves, in hostility against us, or if we have to live with people, individuals, groups, nations who are irreconciled and sick?
This is the situation of all of us, and this situation re-
acts on our personal life, disrupts the concord we may
have reached. The reconciliation in our souls and often
even in our bodies breaks down in the encounter with
reality. Who heals reality? Who brings us a new reality?
Who reconciles the conflicting forces of our whole
existence? We look at those who are most responsible
for our institutions, for our historical reality, the leaders, the statesmen, the wise administrators, the educated,
the good people, the revolutionary masses. There are
healing powers in all of them, otherwise there would be
no more history. And it is understandable that in the
period of Jesus just rulers were called saviours and
healers. They can maintain human life on earth; but can
they make us whole, can they bring us salvation?

They cannot because they themselves need wholeness
and are longing for salvation. Who heals the healer?
There is no answer to this in the old reality. Everybody
and every institution are infected, the healer and the
healed. Only a new reality can make us whole, breaking
into the old one, reconciling it with itself. It is the
humanly incredible, ecstatic, often defeated, but never
conquered faith of Christianity that this new reality

which was always at work in history, has appeared in fullness and power in Jesus, the Christ, the Healer and Saviour. This is said of him because he alone does not give another law for thought or action, because he does not cut off anything or suppress anything that belongs to life, but because he is the reality of reconciliation, because in him a new reality has come upon us in which we and our whole existence are accepted and re-united. We know, even when we confess this faith, that the old reality of conflict and disease has not disappeared. Our bodies ail and die, our souls are restless, our world is a battlefield of individuals and groups. But the new reality cannot be thrown out. We live from it, even if we do not know it. For it is the power of reconciliation whose work is wholeness and whose name is love.

On Healing (II)

The Lord healeth the broken in heart, and bindeth up their wounds – Bless the Lord, O my soul . . . who healeth all thy diseases, who redeemeth thy life from destruction.

PSALM 147:3; 103:2, 3, 4

How do we paint Jesus the Christ? It does not matter whether he is painted in lines and colours, as the great Christian painters in all periods have done or whether we paint him in sermons, as the Christian preachers have done Sunday after Sunday, or whether we paint him in learned books, in biblical or systematic theology, or whether we paint him in our hearts, in devotion, imagination and love. In each case we must answer the question: how do we paint Jesus the Christ? The stories in the Gospel of Matthew contribute to the answer; they add a colour, an expression, a trait of great intensity, they paint him as the healer: it is astonishing that this colour, this vivid expression of his nature, this powerful trait of his character, has more and more been lost in our time. The greyish colours of a moral teacher, the tense expression of a social reformer, the soft traits of a suffering servant have prevailed, at least amongst our painters and theologians and life-of-Jesus novelists; perhaps not so much in the hearts of the people who need somebody to heal them.

The Gospels, certainly, are not responsible for this disappearance of power in the picture of Jesus. They abound in stories of healing; but *we* are responsible, ministers, laymen, theologians, who forgot that 'Saviour' means 'healer', he who makes whole and sane what is broken and insane, in body and mind. The woman who encountered him was made whole, the demoniac who met him was liberated from his mental cleavage. Those who are disrupted, split, disintegrated, are healed by him. And because this is so, because this power has appeared on earth, the kingdom of God has come upon us; this is the answer Jesus gives to the Pharisees when they discuss his power of healing the mentally possessed; this is the answer he gives to the Baptist to overcome his doubts; this is the order he gives to his disciples when he sends them to the towns of Israel. 'And as ye go, preach, saying, the kingdom of God is at hand. Heal the sick, raise the dead, cleanse the lepers, cast out demons.' That is what they shall do and for *this* he gives them authority and power; for in him the kingdom of God has appeared, and its nature is salvation, healing of that which is ill, making whole what is broken.

Are we still able to experience this power? I do not speak of theological inhibitions about the acceptance of such a picture of the Christ. They do not weigh very heavily. Of course we were worried about miracle-stories for many decades; today we know what the New Testament always knew – that miracles are signs pointing to the presence of a divine power in nature and history, and that they are in no way negations of natural laws. Of course, we were and we are worried about the abuse of religious healing for commercial and other selfish purposes or about its distortion into magic and superstition. But abuses occur when the right use is lacking and superstitions arise when faith has become weak. All these are not serious problems; good theology and good practice can solve them.

But the serious problem is, as always, the problem of our own existence. Are we healed, have we received healing forces, here and there from the power of the picture of Jesus as the Saviour? Are we grasped by this power? Is it strong enough to overcome our neurotic trends, the rebellion of unconscious strivings, the split in our conscious being, the diseases which disintegrate our minds and destroy our bodies at the same time? Have we overcome in moments of grace the torturing anxiety in the depth of our hearts, the restlessness which never ceases moving and whipping us, the unordered desires and the hidden repressions which return as poisonous hate, the hostility against ourselves and others, against life itself, the hidden will to death? Have we experienced now and then in moments of grace that we are made whole, that destructive spirits have left us, that psychic compulsions are dissolved, that tyrannical mechanisms in our soul are replaced by freedom; that despair, this most dangerous of all splits, this real sickness unto death, is healed and we are saved from self-destruction? Has this happened to us under the power of the picture of Jesus as the Saviour? This is the real problem, the true Christological problem (theologically speaking), the question of life and death (humanly speaking), for every Christian and of the Christendom of today. Do we go to the physicians alone, or to the psychotherapists alone or to the counsellors alone in order to be healed? Sometimes, of course, we should go to them, but do we also go to or – more precisely – do we also receive the healing power in the picture of Jesus the Christ who is called the Saviour? This is the question before us, and this question is answered by those who can tell us that they have experienced his healing power, that the New Being *has* grasped their bodies and their soul, that they *have* become whole and sane again, that salvation *has* come upon them. Not always, of course, but in those moments which are moments of grace and in which they anticipated the perfect wholeness, the wholeness of God being in all. Can we join this answer?

6. Holy Waste

And while he was at Bethany in the house of Simon the leper, as he sat at table, a woman came with an alabaster jar of ointment of pure nard, very costly, and she broke the jar and poured it over his head. But there were some who said to themselves indignantly, 'Why was the ointment thus wasted? For this ointment might have been sold for more than three hundred denarii, and given to the poor.' And they reproached her. But Jesus said, 'Let her alone; why do you trouble her? She has done a beautiful thing to me. For you always have the poor with you, and whenever you will, you can do good to them; but you will not always have me. She has done what she could; she has anointed my body beforehand for burying. And truly, I say to you, wherever the gospel is preached in the whole world, what she has done will be told in memory of her.'

MARK 14:3-9

What has she done? She has given an example of a waste, which, as Jesus says, is a beautiful thing. It is, so to speak, a holy waste, a waste growing out of the abundance of the heart. She represents the ecstatic element in our relation to God, while the disciples represent the reasonable element. Who can blame the disciples for being angry about the immense waste this woman has created? Certainly not a deacon who has to take care of the poor, or a social worker who knows the neediest cases and cannot help, or a church administrator who collects money for important projects. Certainly the disciples would not be blamed by a balanced person-ality who has his emotional life well under control and for whom it is worse than nonsense, even criminal, to think of doing what this woman did. Jesus felt differ-ently and so did the early Church. They knew that with-out the abundance of the heart nothing great can hap-pen. They knew that religion within the limits of reason-ableness is a mutilated religion, and that calculating love is not love at all. Jesus did not raise the question about how much *eros* and how much *agape*, how much human passion and how much understanding was motivating the woman; he saw the abundant heart and he accepted it without analysing the different elements in it. There are occasions when we must analyse ourselves and others. And certainly we must know about the complexity of all human motives. But this should not prevent us from accepting the waste of an uncalculated self-surrender nor from wasting ourselves beyond the limits of law and rationality.

The history of mankind is the history of men and women who wasted themselves and were not afraid to do so. They did not fear the waste of themselves, of other men, of things in the service of a new creation. They were justified, for they wasted all this out of the fullness of their hearts. They wasted as God does in nature and history, in creation and salvation. The mon-sters of nature to which Jahweh points in his answer to Job – what are they but expressions of the divine abundance? Luther's God, who acts heroically and with-out rules – is he not the wasteful God who creates and destroys in order to create again? Has not Protestantism lost a great deal by losing the wasteful self-surrender of the saints and the mystics? Are we not in danger of a religious and moral utilitarianism which always asks for the reasonable purpose – the same question as that of the disciples in Bethany? There is no creativity, divine or human, without the holy waste which comes out of the creative abundance of the heart and does not ask, 'What use is this?'

We know that lack of love in our early years is mentally destructive. But do we know that the lack of occasions to waste ourselves is equally dangerous? In many people there has been an abundance of the heart. But laws, conventions, and a rigid self-control have repressed it and it has died. People are sick not only because they have not received love but also because they are not allowed to give love, to waste themselves. Do not suppress in yourselves or others the abundant heart, the waste of self-surrender, the Spirit who trespasses all reason. Do not greedily preserve your time and your strength for what is useful and reasonable. Keep yourselves open for the creative moment which may appear in the midst of what seemed to be waste. Do not suppress in yourselves the impulse to do what the woman at Bethany did. You will be reproached by the disciples as the woman was. But Jesus was on her side and he is also on yours. Most of those who are great in the kingdom of God followed her, and the disciples, the reasonable Christians in all periods of history, will remember you as they have remembered her.

Jesus connects this anointing of his body with his death. There is an anointing of kings when they begin their reign and there is an anointing of corpses as a last gift of the living to the dead. Jesus speaks of the latter kind of anointing although he might easily have spoken of the former. In so doing, he turns both the ecstasy of the woman and the reasonableness of the disciples into something else. By his death the reasonable morality of the disciples is turned into a paradox: the Messiah, the Anointed One, must waste himself in order to become the Christ. And the ecstatic self-surrender of the woman is tested by the ignominious perishing of the object of her unlimited devotion. In both cases we are asked to accept an act more radical, more divine, more saving than either ecstatic waste or reasonable service. The Cross does not disavow the sacred waste, the ecstatic surrender. It is the most complete and the most holy waste. And the Cross does not disavow the purposeful act, the reasonable service. It is the fulfilment of all wisdom within the plan of salvation. In the self-surrendering love of the Cross, reason and ecstasy, moral obedience and sacred waste are united. May we have the abundance of heart to waste ourselves as our reasonable service!

7. Principalities and Powers

> For I am sure that neither death, nor life, nor angels, nor principalities, nor things present, nor things to come, nor powers, nor height, nor depth, nor anything else in all creation, will be able to separate us from the love of God in Christ Jesus our Lord.
>
> ROMANS 8:38-39

These words are among the most powerful ever written. Their sound is able to grasp human souls in desperate situations. In my own experience they have proved to be stronger than the sound of exploding shells, of weeping at open graves, of the sighs of the sick, of the moaning of the dying. They are stronger than the self-accusation of those who are in despair about themselves and they prevail over the permanent whisper of anxiety in the depth of our being. What is it that makes these words so powerful?

It is not their literal meaning, for in many respects that is strange to us. The angels and principalities, the height and depth, and even life and death point to the constellations of the stars which, according to ancient beliefs, determine the fate of man and history. Men are in their power, driven by fear and fighting for courage, sometimes victorious, more often defeated. This was the predicament of the men to whom Paul was speaking. Several times in his letters he sums up the meaning of Christianity in the message that Christ has conquered these powers which govern the world, but nowhere does he affirm it as triumphantly as in the beautiful and powerful words to the Romans.

If these words have power over our souls in our time, they must say something which we feel to be true, even if we do not share the ancient belief in the stars and their constellations. They name the powers in whose bondage we all are and with us all men in all periods of history, and the whole of creation. And they show us that which can give us the certainty that these powers do not prevail against us, that they are conquered and that we can participate in the victory over them.

Who, in recent years, and indeed in our whole century, does not feel the irresistible forces which determine our historical and personal destiny? They drive nations and individuals into insoluble conflicts, internal and external; into arrogance and insanity, into revolt and despair, into inhumanity and self-destruction. Each of us is involved in these conflicts and driven to a greater or lesser degree by these forces. The personal life of each of us is in some way determined by them. No security is guaranteed to anyone; no house, no work, no friend, no family, no country anywhere in the world is safe, no plans are certain of fulfilment, all hopes are threatened. This is not a new state of things in human history. But what is new is that during a few years of comparative safety, we had forgotten that this is the true state of things. Now we see it again everywhere because suddenly we are living in its midst in every part of the earth.

Driven by the forces of fate, we ask the question mankind has always asked: what lies behind all this; what is its meaning; how can we endure it?

Long before the Christian era people spoke of the divine providence at work behind the driving forces of life and history. And in Christianity the words of Jesus about the birds of the air and the lilies of the field, and his command not to be anxious about tomorrow, have strengthened the faith in providence. It became the most common belief of Christian people. It gave them courage in danger, consolation in sorrow, hope among ruins. But more and more this faith lost its depth. It became a matter-of-course and was deprived of the overwhelming, surprising and triumphant character it has in the words of Paul.

When the German soldiers went into World War I most of them shared the popular belief in a nice God who would make everything work out for the best. Actually, everything worked out for the worst, for the nation and for almost everyone in it. In the trenches of the war, the popular belief in personal providence was gradually broken and in the fifth year of war nothing was left of it. During and after World War II similar developments took place in this country. In the political tensions and fears of the last decade the belief in historical providence also broke down. The confidence, shared by large groups in this country, that in history everything will eventually turn out for the best, has almost disappeared. Today not much of it is left.

Neither the personal nor the historical belief in providence had depth or a real foundation. These beliefs were products of wishful thinking and not of faith. Faith in providence is not a *part* of the Christian faith – a part which is easier to grasp than the other parts. It is not the case, as an old country parson once told me, that people firmly believe in divine providence, but that the higher contents of the Christian faith, sin and salvation, Christ and the Church, are strange to them. If this is so, then the meaning of providence must also be strange to them and their belief in it is due to break down as such beliefs have in the storms of our century. *Faith in providence is faith altogether.* It is the courage to say yes to one's own life and life in general, in spite of the driving forces of fate, in spite of the insecurities of daily existence, in spite of the catastrophes of existence and the breakdown of meaning.

It is of such courage that Paul speaks in our text. But first he speaks of the powers which try to make this courage impossible. What do these powers do? They separate us from the love of God. This sentence is surprising. We would point to the dangers of pain and death which threaten our life day by day. Paul is certainly not unaware of them. He enumerates them as 'tribulation or distress or persecution or famine or nakedness or peril or the sword'. But he feels himself to be a conqueror of them all. And then he starts again and names the powers which threaten to separate us from the love of God. There is something mysterious about these powers. They do not have evil names like those which Paul has previously listed; most of them have glorious names— 'angels', 'principalities', 'life' and 'height'. Why are they the ones which are most threatening? It is because they are always at work in every moment of our lives and because they have a double face. They are the powers which rule the world and they rule it for good and for evil. They grasp us by the good they bring and they destroy us by the evil they contain. This is the reason that they are more dangerous than the obvious evils. This is the reason that the triumph over them is the ultimate test which proves that Jesus is the Christ, the bringer of the new state of things.

Let us look into their nature, not as if they were strangers to us but as the driving powers of our own being. 'Angels and principalities' are the names of some of them. Both of these words point to the same reality, a reality which has little in common with the nice winged babies who appear in most popular pictures of angels. They point to realities which are simultaneously both glorious and terrible; realities full of beauty and full of destructiveness. What are these realities? We do not have to look far to discover them. They are in all of us, in our own families, in our own nation, in our world. By what signs do we recognize them? By a mixture of irresistible fascination and unconquerable anxiety. The name of one of these powers with an angelic face is love. The poetry of all languages abounds in the praise of this principality ruling over the life of all men. Its angelic face appears in pictures and statues, its angelic beauty sounds through music, its divine fascination is expressed in the figures of pagan gods and goddesses. And at the same time, all works of art, and all myths are full of the tragic and deadly works of the angel of love. Fascination and fear, joy and guilt, creation and destruction are united in this great ruler of our lives. And both the joy and the anxiety of love tend to separate us from the love of God; the one by attracting us away from God to itself, the other by throwing us into the darkness of despair in which we cannot see God any longer.

Another principality, angelic and demonic at the same time, is power. It has the severe manly beauty which we see in some pictures of the great archangels. It is itself a great angel, good and evil, just as love is a mighty principality, and it is the builder and protector of cities and nations, a creative force in every human enterprise, in every human community, in every human achievement. It is responsible for the conquest of nature, the organization of states, the execution of justice. Its mighty ally is another angelic figure, good and evil, namely, knowledge. We are all in their bondage. World history is the realm in which the reign of the angel of power is most manifest in all its glory and in all its tragedy. There is no need to say more about it to the people of our time. Every morning brings us news about this ruler of our world. And we all are grasped both by the angelic fascination of its creativity and by the demonic terror of its destructiveness in our personal lives as well as in the lives of our nations. And when power is allied with knowledge – a knowledge undreamed of ever before in the history of mankind – fascination as well as terror are infinitely increased. Both separate us from the love of God, the one driving us to the adoration of power and knowledge, the other driving us to cynicism and despair.

Paul mentions two other pairs of realities which may separate us from the love of God – 'height and depth', and 'things present and things to come'. Everyone understands their meaning without guidance. But it is hard to exhaust the richness of this meaning. Height and depth are the highest and lowest points in the movements of the stars; they are the points of their greatest and least influence, for good and for evil. Height and depth are the moments in which a life process reaches its strongest realization, in vitality and success and power, and in which it reaches its weakest realization, perhaps its end. Height and depth are the moments of victory and defeat, of fulfilment and emptiness, of elevation and depression, of fascination and of anxiety. And both moments, height as well as depth, try to separate us from the love of God, the one by its light, the other by its darkness, both making God invisible.

'Things present and things to come' – the first points to the impact which the present makes upon us. It points to the seductive power of the present, to our refusal to look back or ahead when we are held in the grip of the acute enjoyment or the acute pain of the present moment. And 'things to come' means the expectation of the new, the joy of the unexpected, the courage of the risk. But it also means the incalculable, the contingent, and the anxiety about the strange and unknown.

Let us close this enumeration with the pair of most threatening powers, with which Paul begins – 'death and life'. These two belong to each other. In every life death is always present; it works in body and soul from the moment of conception to the moment of dissolution. It is present at the beginning of our lives just as much as at their end. At the moment of our birth we begin to die, and we continue to do so daily, throughout our lives. Growth is death, because it undermines the conditions of life even while it is increasing life. But not to grow is immediate death. All of us stand between the fascination of life and the anxiety of death, and sometimes between the anxiety of life and the fascination of death. Death and life are the greatest, the all-embracing powers, which try to separate us from the love of God.

We have looked at the powers which rule the world and over which the faith in providence must triumph. What is this faith? It is certainly not the belief that everything will turn out well in the end. It is not the belief that everything follows a preconceived plan, whether we call the planner God or Nature or Fate. Life is not a machine well-constructed by its builder and running on according to the forces and laws of its own machinery. Life, personal and historical, is a creative and destructive process in which freedom and destiny, chance and necessity, responsibility and tragedy are mixed with each other in everything and in every moment. These tensions, ambiguities and conflicts make life what it is. They create the fascination and the horror of life. They drive us to the question of a courage which can accept life without being conquered by it, and this is the question of providence.

But let us now drop the word 'providence' with all its false connotations and look at what it really means. It means the courage to accept life in the power of that which is more than life. Paul calls it the love of God. This love, certainly, is above the angelic-demonic figure of love of which we spoke. This love is the ultimate power of union, the ultimate victory over separation. Being united with it enables us to stand above life in the midst of life. It enables us to accept the double-faced rulers of life, their fascination and their anxiety, their glory and their horror. It gives us the certainty that no moment is possible in which we can be prevented from reaching the fulfilment towards which all life is striving. This is the courage to accept life in the power of that in which life is rooted and overcome.

And if you now ask how this is possible, we turn again to Paul's hymn and find there two answers. He concludes his list of the ruling powers with the words, '. . . nor anything else in all *creation*'. The powers of this world are *creatures* as we are. They are no more than we, they are limited. We are united with that which is not creature and whose creative ground no creature can destroy; then we know they cannot destroy the *meaning* of our lives even if they can destroy our lives. And this gives us the certainty that no creature can destroy the meaning of life universal, in nature as well as history, of which we are a part, even though history and the whole universe should destroy themselves tomorrow. No creature can keep us from this ultimate courage. None? Perhaps one – ourselves. Against all the powers and principalities, including life and death, the courage to maintain the unity with God stands firm. But it falls when guilt separates us from the love of God. Then we cannot face death, because the sting of death is sin; we cannot face life because guilt drives life into tragic self-destruction; we cannot face love because love is corrupted by greed; and we cannot face power because it is corrupted by cruelty. We shy away from the past because it is polluted by guilt, and we shy away from the future because it may bring the fruits of past guilt, and we cannot rest in the present because it accuses us and expels us. We cannot stand the height because we are afraid of falling, and we cannot stand the depth because we feel responsible for our fall. The rulers of the world cannot achieve what an uneasy conscience can achieve – the undermining of our courage to accept life. Therefore, Paul's final message is: not even your guilty conscience can separate you from the love of God. For the love of

God means that God accepts him who knows that he is unacceptable. This is the meaning of Paul's closing words, 'in Christ Jesus our Lord'. He is the victor over the rulers of the world because he is the victor over our hearts. His image gives us the certainty that even our hearts, our self-accusation, our despair about ourselves cannot separate us from the love of God, the ultimate unity, the source and ground of the courage to accept life.

PART TWO

THE NEW BEING AS FREEDOM

*

8. 'What Is Truth?'

And the Word became flesh and dwelt among us, full of grace and truth; . . . For the law was given through Moses; grace and truth came through Jesus Christ.

JOHN 1:14, 17

Why do you not understand what I say? . . . you are of your father the devil. . . . He was a murderer from the beginning, and has nothing to do with truth, because there is no truth in him. When he lies, he speaks according to his own nature, for he is a liar and the father of lies.

JOHN 8:43, 44

Pilate said to him, 'So you are a king?' Jesus answered, 'You say that I am a king. For this I was born, and for this I have come into the world, to bear witness to the truth. Every one who is of the truth hears my voice.' Pilate said to him, 'What is truth?'

JOHN 18:37, 38

Jesus said to him, 'I am the way, and the truth, and the life.'

JOHN 14:6

He who does what is true, comes to the light.

JOHN 3:21

And I will pray the Father, and he will give you . . . the Spirit of truth, whom the world cannot receive, because it neither sees him nor knows him; you know him, for he dwells with you, and will be in you.

JOHN 14:16, 17

When the Spirit of truth comes he will guide you into all the truth.

JOHN 16:13

Let us love one another; for love is of God, and he who loves is born of God and knows God. He who does not love does not know God; for God is love.

I JOHN 4:7, 8

Jesus then said to the Jews who had believed in him, 'If you continue in my word, you are truly my disciples, and you will know the truth, and the truth will make you free.'

JOHN 8:31, 32

In the above passages there are words in which Jesus speaks about truth. Another of these words shall be the centre of our meditation, the word in which he combines truth and freedom: 'The truth will make you free.'

The question of truth is universally human; but like everything human it was first manifest on a special place in a special group. It was the Greek mind in which the passionate search for truth was most conspicuous; and it was the Greek world in which, and to which, the Gospel of John was written. The words, here said by Jesus, are, according to ancient custom, put into his mouth by the evangelist who wanted to show the answer of Christianity to the central question of the Hellenic mind: the question of truth. The answer is given also to us, for we, too, ask the question of truth. And some of us ask it as passionately, and sometimes as desperately, as the Greeks did.

It is often at an early age that we are moved by the desire for truth. When I, myself, as a fifteen-year-old boy received the words of our text as the motto for my future life from the confirming minister, who happened to be my father, I felt that this was just what I was looking for; and I remember that I was not alone in my group with this longing for truth. But I also observed, in myself and in others, that the early passion for truth is due to be lost in the adolescent and adult years of our lives. How does this happen?

The truth the child first receives is imposed upon him by adults, predominantly by his parents. This cannot be otherwise; and he cannot help accepting it. The passion for truth is silenced by answers which have the weight of undisputed authority, be it that of the mother or the father, or an older friend, or a gang, or the representatives of a social pattern. But sooner or later the child revolts against the truth given to him. He denies the authorities either all together, or one in the name of the other. He uses the teachers against the parents, the gang against the teachers, a friend against the gang, society against the friend.

This revolt is as unavoidable as was his early dependence on authority. The authorities gave him something to live on, the revolt makes him responsible for the truth he accepts or rejects.

But whether in obedience or in revolt, the time comes when a new way to truth is opened to us, especially to those in academic surroundings: the way of scholarly work. Eagerly we take it. It seems so safe, so successful, so independent of both authority and wilfulness. It liberates from prejudices and superstitions; it makes us humble and honest. Where else, besides in scholarly work, should we look for truth? There are many in our period, young and old, primitive and sophisticated, practical and scientific, who accept this answer without hesitation. For them scholarly truth is truth altogether. Poetry may give beauty, but it certainly does not give truth. Ethics may help us to a good life, but it cannot help us to truth. Religion may produce deep emotions, but it should not claim to have truth. Only science gives us truth. It gives us new insights into the way nature works, into the texture of human history, into the hidden things of the human mind. It gives a feeling of joy, inferior to no other joy. He who has experienced this transition from darkness, or dimness, to the sharp light of knowledge will always praise scientific truth and understanding and say with some great medieval theologians, that the principles through which we know our world are the eternal divine light in our souls. And yet, when we ask those who have finished their studies in our colleges and universities whether they have found there a truth which is relevant to their lives they will answer with hesitation. Some will say that they have lost what they had of relevant truth; others will say that they don't care for such a truth because life goes on from day to day without it. Others will tell you of a person, a book, an event outside their studies which gave them the feeling of a truth that matters. But they all will agree that it is not the scholarly work which can give truth relevant for our life.

Where else, then, can we get it? 'Nowhere,' Pilate answers in his talk with Jesus. 'What is truth?' he asks, expressing in these three words his own and his contemporaries' despair of truth, expressing also the despair of truth in millions of our contemporaries, in schools and studios, in business and professions. In all of us, open or hidden, admitted or repressed, the despair of truth is a permanent threat. We are children of our period as Pilate was. Both are periods of disintegration, of a world-wide loss of values and meanings. Nobody can separate himself completely from this reality, and nobody should even try. Let me do something unusual from a Christian standpoint, namely, express praise of Pilate – not the unjust judge, but the cynic and sceptic; and of all those amongst us in whom Pilate's question is alive. For in the depth of every serious doubt and every despair of truth, the passion for truth is still at work. Don't give in too quickly to those who want to alleviate your anxiety about truth. Don't be seduced into a truth which is not really your truth, even if the seducer is your church, or your party, or your parental tradition. Go with Pilate, if you cannot go with Jesus; but go in seriousness with him!

Twofold are the temptations to evade the burden of asking for the truth that matters. The one is the way of those who claim to have the truth and the other is the way of those who do not care for the truth. The first ones are called 'the Jews' in our gospel. They point to their tradition which goes back to Abraham. Abraham is their father; so they have all truth, and do not need to be worried by the question which they encounter in Jesus. Many among us, Christians and secularists, are 'Jews' in the sense of the Fourth Gospel. They point to *their* tradition which goes back to the Church Fathers, or to the popes, or to the Reformers, or to the makers of the American Constitution. Their Church or their nation is their mother, so they have all truth and do not need to worry about the question of truth. Would Jesus tell them, perhaps, what he told the Jews – that even if the Church or the nation is their mother, they carry with them the heritage of the father of untruth; that the truth they have is not the truth which makes free? Certainly there is no freedom where there is self-complacency about the truth of one's own beliefs. There is no freedom where there is ignorant and fanatical rejection of foreign ideas and ways of life. There is not freedom but demonic bondage where one's own truth is called the ultimate truth. For this is an attempt to be like God, an attempt which is made in the name of God.

There is the second way of avoiding the question of truth – the way of not caring for it, of indifference. It is the way of the majority of the people today, as well as at the time of Jesus. Life, they say to themselves, is a mixture of truth, half-truth and falsehood. It is quite possible to live with this mixture, to muddle through most of the difficulties of life without asking the question of a truth that matters ultimately. There may be boundary situations, a tragic event, a deep spiritual fall, death. But as long as they are far removed, the question of truth can also stay far away. Hence, the common attitude – a little bit of Pilate's scepticism, especially in things which it is not dangerous today to doubt, as, for instance, God and the Christ; and a little bit of the Jew's dogmatism, especially in things which one is requested to accept today, as, for instance, an economic or political way of life. In other words, some scepticism and some dogmatism, and a shrewd method of balancing them liberate one from the burden of asking the question of ultimate truth.

But those of us who dare to face the question of truth may listen to what the Fourth Gospel says about it. The first thing which strikes us is that the truth of which Jesus speaks is not a doctrine but a reality, namely, he himself: 'I *am* the truth.' This is a profound transformation of the ordinary meaning of truth. For us, statements are true or false; people may *have* truth or not; but how can they *be* truth, even *the* truth? The truth of which the Fourth Gospel speaks is a true reality – that reality which does not deceive us if we accept it and live with it. If Jesus says, 'I am the truth,' he indicates that in him the true, the genuine, the ultimate reality is present; or, in other words, that God is present, unveiled, undistorted, in his infinite depth, in his unapproachable mystery. Jesus is not the truth because his teachings are true. But his teachings are true because they express the truth which he himself is. He is more than his words. And he is more than any word said about him. The truth which makes us free is neither the teaching of Jesus nor the teaching about Jesus. Those who have called the teaching of Jesus 'the truth' have subjected the people to a servitude under the law. And most people like to live under a law. They want to be told what to think and what not to think. And they accept Jesus as the infallible teacher and giver of a new law. But even the words of Jesus, if taken as a law, are not the truth which makes us free. And they should not be used as such by our scholars and preachers and religious teachers. They should not be used as a collection of infallible prescriptions for life and thought. They *point* to the truth, but they are not a law of truth. Nor are the doctrines about him the truth that liberates. I say this to you as somebody who all his life has worked for a true expression of the truth which is the Christ. But the more one works, the more one realizes that our expressions, including everything we have learned from our teachers and from the teaching of the Church in all generations, is not the truth that makes us free. The Church very early forgot the word of our Gospel that he *is* the truth; and claimed that her doctrines about him are the truth. But these doctrines, however necessary and good they were, proved to be not the truth that liberates. Soon they became tools of suppression, of servitude under authorities; they became means to prevent the honest search for truth – weapons to split the souls of people between loyalty to the Church and sincerity to truth. And in this way they gave deadly weapons to those who attacked the Church and its doctrines in the name of truth. Not everybody feels this conflict. There are masses of people who feel safe under doctrinal laws. They are safe, but it is the safety of him who has not yet found his spiritual freedom, who has not yet found his true self. It is the dignity and the danger of Protestantism that it exposes its adherents to the insecurity of asking the question of truth for themselves and that it throws them into the freedom and responsibility of personal decisions, of the right to choose between the ways of the sceptics, and those who are orthodox, of the indifferent masses, and him who *is* the truth that liberates. For this is the greatness of Protestantism : that it points beyond the teachings of Jesus and beyond the doctrines of the Church to the being of him whose being is the truth.

How do we reach this truth? 'By doing it,' is the answer of the Fourth Gospel. This does not mean being obedient to the commandments, accepting them and fulfilling them. Doing the truth means living out of the reality which is *he* who is the truth, making his being the being of ourselves and of our world. And again, we ask, 'How can this happen?' 'By remaining in him' is the answer of the Fourth Gospel, i.e., by participating in his being. 'Abide in me and I in you,' he says. The truth which liberates is the truth in which we participate, which is a part of us and we a part of it. True discipleship is participation. If the real, the ultimate, the divine reality which is his being becomes our being we are in the truth that matters.

And a third time we ask, 'How can this happen?' There is an answer to this question in our Gospel which may deeply shock us: 'Every one who is of the truth hears my voice.' Being 'of the truth' means, coming from the true, the ultimate reality, being determined in one's being by the divine ground of all being, by that reality which is present in the Christ. If we have part in it, we recognize it wherever it appears; we recognize it as it appears in its fullness in the Christ. But, some may ask in despair: 'If we have *no* part in it, if we are *not* of the truth, are we then forever excluded from it? Must we accept a life without truth, a life in error and meaninglessness? Who tells me that *I* am of the truth, that *I* have a chance to reach it?' Nobody can tell you; but there is one criterion: If you *seriously* ask the question, 'Am I of the truth?' you *are* of the truth. If you do not ask it seriously, you do not really want, and you do not deserve, and you cannot get, an answer! He who asks seriously the question of the truth that liberates, is already on his way to liberation. He may still be in the bondage of dogmatic self-assurance but he has begun to be free from it. He may still be in the bondage of cynical despair, but he has already started to emerge from it. He may still be in the bondage of unconcern about the truth that matters, but his unconcern is already shaken. These all are of the truth and on their road to the truth.

On this road you will meet the liberating truth in many forms. In one form, however, you will never meet it: the form of propositions which you can learn or write down and take home. But you may encounter it in one sentence of a book or of a conversation or of a lecture, or even of a sermon. This sentence is not the truth, but it may open you up for the truth and it may liberate you from the bondage to opinions and prejudices and conventions. Suddenly, true reality appears like the brightness of lightning in a formerly dark place. Or, slowly, true reality appears like a landscape when the fog becomes thinner and thinner and finally disappears. New darknesses, new fogs will fall upon you; but you have experienced, at least once, the truth and the freedom given by the truth. Or you may be grasped by the truth in an encounter with a piece of nature – its beauty and its transitoriness; or in an encounter with a human being in friendship and estrangement, in love, in difference and hate; or in an encounter with yourself in a sudden insight into the hidden strivings of your soul, in disgust and even hatred of yourself, in reconciliation with and acceptance of yourself. In these encounters you may meet the true reality – the truth which liberates from illusions and false authoritities, from enslaving anxieties, desires and hostilities, from a wrong self-rejection and a wrong self-affirmation.

And it may even happen that you are grasped by the picture and power of him who is truth. There is no law that this must happen. Many at all times and in all places have encountered the true reality which is in him without knowing his name – as he himself said. They were of the truth and they recognized the truth, although they had never seen him who is the truth. And those who have seen him, the Christians in all generations, have no guarantee that they participate in the truth which he is. Maybe they were not of the truth. Those, however, who are of the truth and who have encountered him who is the truth have one precious thing beyond the others: they have the point from which to judge all truth they encounter anywhere. They

look at a life which never lost the communion with the
divine ground of all life, and they look at a life which
never lost the union of love with all beings.

And this leads to the last word which the man who
has written the Gospel and the Letters of John has to
say about truth : that the truth which liberates is the
power of love, for God is love. The father of the lie
binds us to himself by binding us to ourselves – or to
that in us which is not our true self. Love liberates from
the father of the lie because it liberates us from our false
self to our true self – to that self which is grounded in
true reality. Therefore, distrust every claim for truth
where you do not see truth united with love; and be
certain that you are of the truth and that the truth has
taken hold of you only when love has taken hold of you
and has started to make you free from yourselves.

9. Faith and Uncertainty

In his book *On the Bondage of the Will*, Martin Luther
writes, 'What is more miserable than uncertainty!' He
challenges the half-sceptical attitude of his great opponent, Erasmus of Rotterdam, who had declared that he
would rather go over at once to the camp of the sceptics,
if the authority of Scripture and the Church would permit him to do so. Luther demands *certainty* in the matter
of our ultimate concern. He demands *assertions* and not
sceptical possibilities or academic probabilities. 'Take
away assertions,' he says, 'and you take away Christianity.' It is not the character of the Christian mind to avoid
assertions, he declares. Every word of the prophets and
the writers of the New Testament confirms his attitude
and disproves that of Erasmus. Neither Jesus nor Paul
nor John speaks in terms of probability or of accumula-
tion of experiences. They make assertions with a certainty and an unshaken confidence about the truth of

their message, which is often hard to stand and harder to understand for the modern mind. Paul writes to the Galatians, '. . . Even if we, or an angel from heaven, should preach to you a gospel contrary to that which we preached to you, let him be accursed.' We feel a kind of resistance and even resentment against this unbroken certainty, the immediate consequence of which is the 'Anathema' against heretics. Have we all become Erasmians, consciously or unconsciously? Do we approach Christianity as just another possibility among so many others? As, perhaps, a probability, but by no means a certainty? Was it not embarrassing for all of us when Karl Barth, following the attitude of the Reformers, said his uncompromising 'No!' to all attempts to approach God in terms of progressive assurance? Did we not hear in his words the voices of ancient and modern dictators? Is the fight between Paul and the Jewish perfectionists, between Augustine and the Pelagian rationalists, between Luther and the Erasmian humanists decided by a compromise in which, in reality, Paul, Augustine and Luther are defeated? I do not speak here of a theological defeat. I speak of a defeat in our hearts, in our lives, in the depths of our souls. Or can we still realize what Luther means when he exclaims, 'What is more miserable than uncertainty!'

But let us look more exactly at the nature of that certainty which Paul and Luther defend. The words of Paul show clearly that it is not *self*-certainty: '. . . Even if *we* . . . should preach to you a gospel contrary to that which we preached to you. . . .' The truth of the gospel Paul has preached is not dependent on Paul. The certainty he has is not dependent on the changes in his personal experience. He can imagine that some day he might preach a distorted gospel; he can even imagine that an angel from heaven might bring another message than that which the Church has already received. He is not sure of himself and he is not even sure of angelic visions. But he is sure of the gospel, so sure that he places himself and the highest spiritual powers under the threat of a divine curse if he or they should distort the gospel. For, he continues, the gospel I preach is not a human affair; no man put it into my head. I, yet not I; my gospel and yet not my gospel; my certainty and yet not my certainty. This is a description of our situation before God which runs through the whole Bible and the confessions of all the great Christian witnesses. It *is* our certainty, but it is lost the moment we begin to regard it as our certainty. We are certain only as long as we look at the content of our certainty and not at the rational or irrational experiences in which we have received it. Looking at ourselves and our certainty as *ours*, we discover its weakness, its vulnerability to every critical thought; we discover the small amount of probability which our reasoning can give to the idea of God and to the reality of the Christ. We discover the contradictions in the emotional side of our religious life, its oscillation between ecstatic confidence and despairing doubt. But looking at God, we realize that all the shortcomings of our experience are of no importance. Looking at God, we see that we do not have him as an object of our knowledge, but that he has us as the subject of our existence. Looking at God we feel that we cannot escape him even by making him an object of sceptical arguments or of irresistible emotions. We realize that in our uncertainty there is one fixed point of certainty, however we may name it and describe it and explain it. *We* may not comprehend, but we *are* comprehended. We may not grasp anything in the depth of our uncertainty, but that we are grasped by something ultimate, which keeps us in its grasp and from which we may strive in vain to escape, remains absolutely certain.

In this sense Luther speaks of Christian certainty. 'By assertion,' he writes, 'I mean a constant adhering, affirming, defending and invincibly persevering.' This certainty was not something he possessed as his own. Nobody has experienced the profundity of doubt more than he. The refuge in authority finally taken by both Augustine and Erasmus was made impossible by Luther. So were all possible arguments for religious truth and all confidence in his vocation as a reformer, in his religious strength and his accumulated experience. All these do not count in the ultimate uncertainty. But sometimes, when, in this worst of all hells, the first commandment, 'I am the Lord, *thy* God,' came to his mind, he knew that one certainty had not left him, and this was the only one which is ultimately needed.

Can we maintain this certainty in spite of the fundamental uncertainties which are the character of our period in religion as well as in all other realms of life? Can we maintain it in spite of our personal doubts and despairs and of our sceptical heritage? The answer to these questions does not depend on us. We can attain the certainty of the reformers and apostles whenever it is given to us to touch the ground of our existence and to look beyond ourselves. When we have left behind all objective probabilities about God and the Christ, and all subjective approximations to God and the Christ, when all preliminary certainties have disappeared, the ultimate certainty may appear to us. And in the power of this certainty, though never secure and never without temptation, we may walk from certainty to certainty.

10. 'By What Authority?'

One day, as he was teaching the people in the temple and preaching the gospel, the chief priests and the scribes with the elders came up and said to him, 'Tell us by what authority you do these things, or who it is that gave you this authority.' He answered them, 'I also will ask you a question; now tell me, Was the baptism of John from heaven or from men?' And they discussed it with one another, saying, 'If we say, "From

heaven," he will say, "Why did you not believe him?"
But if we say, "From men," all the people will stone us;
for they are convinced that John was a prophet.' So
they answered that they did not know whence it was.
And Jesus said to them, 'Neither will I tell you by
what authority I do these things.'

LUKE 20:1-8

The story we have read was very important to the early
Christians who preserved it for us. If we look at it super-
ficially, no reason seems to exist for such a high valuation: the Jewish leaders tried to trap Jesus by a shrewd
question, and Jesus trapped them by an even shrewder
question. It is a pleasant anecdote. But is it more than
this? Indeed, it is infinitely more. It does something surprising: it answers the fundamental question of prophetic religion by not answering it. An answer to the
question of authority is refused by Jesus, but the way
in which he refuses the answer *is* the answer.

Let us imagine that he had answered the question of
the religious leaders about *his* authority by asking them
about the sources of *their* authority! They could have
replied easily and convincingly. The chief priests could
have said, 'The source of our authority is our consecration according to a tradition which goes back without
interruption to Moses and Aaron. The sacred tradition
of which we are a link from the past to the future gives
us our authority.'

And the scribes could have answered, 'The source of
our authority is our knowledge – beyond that of anybody else – of the Scriptures. We have studied them day
and night since our early childhood, as a student of the
Word of God must do. Because we are experts in interpreting the holy Scriptures, we have authority.'

And the elders could have said to Jesus, 'The source
of our authority is our acquisition of wisdom through
many years, and our experience in applying it to the
questions of the day. Our wisdom and our experience

give us our authority.'

And they all together would have said to Jesus, 'But who are you, who are not consecrated and not studied in the Scriptures, and without the wisdom of age and the experience of practice? Which is the source of your authority? You have not only taught and preached, you have also acted as a radical, without our approval. You have driven out of the temple all who sold and bought, you have overturned the tables of the money-changers and the seats of those who sold pigeons. And you know yourself that they are necessary for the preservation of the temple and its cult, and for the performance of the sacrifices! By what authority have you turned against the religion as it has been given to us by Moses and by all generations since his time?'

Thus they could have answered his question. But Jesus does not ask them this question. He asks, 'Was the baptism of John from heaven or from men?' And to this they could not answer. If they had said that it was from men, they would have hurt the popular feeling and perhaps even a feeling within themselves, that John was a prophet. But if they had said that he was from God, they would have established an authority beyond the threefold authority which they could claim for themselves. And this they did not want. *They*, who were called authorities, demanded that all authority be vested in *them*. Therefore, they did not accept John as a prophet, nor Jesus as the Christ. . . . Don't minimize the seriousness of this conflict. It was not simply a conflict between good and evil, between faith and unbelief. The conflict was much more profound and much more tragic than this!

Let us imagine that we ourselves were in the place of those who asked Jesus about the source of his authority. Let us imagine ourselves as the guardians of a great religious tradition, or as the unquestionable experts in a sphere of decisive importance for human existence, or as people who have learned through a long experience to deal with matters of highest value. And let us also assume that we had no function as legally established authorities, and that somebody came and spoke about the same things in quite a different language and acted in the field of our authority in quite a radical way; how would *we* react? And if the people who saw and heard this man said of him what they said about Jesus, that he teaches as one who has authority and not as we the established authorities, how would *we* react? Would we not think: he confuses the masses, he spreads dangerous doctrines, he undermines well-proved laws and institutions, he introduces strange modes of life and thought, he disrupts sacred ties, he destroys traditions from which generations of men have received discipline and strength and hope? It is our duty to resist him and if possible to remove him! For the sake of our people we must defend our consecrated and tested authority against this man who cannot show the source of the authority he claims. Could we be blamed for such a re-action? And if not, can we blame the authorities in Jerusalem for their reaction to Jesus?

We think of the Reformation. This was a moment in the history of the Church in which the question of authority was once more in the centre of events. Luther, and consequently the whole Protestant world, broke away from the Roman Church and from 1500 years of Christian tradition when no agreement about the authority of the pope and the councils could be reached. Here, again, someone had arisen who spoke and acted with an authority the sources of which could not be determined by legal means. And here also we must ask, 'Are the Catholic authorities who rejected him in the name of their established authority to be blamed for it?' But if we do not *blame* them, we can ask them, 'Why do *you* blame the Jewish authorities, who did exactly the same as you did when the people said of the Reformers that they spoke with authority and not like the priests and monks?' Is the same thing so different if it is done by the Jewish high priest and if it is done by the Roman high priest? And one may ask the present-day Protestant authorities in Europe and in this country, 'Are you certain that the insistence on your authority, on your tradition, and on your experience does not suppress the kind of authority which Jesus had in mind?'

And now we ask, 'What does authority mean? What does it mean for man as man? What does it mean for our period and for each of us?'

First of all, it means that we are finite and in need of what the word 'authority' really says: to be started and increased. It means that we are born, that we were infants and children, that we were completely dependent on those who gave us life and home and guidance and contents for soul and mind. We were not able to decide for ourselves for many years, and that made us dependent on authority and made authority a benefit for us. We accepted this authority without resistance, even if we rebelled on special occasions. And this authority became the basis for all other authorities. It gave strength to the authority of the older brother or sister, of the more mature friend or teacher, of the official, of the ruler, of the minister. And through them we have been introduced into the institutions and traditions in society, state and Church. Authority permeates, guides, shapes our lives. The acceptance of authority is the acceptance of what is given by those who have more than we. And our subjection to them and to what they stand for enables us to live in history, as our subjection to the laws of nature enables us to live in nature. And from the authority of the law is derived the authority of those who represent and administer it and who, for this reason, are called 'the authorities'.

Our daily life would be impossible without traditions of behaviour and customs and the authority of those who have received them and surrendered them to us. Man's control of nature would be impossible without the tradition of knowledge and skill into which every new generation is introduced and which gives authority to those who are able to introduce us. Man's intellectual life – the language he uses, the songs he sings, the music he plays, the houses he builds, the pictures he paints, the symbols he creates – he has received through the authority of those who have participated in it before him. Man's religious life – the faith he holds, the cult he loves, the stories and legends he has heard, the commandments he tries to obey, the texts he knows by heart – all this is not created by him; he takes it from those who represent to him religious authority.

And if he revolts against the authorities which have shaped him, he does it with the tools he has received from them. The language of the revolutionary is formed by those against whom he revolts. The protest of the reformer uses the tradition against which he protests. Therefore, no absolute revolution is possible. If it is attempted, it fails immediately; and if a revolution succeeds, its leaders soon have to use forms and ideas created by the authorities of the past. This is true of the rebellion of the adolescent against the family authority as well as of the rebellion of new social groups against the authority of the established powers.

When we speak of human finitude, we usually think of man's transitoriness in time, of birth and death, of the vicissitudes which threaten him in every moment. But we are not only finite in that we are temporal, we are also finite in that we are historical and that means subject to authority, even if we rebel against it. We are thrown into existence, not only bodily, but also mentally. In no respect are we by ourselves, in no moment can we be by ourselves. He who tries to be without authority tries to be like God, who alone is by himself. And like everyone who tries to be like God, he is thrown down to self-destruction, be it a single human being, be it a nation, be it a period of history like our own.

In our story, Jesus as well as his foes acknowledges authority. They struggle about *valid* authority, not about authority as such. And this is what we find everywhere in the Bible and the life of the Church. Paul fights with the original disciples, including Peter, about the foundations of apostolic authority. The bishops fight with the enthusiasts about the leadership in the Church. The popes fight with the princes about the ultimate source of political authority. The reformers fight with the hierarchs about the interpretation of the Bible. The theologians fight with the scientists about the criteria of ultimate truth. None of the struggling groups denies authority, but each of them denies the authority of the other group.

But if the authority is split in itself, which authority decides? Is not split authority the end of authority? Was not the split produced by the Reformation the end of the authority of the Church? Is not the split about the interpretation of the Bible the end of the biblical authority? Is not the split between theologians and scientists the end of intellectual authority? Is not the split between father and mother the end of parental authority? Was not the split between the gods of polytheism the end of their divine authority? Is not the split in one's conscience the end of the authority of one's conscience? If one has to choose between different authorities, not *they* but *oneself* is ultimate authority for oneself, and this means: there is no authority for him.

This, however, creates the dreadful alternative of *our* historical period. If there is no authority, we must decide ourselves, each for himself. As finite beings we must act as if we were infinite, and since this is impossible, we are driven into complete insecurity, anxiety and despair. Or, unable to stand the loneliness of deciding for ourselves, we suppress the fact that there is a split authority. We subject ourselves to a definite authority and close our eyes against all other claims. The desire of most people to do this is very well known to those in power. They use the unwillingness of human beings to decide for themselves in order to preserve their power and to increase it. This is true of religious as well as of political powers. On this ground of human weakness the systems of authority are built in past and present.

'By what authority do you do this?' Jesus is asked. And he answers not by answering but by pointing to the acting and speaking of John. Here, he tells the leaders of his nation, you see the rise of an authority without ritual or legal foundation. But you deny the possibility of it. So you deny both the Baptist and myself. You deny the possibility of an authority guaranteed by its inner power. You have forgotten that the only test of the prophets was the power of what they had to say. Listen to what the *people* say about us, namely, that *we* speak with authority and not as *you*, who are called the 'authorities'. That is what he tells them.

What would he say to us? He would not have to fight about his authority with the chief priests and the scribes and the elders of our day. In our time they all acknowledge him. He would have to ask a quite different question of them. He would have to ask: 'What is the nature of *my* authority for you? Is it like that of John the Baptist, or is it like that of the authorities who tried to remove me? Have you made the words of those who have witnessed to me, the Bible, the Church Fathers, the popes, the reformers, the creeds, into ultimate authorities? Have you done this in my name? And if so, do you not abuse my name? For whenever my name is remembered, my fight with those who were in authority is also remembered.'

There is something in the Christian message which is opposed to established authority. There is something in the Christian experience which revolts against subjection to even the greatest and holiest experiences of the past. And this something is indicated in the question of Jesus, 'Was the baptism of John from God or man?' and in his refusal to give an answer! That which makes an answer impossible is the nature of an authority which is derived from God and not man. The place where God gives authority to a man cannot be circumscribed. It cannot be legally defined. It cannot be put into the fences of doctrines and rituals. It is here, and you do not know where it comes from. You cannot derive it. You must be grasped by it. You must participate in its power. This is the reason why the question of authority never can get an ultimate answer. Certainly there are many preliminary answers. There is no day in our lives in which we do not give, silently or openly, answers to the question of authority, saying mostly 'yes' and sometimes 'no'.

But an ultimate answer we cannot give. We only can point to a reality, as Jesus does. And this is what our religious leaders could and should do – the churches, and the ministers, and the theologians, and every Christian who acts as a priest to other Christians. They all can raise their finger as Jesus did to John, and as John did to Jesus. We all can point passionately, but not as established authorities, to the Crucified – as does the Baptist, in the tremendous picture by the old painter Matthias Grünewald. There his whole being is in the finger with which he points to the Cross. This is the greatest symbol of which I know for the true authority of the Church and the Bible. They should not point to themselves but to the reality which breaks again and again through the established forms of their authority and through the hardened forms of our personal experiences.

And once more we ask : 'What does it mean that the question of authority cannot get an ultimate answer?' It would sound like a blasphemy if I said, 'Because God himself cannot give an answer'. It would sound not blasphemous but conventional if I said, 'Because God is Spirit'. Yet both sentences mean the same. God who is Spirit cannot give an ultimate answer to the question of authority. The churches, their leaders and members, often ignore the infinite significance of the words 'God is Spirit'. But the sharp eyes of the enemy see what these words mean. Nietzsche calls the man who first said that God is Spirit the first one of those who have killed God. His profound insight into the human soul made it certain to him that a God who is not circumscribed on a definite place, who does not answer definitively the question of authority, cannot be accepted by most human beings. If he were right, we either had to agree with him that there is no God left, or we had to return to a God who tells us a definite answer to the question of authority, and subjects us by divine order to an established religious authority as the earthly representative of his own heavenly authority. But this God is not the God who is Spirit. Actually, such a God is the heavenly image of the earthly authorities which use him for the consecration of their own power. This God is not the God of whom Jesus speaks in our story.

The God who cannot answer the question of ultimate authority because he is Spirit does not remove the preliminary authorities with whom we live our daily lives. He does not condemn us to the emptiness of an adolescent who feels that the world must start with himself. He does not deprive us of the protection of those who have more wisdom and power than we have. He does not isolate us from the community to which we belong and which is a part of ourselves. But he denies ultimate significance to all these preliminary authorities, to all those who claim to be images of his authority and who distort God's authority into the oppressive power of a heavenly tyrant.

The God who does not answer the question of ultimate authority transforms the preliminary authorities into media and tools of himself – of the God who is Spirit. Parental authority on earth is not the consecrated image of a parental authority in heaven, but it is the earliest tool through which the spiritual qualities of order and self-control and love are mediated to us. Therefore, the parents must be and remain subjects of honour, but not of unconditional authority. Even God whom we call the Father in heaven cannot answer the ultimate question of authority. How could the parents?

The authority of wisdom and knowledge on earth is not the consecrated image of the authority of heavenly omniscience, but it is the tool through which the spiritual qualities of humility and knowledge and wisdom are mediated to us. Therefore, the wise ones should be honoured but not accepted as unconditional authorities.

The authorities in community and society, in nation and state, are not consecrated images of heavenly power and justice, but they are tools through which the spiritual qualities of mutuality, understanding, righteousness, and courage can be mediated to us. Therefore, the social authorities should be accepted as guarantees of external order but not as those which determine the meaning of our lives.

The authority of the Church is not the consecrated earthly image of the heavenly ruler of the Church, but it is a medium through which the spiritual substance of our lives is preserved and protected and reborn.

Even the authority of Jesus the Christ is not the consecrated image of the man who rules as a dictator, but it is the authority of him who emptied himself of all authority; it is the authority of the man on the Cross. It is one and the same thing, if you say that God is Spirit and that he is manifest on the Cross.

And you who are fighting *against* authorities and you who are searching *for* authorities, listen to the story in which Jesus fights against them and establishes an authority which cannot be established! Here is an answer, namely, that no answer can be given except the one that, beyond all preliminary authorities, you must keep yourselves open to the power of him who is the ground and the negation of everything which is authority on earth and in heaven! . . .

11. Has the Messiah Come?

Now there was a man in Jerusalem, whose name was Simeon, and this man was righteous and devout, looking for the consolation of Israel, and the Holy Spirit was upon him. And it had been revealed to him by the Holy Spirit that he should not see death before he had seen the Lord's Christ. And inspired by the Spirit he came into the temple; and when the parents brought in the child Jesus, to do for him according to the custom of the law, he took him up in his arms and blessed God and said,

'Lord, now lettest thou thy servant depart in
    peace, according to thy word;
for mine eyes have seen thy salvation
which thou has prepared in the presence of
    all peoples,
a light for revelation to the Gentiles,
and for glory to thy people Israel.'

LUKE 2:25-32

Then turning to the disciples [Jesus] said privately, 'Blessed are the eyes which see what you see! For I tell you that many prophets and kings desired to see what you see, and did not see it, and to hear what you hear, and did not hear it.'

LUKE 10:23-24

A few days ago I had a talk with a Jewish friend about the idea of the Messiah in Judaism and Christianity. We finally stated the difference in a way similar to the alternative put before Jesus by the disciples of John the Baptist: 'Are you the Coming One? Or are we to look out for someone else?' We agreed that the Jews are looking for someone else while the Christians assert that the 'Coming One' has already come. The Christians say with Simeon: 'Our eyes *have* seen his salvation.' The Jews reply: 'We have *not* seen his salvation, we are waiting for it.' The Christians feel blessed, according to the words of Jesus, because they have seen the presence of the saving power within the world and history. The Jews consider such a feeling almost blasphemous, since, according to their faith, nothing of what they expect to happen in the Messianic age has actually happened. And when we defend our Christian faith they point to the fact that the world has not become better since the days of Hosea and Jeremiah, that the Jews – and with them the largest part of mankind – are suffering not less than they did two thousand years ago; that the prophetic visions of doom are more realistic today than they were in those days. It is hard to answer this; but we *must* answer it for not only the Jews, but also innumerable Christians and non-Christians, our friends and our children, and something in ourselves ask these questions.

It is hard to answer them. What, for instance, *can* we answer when our children ask us about the child in the manger while in some parts of the world all children 'from two years old and under' have died and are dying, not by an order of Herod, but by the ever-increasing cruelty of war and its results in the Christian era and by the decrease of the power of imagination in the Christian people. Or, what can we answer the Jews when the remnants of the Jewish people, returning from death-camps, worse than anything in Babylon, cannot find a resting place anywhere on the surface of the earth, and certainly not amongst the great Christian nations? Or, what can we answer Christians and non-Christians who have realized that the fruit of centuries of Christian technical and social civilization is the imminent threat of a complete and universal self-destruction of humanity? And what answer can we give to ourselves when we look at the unhealed and unsaved stage of our own lives after the message of healing and salvation has been heard at every Christmas for almost two thousand years?

Should we say that *the world*, of course, is unsaved but that there are men and women in all generations who are saved *from* the world? But this is not the message of Christmas. All those in the Christmas legend who expect the Christ and receive the divine are looking out for the salvation of Israel and of the Gentiles and of the world. For all of them, and for Jesus himself, and for the apostles, the kingdom of God, the universal salvation is at hand. But if this was the expectation, has it not been utterly refuted by reality?

This question is as old as the Christian message itself and the answer is equally old, as our texts indicate. Jesus takes his disciples aside and speaks privately to them when he praises them because they see what they are seeing. The presence of the Messiah is a mystery; it cannot be said to everybody, and it cannot be seen by everybody, but only by those like Simeon who are driven by the Spirit. There is something surprising, unexpected about the appearance of salvation, something which contradicts pious opinions and intellectual demands. *The mystery of salvation is the mystery of a child*. So it was anticipated by Isaiah, by the ecstatic vision of the sibyl and by the poetic vision of Virgil, by the doctrines of mysteries and by the rites of those who celebrated the birth of the new aeon. They all felt as did the early Christians, that the event of salvation is the birth of a child. A child is real and not yet real, it is *in* history and not yet historical. Its nature is visible and invisible, it is here and not yet here. And just this is the character of salvation. *Salvation has the nature of a child*. As Christendom remembers every year, in the most impressive of its festivals, the child Jesus, so salvation, however visible it may be, remains always *also* invisible. He who wants a salvation which is *only* visible cannot see the divine child in the manger as he cannot see the divinity of the Man on the Cross and the paradoxical way of all divine acting. Salvation is a child and when it grows up it is crucified. Only he who can see power under weakness, the whole under the fragment, victory under defeat, glory under suffering, innocence under guilt, sanctity under sin, life under death can say: mine eyes have seen the salvation.

It is hard to say this in our days. But it always has been hard and it always will be hard. It was and is and will be a mystery, the mystery of a child. And however deep the world might fall, even into utter self-destruction, as long as there are men they will experience this mystery and say: 'Blessed are the eyes which see the things that we see.'

12. 'He Who Believes in Me . . .'

And Jesus cried out and said, 'He who believes in me, believes not in me but in him who sent me. And he who sees me sees him who sent me. I have come as light into the world, that whoever believes in me may not remain in darkness. If any one hears my sayings and does not keep them, I do not judge him; for I did not come to judge the world but to save the world. He who rejects me and does not receive my sayings has a judge; the word that I have spoken will be his judge on the last day. For I have not spoken on my own authority; the Father who sent me has himself given me commandment what to say and what to speak. And I know that his commandment is eternal life. What I say, therefore, I say as the Father has bidden me.'

JOHN 12:44-50

'He who believes in me, believes not in *me* but in him who sent me. . . .' These words follow a bitter complaint of the evangelist about the unbelief and half-belief of the people and their leaders. The words are introduced by the phrase: 'Jesus cried out. . . .' He is making an almost desperate effort to be understood. And what he cries out is that believing in him means not believing in *him*. The argument of the unbelievers was – and is in all periods – that it is impossible to believe in Jesus of Nazareth as Jesus of Nazareth. Jesus declares: 'This argument is valid. If people are asked to believe in me, they should not do so. But they are not asked any such thing! They are asked to believe in him who has sent me, who is greater than I and with whom I am one. I have not spoken on my own authority.' He continues, 'If I did so, the unbelievers would be right.'

There are many authorities in past and present. Why accept one and not another? Why accept any authority? As Jesus the man Jesus is neither an authority nor an object of faith. None of his superior qualities – neither his religious life, nor his moral perfection, nor his profound insights – make him an object of faith or the ultimate authority. On this basis, he says, he does not judge anyone. If he did, he would be a tyrant who imposes himself and his greatness on others, thus destroying instead of saving them.

What about our preaching? When we use the name of Jesus, do we not often try to force upon those to whom we are speaking and upon ourselves something great besides God? Do we always make it clear that believing in him does not mean believing in *him*? If not, are we not working for destruction more than for salvation?

It seems that the Christian painters knew more about this than we often do. They did not present a picture of Jesus of Nazareth as Jesus of Nazareth. They painted him as the infant of Bethlehem who contains the whole universe, though 'lying now in Mary's lap,' as Luther sings. Through his infantile traits shines the power of the Lord of the world. Or they painted him as the visible bearer of the divine majesty in those great mosaics where every piece of his gown is transparent for the infinite depth he represents and expresses. Or they

H

painted him as the Crucified who does not suffer as an individual man, but as he who stands for both the suffering universe and the divine love which participates in its suffering. Or they painted him as the bringer of the new aeon who controls the powers of nature, the souls of men, the demonic forces of disease, insanity, and death. But they did not give him individual traits, did not make him a representative of a psychological type or of a sociological group.

Look at the pictures of the Sistine Chapel. Michaelangelo gave a special character to every prophet, to every sibyl. But when he painted Jesus as the ultimate judge, only an irresistible divine-human power appears.

When in our time Jesus became an object of biographical and psychological essays and was portrayed as a fanatic and neurotic, or as a pious sufferer, or as a social benefactor, or as a moral example, or as a religious teacher, or as a mass leader – he ceased to be the one in whom we can believe, for he ceased to be the one in whom we do *not* believe, if we believe in him. He was no longer the Jesus who is the Christ.

We cannot pray to anyone except to God. If Jesus is someone besides God, we cannot and should not pray to him. Many Christians, many among us, cannot find a way of joining honestly with those who pray to Jesus Christ. Something in us is reluctant, something which is genuine and valid, the fear of becoming idolatrous, the fear of being split in our ultimate loyalty, the fear of looking at two faces instead of at the one divine face.

But he who sees *him* sees the Father. There are not two faces. In the face of Jesus the Christ, God 'makes his face to shine upon us'. For nothing is left in the face of Jesus the Christ which is only Jesus of Nazareth, which is only the face of *one* individual besides others. Everything in his countenance is transparent to him who has sent him. Therefore, and therefore alone, can we sing at Christmas-time: 'O come, let us adore him!'

13. Yes and No

> Jesus Christ . . was not Yes and No; but in him it is
> always Yes. For all the promises of God find their Yes
> in him.
>
> 2 CORINTHIANS 1:19, 20

A change in his travelling plans and the angry reaction
of the Corinthian Christians to this change is used by
Paul for profound and far-reaching assertions about Jesus
'the Christ': 'In him it is always Yes, he is not Yes and
No.' This reminds us by contrast of the words of a great
Protestant mystic who has said that in Yes and No all
things consist, and of philosophers and theologians who
are convinced that truth can only be expressed through
No and Yes, and above all of Paul's own central doctrine
that God justifies the sinner, that he says 'yes' to him
to whom he says a radical 'no' at the same time. And
does not Paul in this second letter to the Corinthians formulate the Yes and No in a most paradoxical way:
'Unknown and yet well known, dying and behold we
live, having nothing and yet possessing everything.'
This certainly is Yes and No. But in the Christ, he says,
there is not Yes and No. Really not? Do we not come
from Good Friday to Easter, which point to the deepest
No and the highest Yes – that of the death and life of
the Christ?

Yes and No: this certainly is the law of all life, but
not Yes alone and not No alone. Yes alone is the advice
of a self-deceiving confidence which soon will be shaken
by the No of the three grey figures: emptiness, guilt,
death. No alone is the advice of a self-deceiving despair
whose hidden Yes to itself is manifest in its self-seclusion and its resistance against the Yes of love and communion. And further, Yes and No is the law of all truth.
Not Yes alone and not No alone! Yes alone is the arro-

gance which claims that its limited truth is the ultimate truth, but which reveals by its fanatical self-affirmation how many hidden No's are present in its ground. No alone is the resignation which denies any ultimate truth but which shows by its self-complacent irony against the biting power of every word of truth how strong the Yes to itself is that underlies its ever-repeated No.

Truth as well as life unites Yes and No, and only the courage which accepts the infinite tension between Yes and No can have abundant life and ultimate truth. How is such a courage possible? It is possible because there is a Yes above the Yes and No of life and of truth. But it is a Yes which is not ours. If it were ours, even our greatest, our most universal and most courageous Yes, it would be contrasted by another No. This is the reason why no theology and no philosophy, not even a theology or philosophy of 'Yes and No' is ultimate truth. In the moment in which it is expressed, it is contradicted by another philosophy and another theology. Not even the message of Yes and No, be it said by Kierkegaard or by Luther or by Paul, can escape its No. There is only one reality where there is not Yes and No but only Yes: Jesus as the Christ. First he also stands under the No, as completely as a being can stand; this is the meaning of the Cross. Everything of him which is only the expression of a finite life or a finite truth stands with all life and all truth under the No. Therefore, we are not asked to accept him as the unquestionable teacher or as the always fitting example, but we are told that in him all promises of God have become real, and that in him a life and a truth which are beyond Yes and No have become manifest. This is the meaning of 'resurrection'. The No of death is conquered and the Yes of life is transcended by that which has appeared in him. A life which is not balanced by death, a truth which is not balanced by error is visible in his being. He shows the final Yes without another No. This is the Easter message; this is the Christian message altogether. And this is the ground of a courage which can stand the infinite tension between Yes and No in everything finite, even in everything religious and in everything Christian.

Paul points to the fact that the Christians say Amen through Christ. One cannot say Amen to anything except the reality which is the Christ. Amen is the formula of confirmation, the expression of ultimate certitude. There is no ultimate certitude except the life which has conquered its death and the truth which has conquered its error, the Yes which is beyond Yes and No.

Paul points to that which gives us such a certainty: it is not an historical report, but it is the participation *in* Christ, in whom we are established, as he says, who has given us the guarantee of his spirit in our hearts. We can stand the Yes and No of life and truth because we participate in the Yes beyond Yes and No, because we are *in* it as it is *in* us. We are participants of his resurrection; therefore, we can say the ultimate Yes, the Amen beyond *our* Yes and *our* No.

14. 'Who Are My Mother and My Brothers . . .?'

Then he went home; and the crowd came together again, so that they could not even eat. And when his friends heard it, they went out to seize him; for they said, 'He is beside himself.'

MARK 3:19-21

And his mother and his brothers came; and standing outside they sent to him and called him. And a crowd was sitting about him; and they said to him, 'Your mother and your brothers are outside, asking for you.' And he answered, 'Who are my mother and my brothers?' And looking around on those who sat about him, he said, 'Here are my mother and my brothers! Whoever does the will of God is my brother, and sister, and mother.'

MARK 3:31-35

For most of those who go away to a university to study, it is not the first time that they leave the home of their parents. But for all of them it is an important step on their own independent way of life. Every step on this road brings them farther away from the place from which they came, the family into which they were born. The first moves towards independence occur very early in life – as exemplified in the story of the twelve-year-old Jesus in the temple. And none of these moves is without pain and tragic guilt – as indicated in the anxiety of the parents of Jesus and the reproaches they made to him. But only after Jesus has begun his public activities the depth of the gap between him and his family becomes fully manifest. In the story which we have just read and which is recorded by the three first Gospels, Jesus uses the family relations as symbols for a relation of a higher order, for the community of those who do the will of God. Something unconditional breaks into the conditional relations of the natural family and creates a community which is as intimate and as strong as the family relations, and at the same time infinitely superior to it. The depth of this gap is emphasized in the attempt of his family to seize him and to bring him home because of his extraordinary behaviour which makes them believe that he is out of his mind. And the gap is strongly expressed in his saying that he who loves father and mother more than him cannot be his disciple, words even sharpened in Luke's version, where everyone is rejected by him who does not 'hate' father and mother and wife and children and brothers and sisters – and his own life.

All these words cut with divine power through the natural relation between the members of the family whenever these relations claim to be ultimates. They cut through the bondage of age-old traditions and conventions and their unconditional claims; they cut through the consecration of the family ties by sacramental or other laws which make them equal to the ties between those who belong to the new reality in the Christ. The family is no ultimate! The family relations are not unconditional relations. The consecration of the family is not a consecration for the final aim of man's existence. We can imagine the revolutionary character of such sayings in face of the religions and cultures of mankind. We can hardly measure their disturbing character in face of what has happened century after century within the so-called Christian nations – with the support of the Christian churches who could not stand the radical nature of the Christian message in this as in other respects. However, in spite of its radicalism, the Christian message does not request the dissolution of the family. It affirms the family and limits its significance. Jesus takes up the prophecy of Micah, that in the last days 'brother will deliver up brother to death, and the father his child, and children will rise against parents and have them put to death'. It belongs to periods in which the demonic powers get hold of the world, that the family community is turned into its opposite. But when Jesus uses this prophecy, he adds, 'And you will be hated by all for my name's sake'. The same words which point to the demonic disruption of the family are used to describe its inescapable divine disruption. This is the profound ambiguity of the biblical teaching about the family.

Now let us look into our own situation. We cannot cut the ties with our family without being guilty. But the question is: is it wilfulness which demonically disrupts the family communion, or is it the step toward independence and one's own understanding of the will of God which divinely liberates us from the bondage to our family? We never know the answer with certainty. We must risk tragic guilt in becoming free from father and mother and brothers and sisters. And we know today better than many generations before us what that means, how infinitely difficult it is and that nobody does it without carrying scars in his soul his whole life. For it is not only the real father or mother or brother or sister from whom we must become free in order to come into our own. It is something much more refined, the image of them, which from our earliest childhood has impregnated our souls. The real father, the real mother may let us go free, although this is by no means the rule in Christian families. But even if they have the wisdom to do it, their images can prevent us from doing what the will of God is in a concrete situation, namely, to do acts in which love, power and justice are united. Their image may prevent us from love by subjection to law. It may prevent us from having power by weakening our personal centre. It may prevent us from exercising justice by blinding us to a concrete situation and its demands. And the same happens with the images of brothers and sisters. Although it is easier to become free from them in an external sense, they may hiddenly produce decisions which determine for the worse whole periods of our lives.

But do not mistake me! Opposition and revolt are not yet freedom. They are unavoidable stages on the way to freedom. But they create another servitude if they are not overcome as much as the early dependence must be overcome. How can this happen? Certainly, in pathological cases, psychotherapy is needed, as Jesus himself acted as a healer, bodily and mentally. But more is necessary, namely, the dependence on that which gives ultimate independence, the image of that which includes and transcends all father and mother images, the life of that which makes it possible to hate and to love every life, including our own. No human problem and certainly not the family problem can be solved on a finite level. This is true although we know that even the image of God can be distorted by the images of father and mother, so that its saving power is almost lost. This is the danger of all religion and a serious limit for our religious work. But it is not a limit for God, who again and again breaks through the images we have

made of him, and who has shown in Christ that he is
not only father and mother to us, but also child, and
that therefore in him the inescapable conflicts of every
family are overcome. The Father who is also child is
more than a father as he is more than a child. Therefore
we can pray to the Father in heaven without transfer-
ring our hostility against the father image to him. Because God has become child, it is possible for us to say
the 'Our Father'.

15. 'All Is Yours'

If anyone among you thinks that he is wise in this age,
let him become a fool that he may become wise. For
the wisdom of this world is folly with God.

                                    I CORINTHIANS 3:18-19

When a speaker in a morning chapel service used this as
his text, I got a written question in class: 'What do you
think about this morning's sermon?' And this was the
implication: how can philosophy stand in view of
Paul's depreciating words? I want to answer by trying
to interpret what I believe Paul means, not only in the
passage above but in the whole context. At the end of
his discussion he gives the key by saying: *Let no one
boast of men. For all things are yours, whether Paul or
Apollos or Cephas or the world or life or death or the
present or the future, all are yours; and you are Christ's
and Christ is God's.* (1 Corinthians 3:21-23.)

Paul has asked, 'Has not God made foolish the wisdom
of the world?' And now he exclaims, 'World and life
and Apollos are yours.' This means that the wisdom of
the world is ours also. How could it be otherwise? We
could not even read Paul's words without the wisdom of
the world which enables us to understand ancient texts,
which gives us the technical tools to spread the Christian message all over the earth, which produces and sus-

tains the political and educational and artistic institutions which serve and protect the Church. All this is ours. And even the different theologies are ours: the more dialectical one of Paul, the more ritualistic one of Peter, the more apologetic one of Apollos. There is only one type of theology which Paul dislikes – that which wants to monopolize the Christ and call itself the party of Christ. For each of these theologies wisdom of the world is needed; scribes are needed, debaters are needed, philosophers are needed, a language is needed to which everybody contributes. It is impossible to deny all this. But it is possible to discredit through loose talk what one cannot avoid using at the same time. There is a deep dishonesty in the accusation against the use of historical research and philosophical thought in theology. In daily life one calls somebody dishonest who brings defamation upon those whom he uses. We should not commit this dishonesty in our theological work. And we cannot escape using the wisdom of this world. It is no escape if we say : let us use a little of it, but not much, in order to escape the dangers implied in it. This certainly is not what Paul means. The whole world is yours, he says, the whole life, present and future, not parts of it. These important words speak of scientific knowledge and its passion, artistic beauty and its excitement, politics and their use of power, eating and drinking and their joy, sexual love and its ecstasy, family life and its warmth and friendship with its intimacy, justice with its clarity, nature with its might and restfulness, the man-made world above nature, the technical world and its fascination, philosophy with its humility – daring only to call itself love of wisdom – and its profundity – daring to ask ultimate questions. In all these things is wisdom of this world and power of this world and all these things are ours. They belong to us and we belong to them; we create them and they fulfil us.

But . . . and this 'but' of Paul's is not one of those 'buts' in which everything is taken back that was given before. The great 'but' to the world which is ours gives both the foundation and the limit of the world that is ours: 'And you are Christ's', namely, that Christ whose Cross is foolishness and weakness to the wisdom of the world. The wisdom of this world in all its forms cannot know God, and the power of this world with all its means cannot reach God. If they try it, they produce idolatry and are revealed in their foolishness which is the foolishness of idolatry. No finite being can attain the infinite without being broken as he who represented the world, and its wisdom and its power, was broken on the Cross. This is the foolishness and the weakness of the Cross which is ultimate wisdom and which is the reason that Christ is not another bearer of wisdom and power of this world but that he is God's. The Cross makes him God's. And out of this foolishness we win the wisdom to use what is ours, the wisdom of the world, even philosophy. If it be unbroken, it controls us. If it be broken, it is ours. 'Broken' does not mean reduced or emaciated or controlled, but it means undercut in its idolatric claim.

Paul's courage is affirming everything given, his openness towards the world, his sovereignty towards life should put to shame each of us as well as all our churches. We are afraid to accept what is given to us; we are in compulsive self-seclusion towards our world, we try to escape life instead of controlling it. We do not behave as if everything were ours. And the churches do so even less. The reason for this is that we and our churches do not know as Paul did what it means to be Christ's and because of being Christ's, to be God's.

16. 'Is There Any Word from the Lord?'

I did not send the prophets, yet they ran; I did not speak to them, yet they prophesied. But if they had stood in my council, then they would have proclaimed

my words to my people, and they would have turned
them from their evil way, and from the evil of their
doings.

Am I a God at hand, says the Lord, and not a God
afar off? Can a man hide himself in secret places so
that I cannot see him? says the Lord. Do I not fill
heaven and earth? says the Lord. I have heard what
the prophets have said who prophesy lies in my name,
saying, 'I have dreamed, I have dreamed!' How long
shall there be lies in the heart of the prophets who prophesy lies, and who prophesy the deceit of their own
heart, who think to make my people forget my name
by their dreams which they tell one another, even as
their fathers forgot my name for Baal? Let the prophet
who has a dream tell the dream, but let him who has
my word speak my word faithfully. What has straw
in common with wheat? says the Lord. Is not my
word like fire, says the Lord, and like a hammer which
breaks the rock in pieces? Therefore, behold, I am
against the prophets, says the Lord, who steal my
words from one another. Behold, I am against the prophets, says the Lord, who use their tongues and say,
'Says the Lord.'

JEREMIAH 23:21-31

Then Zedekiah the king asked Jeremiah secretly in his
house and said: 'Is there any word from the Lord?'
And Jeremiah said: 'There is: for thou shalt be
delivered into the hand of the king of Babylon.'

JEREMIAH 37:17

Is there any word from the Lord? This is a question
asked by kings in moments of danger. They asked it of
priests and prophets. It has been asked by people in all
ages and places in times of unrest. They asked it of
extraordinary men and women, often of those considered to be abnormal, of ecstatics and hysterics. It has
been asked by individuals in moments of great personal
decisions. They asked it of holy Scriptures which should
give a special word to them, from saints and inner voices.

What about ourselves? Have we never asked for a word from the Lord? Many, certainly, will answer with a definite 'No'. They will tell us that they always decided for themselves, using their own reasonable judgment, based on experience, knowledge, and intelligence. Perhaps they impress us. Perhaps we are ashamed to confess that sometimes we *have* asked for a word from the Lord. But let us wait with our answer until we have found out what these words mean.

We should not be misled by the phrase, 'word from the Lord'. It sounds as if we turned to a heavenly authority after all others, including the authority of reason, have failed. It sounds as if we asked the Lord of providence to give us for a moment a glimpse into what he plans for us, individually and in history. But such a favour is not granted. The answers given by seers, ecstatics, books and inner voices are mostly ambiguous, open to different interpretations, so that we would have to ask for a second divine word to interpret the first, and so on indefinitely. Or, these answers are clear and agree with the best wisdom we can have without them. Therefore, I repeat: let us not be misled by the phrase 'word from the Lord'. It is not an oracle-word telling us what to do or to expect. Then what is it?

It is the voice from another dimension than that in which we ordinarily live. It cuts into the dimension of things and events which we call our world. It does not help us to manage things within this dimension more successfuly than before. It does not add to our knowledge of the factors which influence a situation, it does not remove the responsibility for our decisions. It does something else. It elevates the situation in which we have to decide, into the light of a new dimension, the dimension of that which is ultimately important and infinitely significant and for which we use the word 'Divine'.

So it was in the case of the king Zedekiah and of the false prophets with whom Jeremiah had to fight. The

king came to Jeremiah in a hopeless situation, in a
situation into which he had brought himself and his
people through guilt and error and disregard of the
warnings of the prophet. He was supported in his wrong
decision by nationalistic politicians who called themselves 'prophets' without having received a word from
God. They did not interpret the situation of Judah in the
midst of threatening empires in its seriousness. They
lacked the realism which is the quality of true prophet-
ism. They were not able to look beyond political chances
and military calculations. And so disaster approached
and brought about Zedekiah's desperate attempts to get
a consoling or helping word from the prophet. But he
did not get it. Out of his prison Jeremiah tells him the
only thing he did *not* want to hear : you shall be delivered into the hand of the king of Babylon ! God will
not save you ! And the king felt : so it is ! He did not
slay the prophet of doom, as present-day dictators or
nationalistic mobs would do. On the contrary, he helped
him out of his miserable prison. But he did not do anything to change the situation. It was too late for this
politically and psychologically, and the threat of the
prophet, the word he had received from the Lord for
Zedekiah, became a terrible reality. Yet it was spoken
in vain. It has been remembered ever since, not as an
interesting historical report but as an event in which
the eternal gives ultimate meaning to an historical catastrophe.

The many words from the Lord which are recorded in
the Old Testament have the same quality. They are not
promises of an omnipotent ruler replacing political or
military strength. They are not lessons handed down by
an omniscient teacher, replacing sound judgments. They
are not advices of a heavenly counsellor, replacing in-
telligent human counsel. But they are manifestations of
something ultimate breaking into our existence with all
its preliminary concerns and insights. They do not add
something to our situation, but they add a dimension to

the dimension in which we ordinarily live. The word from the Lord is the word which speaks out of the depth of our situation. It is, one could say, the deepest meaning of the situation, of every situation which comes to us in such words.

It is also the depth of our own situation that speaks to us when we receive a word from the Lord.

Let us imagine an hour in which we have to make an important decision, be it the choice of a vocation, be it the choice of a mate for life. We know most of the factors which could determine our decision, and we know the ways our souls work in relation to these factors. Nevertheless, we cannot decide. *The anxiety of the possible* makes us restless. We see one, two, perhaps more possibilities. We realize a disturbing number of possible consequences in each of them. We ask friends, counsellors; we seek for counsel in ourselves. But the anxiety of having to decide increases. And a longing grows in our souls, a longing for something that liberates us from the anxiety of the possible and gives us the courage toward the real. It is the question of our text: is there a word from the Lord? And perhaps an answer has been received. But it was not an oracle-word pointing to the right vocation to choose, or the right man or woman to join with. It was a voice out of the depth of our situation, elevating our concrete problems into an ultimate perspective. In doing so, it probably has devaluated some factors determining our decision and has stressed others. Or it has left the balance of possibilities unchanged, but has given us the courage to make a decision with all the risks of a decision, including error, failure, guilt. The word from the Lord, the voice out of the depth of our situation, ends the anxiety of the possible and gives the courage to affirm the real with its many questionable elements.

Some of you may say: if this is what 'word from the Lord' means, how can it help me in moments of decision? But would you really want me to tell you where to turn for an oracle which would liberate you from the burden of decision? Certainly, that which is weak in you would like it. But that which is strong in you would reject it. The Lord from whom you derive a word wants you to decide for yourselves. He does not offer you a safe way. You may be wrong in your decision. But if you realize that in relation to God man is always wrong, your wrong may turn out to be right. If in the presence of the eternal you risk defeat, through your very defeat a word from the Lord has come to you.

Let us now look at a quite different situation, one in which we do not have to make a great decision, and in which the small decisions we have to make daily do not give us much anxiety. There are not concrete threats against life and well-being, there is not a depressing guilt feeling or a despair about ourselves. There is not a disintegrating doubt or an intolerable emptiness. There is not an extreme situation. Does this mean that there is no desire to ask for a word from the Lord? Are the situations which are not extreme situations, deprived of a word out of the dimension of the eternal? Is God silent if the foundations of our existence are *not* shaken? A hard question, and answered in many different ways! How would we answer? I shall never forget the word of a wise old man who said to my grandfather when I was still a child, 'I need somebody whom I can thank when a great joy is given to me.' Can we share this experience? Do we remember such moments in which the eternal made itself felt to us through the abundance or greatness or beauty of the temporal? I believe that none of us is completely without such experiences. But did we not say that a word from the Lord is the eternal cutting into the temporal? Certainly that is what it is! But cutting into the temporal does not mean negating it. This it *can* mean, and this it *does* mean whenever we are driven into an ultimate situation. There are in everybody's life such situations, and they are frequent in man's tragic history. But the eternal can also cut into the temporal by affirming it, by elevating a piece of it out of the ordinary context of temporal things and events, making it translucent for the divine glory. Without such moments, life would be poor and sad; there would be no creations in which the greatness of life is expressed. But they exist, and the eternal shines through them; they can become a word from the Lord to us.

But still some of you are thinking: all this may be as you say, but it remains strange to us. Neither in ultimate situations nor in moments of a great elevation has the eternal cut into our temporal existence. We never got a word from the Lord. Maybe you did not hear it. But certainly it was spoken to you. For there is always a word from the Lord, a word that *has* been spoken. The problem of man is not that God does not speak to him: God *does* speak to everyone who has a human countenance. For this is what makes him man. He who is not able to perceive something ultimate, something infinitely significant, is not a man. Man is man because he is able to receive a word from the dimension of the eternal. The question is not that mankind has not received any word from the Lord; the question is that it has been received and resisted and distorted. This is the predicament of all of us. Human existence is never without that which breaks vertically into it. Man is never without a manifestation of that which is ultimately serious and infinitely meaningful. He is never without a word from the Lord and he never ceases resisting and distorting it, both when he has to hear it and when he has to say it.

Every Christian, and especially every Christian minister, should be aware of this: we resist and distort the word from the Lord not only when we hear it, but also when we say it. When we ask why our message of the Word of God is rejected, we often find that one does not reject that for which we stand, but the *way* in which we stand for it. Many of those who reject the Word of God reject it because the way we say it is utterly meaningless to them. They know the dimension of the eternal, but they cannot accept our names for it. If we cling to their words, we may doubt whether they have received a word from the Lord. If we meet them as persons, we know they have.

There is always a word from the Lord, a word that has been spoken. The Christian Church believes that this word has a central content, and that it has the name Jesus the Christ. Therefore, the Church calls not his *words* but his *Being* the Word of God. The Church believes that in his Being, the eternal has broken into the temporal in a way which once for all gives us *a* word, nay, *the* word from the Lord. It believes that whatever word from the Lord has been said in all history and in every individual life, is implied in this Word, which is not words but reality, a new reality, the reality of the eternal in the temporal, conquering the resistance and the distortions of the temporal.

So we have not *a*, but *the* word from the Lord? As Christians we can boast that we have it? Can we really? Did we not receive the message through men, and are not we who heard it men? And does that not mean that the message, while it went through the mouths of those who said it and through the ears of us who heard it, lost its power to cut into our world and our soul?

Those who said it – the Church and its servants in all periods – made it a matter of law and tradition, of habit and convention. They made it into something we believe we know and have tried to follow. It does not cut any more into our ordinary world. It has become a part of our ordinary world. Like the prophets with whom Jeremiah fights in our text, the ministers of the word have ceased to ask, to cry for, a word from the Lord. They claim to have it as their possession, and since the Word of God can never be a possession, the words they say are not a word from the Lord. We have received it. But as it has been distorted in the mouths of the preachers, so it has been resisted in the ears of the listeners, that is, in all of us. We hear it, but we cannot perceive it. As Christians we do not reject it, but it has lost its voice, that voice with which Jahweh spoke into the hearts of the prophets, that voice with which the Spirit spoke into the hearts of the disciples. We hear the words which have been said before. But we do not feel that they speak *to* our situation, and *out of* the depth of our situation. They may even produce torturing doubts and drive us to ask passionately for a word from the Lord *against* what we have received as the Word of God, in Bible and Church.

For there is no word from the Lord except the word which is spoken now. How can we get such a word that is spoken now and is spoken to us?

There is only one answer: by keeping ourselves open when it comes to us! This is not easy. We try to resist it, and if it is too strong for us we try to falsify it. We may be in a situation out of which we cannot extricate ourselves. It is too late for this. So the word from the Lord comes as a word of judgment and we cannot take it. Or the word which comes to us requests a radical change in our ways of life and thought. But this we cannot achieve, and we back into our habits of good and evil, of right and wrong. Or we are in doubt and guilt and despair, and the word comes to us and tells us that we can say yes to ourselves because an eternal yes has been said to us and of us. But we resist the word which demands of us the courage to say yes to ourselves because we are in love with our doubt and our guilt and our despair.

It is not easy to keep oneself open for a word from the Lord. And nobody can make it easier for us by giving us the direction in which to listen. No fixed place can be named, either in our religious tradition or in our cultural creations, or in the depth of our souls. But for this very reason, no place is excluded from communicating to us a word from the Lord. It is always present and tries always to be perceived by us. It is like the air, surrounding us, omnipresent, trying to enter every empty space. It is the empty space in our souls into which it tries to enter here and now. So the last question is: is there an empty space in *your* soul? Or is everything filled with that which is transitory, preliminary, ultimately insignificant, however important it tries to be? Without a soul opened for it, no word from the Lord can be received. Listening with an open soul, keeping an empty space in our inner life, sharpening our spiritual hearing: this is the only thing we can do. But this is much. And blessed are those whose minds and hearts are open.

Therefore, let us keep open our ears and let us keep open our hearts, and ask with great seriousness and great passion: is there a word from the Lord, a word for me, here and now, a word for our world in this moment? It *is* there, it tries to come to you. Keep open for it!

17. Seeing and Hearing

Jesus said, 'For judgment I came into this world, that those who do not see may see, and that those who see may become blind.' Some of the Pharisees near him heard this, and they said to him, 'Are we also blind?' Jesus said to them, 'If you were blind, you would have no guilt; but now that you say, "We see," your guilt remains.'

JOHN 9:39-41

The Bible of both Testaments, like much other religious literature, speaks again and again of 'seeing'. 'Come and see.' These words of the disciple sound through the writings of prophets and apostles. We *have* seen: this is the message of Gospels and Epistles. It is not true that religious faith is belief in things without evidence. The word 'evidence' means 'seeing thoroughly'. And we are asked to *see*. We have present with us what we see; therefore, we want to see what we love, what is significant for us. The great men of God wanted to see God; Moses asked this as the highest of all favours of Jahweh. Isaiah was made the most powerful of the prophets after he had seen God in the temple. Jesus blesses the pure in heart as those who will see God. In the Fourth Gospel he says about himself that he has seen the Father, and that whoever has seen him has also seen the Father. In pious imagery the angels and the saints are described as those who see God face to face. And the ultimate fulfilment, the end of all moving and striving, is pictured as the eternal vision of God.

But doubts and questions arise when we look at our present human predicament. Is faith not the opposite of vision? Must we not believe without seeing? Does Jesus not bless those who have not seen and yet believe? Is not faith defined as the evidence of things not seen? And does not Paul write, 'We walk by faith, not by sight'? 'We look not at the things which are seen, but at the things which are not seen. For the things which are seen are temporal, but the things which are not seen are eternal'? All this seems to indicate that faith must be based on *hearing* and not on seeing. You *hear* about something you do not see. You believe him who tells you. You accept the word of the authorities in humility and obedience. You believe what the Bible says because the Bible says it. You accept what the Church teaches because it is taught by the Church. 'Word of God'. You hear, you believe, you obey, but you do not see.

In former centuries there was a long-lasting struggle in the Church about the religious significance of hearing and seeing. First, seeing prevailed, but then hearing became more and more significant. Finally, in the days of the Reformation hearing became completely victorious. The typical Protestant church-buildings bear witness to this victory. They are halls to hear sermons, emptied of everything to be seen of pictures and sculptures, of lights and stained windows, of most of the sacramental activities. Around the desk of the preacher a room was built to listen to the words of the law and the gospel. The eye could not find a place to rest in contemplation. Hearing replaced seeing, obedience replaced vision.

But Jesus says, 'I came into this world, that those who do not see may *see*.' And the apostle says, 'That which we have *seen with our eyes*, which we have looked upon – we proclaim to you.' Both speak not about the future, but about something they *have* seen and *still* see. And they certainly do not feel as do old and new theologians that there is a conflict between seeing and hearing, between seeing and believing. 'That which we have seen *and* heard,' writes the apostle. 'Everyone who *sees* the Son and *believes* in him,' says Jesus. And most important and surprising: that which we have seen with our eyes according to our gospel is the Word, the eternal Word or Logos in whom God speaks, who can be seen through the works of creation and who is visible in the man Jesus. The Word can be *seen*, this is the highest unity of hearing and seeing, that is the truth which can bridge the Protestant and the Catholic half-truths.

Seeing is the most astonishing of our natural powers. It receives the light, the first of all that is created, and as the light does it conquers darkness and chaos. It creates for us an ordered world, things distinguished from each other and from us. Seeing shows us their unique countenance and the larger whole to which they belong. Wherever we see, a piece of the original chaos is transformed into creation. We distinguish, we recognize, we give a name, we know. 'I have seen' – that means in Greek 'I know'. From seeing, all science starts, to seeing it must always return. We want to ask those who have seen with their eyes and we ourselves want to see with our eyes. Only the human eye is able to see in this way, to see a world in every small thing and to see a universe of all things. Therefore the human eye is infinite in reach and irresistible in power. It is the correlate to the light of creation.

But seeing means more than the creation of a world. Where we see we unite with what we see. Seeing is a kind of union. As poetry has described it, we *drink* colours and forms, forces and expressions. They become a part of ourselves. They give abundance to the poverty of our loneliness. Even when we are unaware of them they stream into us; but sometimes we notice them and welcome them and desire more of them.

Not all seeing has this character of union. If we look at things and observe them merely to control and to use them, no real union takes place. We keep them at a distance. We try to bring them into our power, to use them for our purposes, as means for our ends. There is no love in this kind of seeing. We glimpse the beings that shall serve us coldly; we have for those which we use a look, curious or indifferent, sensational or aggressive, hostile or cruel. There is abuse in the looking at those which we *use*. It is a seeing that violates and separates. This is the look of the masses who in medieval paintings are looking at the Crucified. But even this kind of seeing creates some union, though union through separation. But the seeing that really unites is different. Our language has a word for it: intuition. This means seeing *into*. It is an intimate seeing, a grasping and being grasped. It is a seeing shaped by love. Plato, the teacher of the centuries, whose visions and words have deeply influenced the Fourth Gospel and the Church, knew about the seeing which unites. He called the love which drives us to a genuine intuition the 'child of poverty and abundance'. It is the love which fills our want with the abundance of our world. But it fills us in such a way that the disrupted multitude is not the last we see – a view which disrupts ourselves. The last we see lies in that which unites, which is eternal *in* and *above* the transitory things. Into this view Plato wanted to initiate his followers.

This leads us to another characteristic of seeing, the most significant of all. We never see only what we see; we always see something else with it and through it! Seeing creates, seeing unites, and above all seeing goes beyond itself. If we look at a stone we see directly only the colours and forms of the side which is turned towards us. But with and through this limited surface we are aware of the roundness, of the extension and mass of the structure of the whole thing. We see beyond what we see. If we look at an animal we see directly the colours and forms of its skin. But with it and through it we are aware of the tension and power of its muscles, of its inner strivings which are covered as well as revealed by the skin. We see not colour spots, but a living being. If we look at a human face, we see lines and shades, but with it and through it we see a unique, incomparable personality whose expressions are visible in his face, whose character and destiny have left traces which we understand and in which we can even read something of his future. With and through colours and forms and movements we see friendliness and coldness, hostility and devotion, anger and love, sadness and joy. We see infinitely more than we see when we look into a human face. And we see even beyond this into a new depth. Again the language gives us a help when it speaks of con-templation. Con-templation means going into the temple, into the sphere of the holy, into the deep roots of things, into their creative ground. We see the mysterious powers which we call beauty and truth and goodness. We cannot see them as such, we can see them only in things and events. We see them with and through the shape of a rose and the movements of the stars and the image of a friend. We *can* see them, but it is not *necessary* that we see them. We can close our eyes, we can become blind. Some are blind to any beauty which is more than a pleasant feeling, some are blind to any truth which is more than correct observation and calculation, some are blind to any goodness which is

more than usefulness. And some are blind to any ground
which is the unity of these powers and which we call
'holy'. It is the ultimate, the last which we can see with
and through all things; and therefore it is the end of all
seeing. It is the light itself and therefore it is darkness for
our eyes. Only 'with and through' can we see it, through
things and men, through events and images. This seeing
and not seeing at the same time is what we call faith.
Nobody can see God; but we can see him 'with and
through'. Here the conflict ends between seeing and
hearing. The word tells us where to see and when we
have seen we pronounce what we have seen and heard.
In the state which we call faith, sound and vision are
united and perhaps this is the reason why the 'holy'
likes to be expressed in music more than in any other
medium. Music gives wings to both, word and image,
and goes beyond both of them.

But for a second time we are called down from the
flight above to the lowliness of our human situation.
Our gospel calls us blind, all of us. And Jesus says that
we are blind because we believe we see and do not know
that we are blind; and he threatens that we shall be
thrown into more blindness if we insist that we are
seeing. The question is: where of all places can and shall
we see into the ground of all Being? Who can lead our
contemplation into the temple, into the holy itself?

Seeing gives us a 'world', the order and unity of the
many. But we see within this order, disorder; within
the unity, conflict threatening to explode the world
itself and to bring back the old darkness of the chaos.
And order and chaos are so mixed with each other that
we often feel dizzy, without ground and meaning, de-
siring to keep our eyes closed. Seeing unites us with what
we see. But we see so many things and beings with
which we do not want to be united, towards which we
are indifferent or hostile, which are indifferent or hostile
to us, which are repulsive and which we hate to see just
because every seeing unites, even if it is through hate.

And it may be even our own self that we do not want to see because we are repelled by our image and because we hate it if we see it. Not in love but in hate are we united with ourselves, and perhaps we want to deprive ourselves of our eyes like Oedipus, of our eyes which first did not see what they ought to see and now cannot stand to see what they must see. And is not that which we love to see and that which we hate to see so mixed that we often praise the poverty of not seeing? Seeing is seeing with and through beings into their depth, into the good and the true and into their holy ground. But which are the beings and images that shall lead us to this temple? Those whom Jesus called blind believed they knew the way to the temple, to the holy and the holiest. Innumerable temples all over the world contain things and images with and through which we can see God. But what we see are idols, fascinating, horrible, overwhelming in seductive beauty or destructive power, demanding what cannot be fulfilled, promising what cannot be given, giving what elevates and lowers at the same time. And this is so because they hold us fast to themselves and do not lead us beyond. Our eyes are bound by them, often bound by the demonic fascination they exercise and with which they take possession of us. We contemplate them, we go into their temples, we unite with them in self-surrender, and we leave them emptied, despairing, destroyed. This is the great temptation of seeing. This is the reason why hearing was put against seeing. It is the reason why images were destroyed again and again and every image forbidden, why the temples were burned and God was called the Infinite Void. But this cannot be the last word. Emptiness can be both light and darkness; and we want light, the light which is life and vision.

Jesus also could have become an idol, a national and religious hero, fascinating and destructive. This is what the disciples and the masses wanted him to be. They saw him, they loved him, they saw with and through him the good and the true, the holy itself. But they succumbed to the temptation of seeing. They kept to that which must be sacrificed if God shall be seen with and through any mortal being. And when he sacrificed himself, they looked away in despair like those whose image and idol is destroyed. But he was too strong; he drew their eyes back to him, but now to him crucified. And they could stand it, for they saw with him and through him the God who is really God. He who has seen him has seen the Father: this is true only of the Crucified. But of him it *is* true. Certainly he is not the only one to look at in intuition and contemplation. We are not asked to stare at him, as some do. We are not asked to look away from everything for his sake, as some do. We are not asked to give up the abundance of his creation as some do. We are not asked to refuse union with what we see as some do. But we are asked to see with and through everything into the depth into which he shows the way. We shall see into it unimpeded by that which tries to keep us, away from the last depth. And when we are tired of seeing the abundance of the world with all its disorder, its hate and separation, its demonic destruction, and if we are also unable to look into the blinding light of the divine ground, then let us close our eyes. And then it might happen that we see the picture of someone who looks at us with eyes of infinite human depth and therefore of divine power and love. And these eyes say to us, 'Come and see.'

18. The Paradox of Prayer

Likewise the Spirit helps us in our weakness; for we do not know how to pray as we ought, but the Spirit himself intercedes for us with sighs too deep for words. And he who searches the hearts of men knows what is the mind of the Spirit, because the Spirit intercedes for the saints according to the will of God.

ROMANS 8:26-27

This passage of Romans about the Spirit interceding for us 'with sighs too deep for words' belongs to the most mysterious of Paul's sayings. It expresses the experience of a man who knew how to pray and who, because he knew how to pray, said that he did *not* know how to pray. Perhaps we may draw from this confession of the apostle the conclusion that those amongst us who act as if they knew how to pray, do not know how at all. For this conclusion we could find much evidence in our daily experience. Ministers are used to praying publicly on all kinds of occasions, some of which offer themselves naturally to a prayer, others only artificially and against good taste. It is not unimportant to know the right hour for praying and the right hour for not praying. This is a warning, on the periphery of what Paul wants to say, but a necessary warning, especially to ministers and laymen who are leaders in the Church.

The next step leads us nearer to the centre of Paul's problem: there are two main types of prayer, the fixed liturgical and the free spontaneous prayer. Both of them show the truth of Paul's assertion, that we do not know how 'to pray as we ought'. The liturgical prayer often becomes mechanical or incomprehensible or both. The history of the Church has shown that this was the fate even of the Lord's Prayer. Paul certainly knew the 'Our Father' when he wrote that we do not know how to pray. It does not prove that we know how to pray when we make a liturgical law out of the example of praying which Jesus gave to his disciples.

But if we turn from the formulated to the spontaneous prayer, we are not better off. Very often the spontaneous prayer is an ordinary conversation with somebody who is called 'God', but who is actually another man to whom we tell things, often at great length, to whom we give thanks and of whom we ask favours. This certainly does not prove that we know how to pray.

The liturgical churches which use classical formulas should ask themselves whether they do not prevent the people of *our* time from praying as they honestly can. And the non-liturgical churches who give the freedom to make up prayers at any moment, should ask themselves whether they do not profane prayer and deprive it of its mystery.

And now let us take a third step, into the centre of Paul's thought. Whether at the right time or not, whether a formulated or a spontaneous prayer, the question is decisive whether a prayer is possible at all. According to Paul, it is humanly impossible. This we should never forget when we pray: we do something humanly impossible. We talk to somebody who is not somebody else, but who is nearer to us than we ourselves are. We address somebody who can never become an object of our address because he is always subject, always acting, always creating. We tell something to him who knows not only what we tell him but also all the unconscious tendencies out of which our conscious words grow. This is the reason why prayer is humanly impossible. Out of this insight Paul gives a mysterious solution to the question of the right prayer: it is God himself who prays through us, when we pray to him. God himself in us: that is what Spirit means. Spirit is another word for 'God present', with shaking, inspiring, transforming power. Something in us, which is not we ourselves, intercedes before God for us. We cannot bridge the gap between God and ourselves even through the most intensive and frequent prayers; the gap between God and ourselves can be bridged only by God. And so Paul gives us the surprising picture of God interceding for us before himself. Such symbols – like all symbols concerning God – are absurd if taken literally. They are profound if taken as genuine symbols. The symbol of God interceding before himself for us says that God knows more about us than that of which we are conscious. He 'searches the hearts of men'. These are words which anticipate the present-day insight, of which we are rightly proud, that the small light of consciousness rises on a large basis of unconscious drives and images. But if this is so, who else can bring our whole being before God except God himself, who alone knows the deep things in our soul?

This may help us also to understand the most mysterious part of Paul's description of prayer, namely, that the Spirit 'intercedes with sighs too deep for words'. Just because every prayer is humanly impossible, just because it brings deeper levels of our being before God than the level of consciousness, something happens in it that cannot be expressed in words. Words, created *by* and used *in* our conscious life, are not the essence of prayer. The essence of prayer is the act of God who is working in us and raises our whole being to himself. The way in which this happens is called by Paul 'sighing'. Sighing is an expression of the weakness of our creaturely existence. Only in terms of wordless sighs can we approach God, and even these sighs are his work in us.

This finally answers a question often asked by Christians: which kind of prayer is most adequate to our relation to God? The prayer in which we thank or the prayer in which we beg, the prayer of intercession or of confession or of praise? Paul does not make these distinctions. They are dependent on words; but the sighing of the Spirit in us is too deep for words and for the distinction of kinds of prayer. The spiritual prayer is elevation to God in the power of God and it includes all forms of prayer.

A last word to those who feel that they cannot find the words of prayer and remain silent towards God. This may be lack of Spirit. It also may be that their silence is silent *prayer*, namely, the sighs which are too deep for words. Then he who searches the hearts of men, knows and hears.

PART THREE

THE NEW BEING AS FULFILMENT

•

19. The Meaning of Joy

When the Lord restored the fortunes of Zion, we were like those who dream. Then our mouth was filled with laughter, and our tongue with shouts of joy; then they said among the nations, 'The Lord has done great things for them.' The Lord has done great things for us; we are glad.

Restore our fortunes, O Lord, like the water-courses in the Negeb! May those who sow in tears reap with shouts of joy! He that goes forth weeping, bearing the seed for sowing, shall come home with shouts of joy, bringing his sheaves with him.

PSALM 126

Truly, truly, I say to you, you will weep and lament, but the world will rejoice; you will be sorrowful, but your sorrow will turn into joy. When a woman is in travail she has sorrow, because her hour has come; but when she is delivered of the child, she no longer remembers the anguish, for joy that a child is born into the world. So you have sorrow now, but I will see you again and your hearts will rejoice, and no one will take your joy from you.

JOHN 16 : 20-22

These things I have spoken to you, that my joy may be in you, and that your joy may be full.

JOHN 15 : 11

The Bible abounds in admonitions to rejoice. Paul's word to the Philippians, 'again I will say, Rejoice,' represents an ever-present element in biblical religion. For the men of the Old and New Testaments the lack of joy is a consequence of man's separation from God, and the presence of joy is a consequence of the reunion with God.

Joy is demanded, and it can be given. It is not a thing one simply has. It is not easy to attain. It is and always was a rare and precious thing. And it has always been a difficult problem among Christians. Christians are accused of destroying the joy of life, this natural endowment of every creature. The greatest of the modern foes of Christianity, Friedrich Nietzsche, himself the son of a Protestant minister, has expressed his judgment about Jesus in the words, 'His disciples should look more redeemed.' We should subject ourselves to the piercing force of these words and should ask ourselves, 'Is our lack of joy due to the fact that we are Christians, or to the fact that we are not sufficiently Christian?' Perhaps we can defend ourselves convincingly against the criticism that we are people who despise life, whose behaviour is a permanent accusation of life. Perhaps we can show that this is a distortion of the truth.

But let us be honest. Is there not enough foundation for criticism? Are not many Christians – ministers, students of theology, evangelists, missionaries, Christian educators and social workers, pious laymen and laywomen, even the children of such parents – surrounded by an air of heaviness, of oppressive sternness, of lack of humour and irony about themselves? We cannot deny this. Our critics outside the Church are right. And we ourselves should be even more critical than they, but critical on a deeper level.

As Christians we know our inner conflicts about accepting or rejecting joy. We are suspicious of the gifts of nature which contribute to joy, because we are suspicious of nature itself, although we confess that it is divine creation, knowing what God has spoken about his creation: 'Behold, it was very good!' We are suspicious of the creations of culture which contribute to joy because we are suspicious of man's creativity, although we confess that God has commanded man to cultivate the garden of the earth which he has made subject to him. And even if we overcome our suspicions and affirm and accept the gifts of nature and the creations of culture, we often do so with an uneasy conscience. We know that we *should* be free for joy, that as Paul says, 'all is ours', but our courage is inferior to our knowledge. We do not dare to affirm our world and ourselves; and if we dare to, in a moment of courage, we try to atone for it by self-reproaches and self-punishments, and we draw upon ourselves malicious criticism by those who never have dared. Therefore, many Christians try to compromise. They try to hide their feeling of joy, or they try to avoid joys which are too intense, in order to avoid self-accusations which are too harsh. Such an experience of the suppression of joy, and guilt about joy in Christian groups, almost drove me to a break with Christianity. What passes for joy in these groups is an emaciated, intentionally childish, unexciting, unecstatic thing, without colour and danger, without heights and depths.

It is difficult to deny that this is the state of things in many Christian churches. But now we hear the question from both the Christian and the non-Christian sides: 'Is not joy, as observed in the Bible, something completely different from the joy of life, which is lacking in many Christians? Do not the Psalmist and Paul and the Jesus of the Fourth Gospel speak of a joy which transcends the natural joy of life? Do they not speak about the joy in God? Is not the decision to be a Christian a decision for the joy in God instead of for the joy of life?'

The first and simplest answer to these questions is that life is God's, and God is the creative Ground of life. He is infinitely more than any life process. But he works creatively through all of them. Therefore, no conflict is necessary between the joy in God and the joy of life. But this first answer, great and joyful as it is, is not sufficient; for 'joy of life' can mean many things.

Joy seems to be the opposite of pain. But we know that pain and joy can exist together. Not joy but pleasure is the opposite of pain. There are people who believe that man's life is a continuous flight from pain and a persistent search for pleasure. I have never seen a human being of whom that is true. It is true only of beings who have lost their humanity, either through complete disintegration or through mental illness. The ordinary human being is able to sacrifice pleasures and to take pain upon himself for a cause, for somebody or something he loves and deems worthy of pain and sacrifice. He can disregard both pain and pleasure because he is directed *not* towards his pleasure but towards the things he loves and with which he wants to unite. If we desire something because of the pleasure we may get out of it, we may get the pleasure but we shall not get joy. If we try to find someone through whom we may get pleasure, we may get pleasure but we shall not have joy. If we search for something in order to avoid pain, we may avoid pain, but we shall not avoid sorrow. If we try to use someone to protect us from pain, he may protect us from pain but he will not protect us from sorrow. Pleasures *can* be provided and pain *can* be avoided, if we use or abuse other beings. But joy cannot be attained and sorrow cannot be overcome in this way. Joy is possible only when we are driven towards things and persons because of what they are and not because of what we can get from them. The joy about our work is spoiled when we perform it not because of what we produce but because of the pleasures with which it can provide us, or the pain against which it can protect us. The pleasure about the fact that *I* am successful spoils the joy about the success itself. Our joy about knowing truth and experiencing beauty is spoiled if we enjoy not the truth and the beauty but the fact that it is *I* who enjoys them.

Power can give joy only if it is free from the pleasure about having power and if it is a method of creating

something worthwhile. Love relations, most conspicu-
ously relations between the sexes, remain without joy if
we use the other one as a means for pleasure or as a
means to escape pain. This is a threat to all human relations. It is not an external law which warns us about
certain forms of these relations, but the wisdom born
out of past experiences which tells us that some of these
relations may give pleasure, but that they do not give
joy. They do not give joy because they do not fulfil what
we are, and that for which we strive. Every human relation is joyless in which the other person is not sought
because of what he is in himself, but because of the
pleasure he can give us and the pain from which he can
protect us.

To seek pleasure for the sake of pleasure is to avoid
reality, the reality of other beings and the reality of ourselves. But only the fulfilment of what we really are can
give us joy. Joy is nothing else than the awareness of
our being fulfilled in our true being, in our personal
centre. And this fulfilment is possible only if we unite
ourselves with what others really are. It is reality that
gives joy, and reality alone. The Bible speaks so often
of joy because it is the most realistic of all books.
'Rejoice!' That means: 'Penetrate from what *seems* to
be real to that which is *really* real.' Mere pleasure, in
yourselves and in all other beings, remains in the realm
of illusion about reality. Joy is born out of union with
reality itself.

One of the roots of the desire for pleasure is the feeling of emptiness and the pain of boredom following from
it. Emptiness is the lack of relatedness to things and persons and meanings; it is even the lack of being related to
oneself. Therefore we try to escape from ourselves and
the loneliness of ourselves, but we do not reach the
others and their world in a genuine relation. And so we
use them for a kind of pleasure which can be called 'fun'.
But it is not the creative kind of fun often connected
with play; it is, rather, a shallow, distracting, greedy way

of 'having fun'. And it is not by chance that it is that type of fun which can easily be commercialized, for it is dependent on calculable reactions, without passion, without risk, without love. Of all the dangers that threaten our civilization, this is one of the most dangerous ones: the escape from one's emptiness through a 'fun' which makes joy impossible.

Rejoice! This biblical exhortation is more needed for those who have much 'fun' and pleasure than for those who have little pleasure and much pain. It is often easier to unite pain and joy than to unite fun and joy.

Does the biblical demand for joy prohibit pleasure? Do joy and pleasure exclude each other? By no means! The fulfilment of the centre of our being does not exclude partial and peripheral fulfilments. And we must say this with the same emphasis with which we have contrasted joy and pleasure. We must challenge not only those who seek pleasure for pleasure's sake, but also those who reject pleasure because it is pleasure. Man enjoys eating and drinking, beyond the mere animal need of them. It is a partial ever-repeated fulfilment of his striving for life; therefore, it is pleasure and gives joy of life. Man enjoys playing and dancing, the beauty of nature, and the ecstasy of love. They fulfil some of his most intensive strivings for life; therefore, they are pleasure and give joy of life. Man enjoys the power of knowledge and the fascination of art. They fulfil some of his highest strivings for life; therefore, they are pleasure and give joy of life. Man enjoys the community of men in family, friendship, and the social group. They fulfil some fundamental strivings for life; therefore, they are pleasure and give joy of life.

Yet in all these relations the question arises: is our way of having these pleasures right or wrong? Do we use them for pleasure's sake or because we want to unite in love with all that to which we belong? We never know with certainty. And those of us together with those in the past history of Christianity who have an anxious conscience, prefer to renounce pleasures although they are established as good by creation itself. They hide their anxiety behind parental or social or ecclesiastical prohibitions, calling these prohibitions divine commands. They justify their fear to affirm the joy of life by appealing to their conscience, calling it the voice of God, or to the need of discipline and self-control, and selflessness, calling them the 'imitation of Christ'. But Jesus, in contrast to John the Baptist, was called a glutton and a drunkard by his critics. In all these warnings against pleasure, truth is mixed with untruth. Insofar as they strengthen our responsibility, they are true; insofar as they undercut our joy, they are wrong. Therefore let me give another criterion for accepting or rejecting pleasures, the criterion indicated in our text: those pleasures are good which go together with joy; those are bad which prevent joy. In the light of this norm we should risk the affirmation of pleasures, even if our risk may prove to have been an error. It is not more Christian to reject than to accept pleasure. Let us not forget that the rejection implies a rejection of creation, or as the Church Fathers called it, a blasphemy of the Creator-God. And every Christian should be aware of a fact of which many non-Christians are keenly aware: the suppression of the joy of life produces hatred of life, hidden or open. It can lead to a self-destruction, as many physical and mental diseases prove.

Joy is more than pleasure; and it is more than happiness. Happiness is a state of mind which lasts for a longer or shorter time and is dependent on many conditions, external and internal. In the ancient view it is a gift of the gods which they give and take away again. in the American Constitution, 'the pursuit of happiness' is a basic human right. In economic theory the greatest happiness of the greatest possible number of people is the purpose of human action. In the fairy tale, 'they lived happily ever after.' Happiness can stand a large amount of pain and lack of pleasure. But happiness cannot stand the lack of joy. For joy is the expression of our essential and central fulfilment. No peripheral fulfilments and no favourable conditions can be substituted for the central fulfilment. Even in an unhappy state a great joy can transform unhappiness into happiness. What, then, is this joy?

Let us first ask what is its opposite. It is sorrow. Sorrow is the feeling that we are deprived of our central fulfilment, by being deprived of something that belongs to us and is necessary to our fulfilment. We may be deprived of relatives and friends nearest to us, of a creative work and a supporting community which gave us a meaning of life, of our home, of honour, of love, of bodily or mental health, of the unity of our person, of a good conscience. All this brings sorrow in manifold forms, the sorrow of sadness, the sorrow of loneliness, the sorrow of depression, the sorrow of self-accusation. But it is precisely this kind of situation in which Jesus tells his disciples that his joy shall be with them and that their joy shall be full. For, as Paul calls it, sorrow can be the 'sorrow of the world' which ends in the death of final despair, and it can be divine sorrow which leads to transformation and joy. For joy has something within itself which is beyond joy and sorrow. This something is called blessedness.

Blessedness is the eternal element in joy, that which makes it possible for joy to include in itself the sorrow out of which it arises, and which it takes into itself. In the Beatitudes, Jesus calls the poor, those who mourn, those who hunger and thirst, those who are persecuted, 'blessed'. And he says to them: 'Rejoice and be glad!' Joy within sorrow is possible to those who are blessed, to those in whom joy has the dimension of the eternal.

Here we must once more reply to those who attack Christianity because they believe that it destroys the joy of life. In view of the Beatitudes they say that Christianity undercuts the joy of *this* life by pointing to and preparing for another life. They even challenge the blessedness in the promised life as a refined form of seeking for pleasure in the future life. Again we must confess that in many Christians, joy in this way is postponed till after death, and that there are biblical words which seem to support this answer. Nevertheless, it is wrong. Jesus will give his joy to his disciples *now*. They shall get it after he has left them, which means in *this* life. And Paul asks the Philippians to have joy *now*. This cannot be otherwise, for blessedness is the expression of God's eternal fulfilment. Blessed are those who participate in this fulfilment here and now. Certainly eternal fulfilment must be seen not only as eternal which is present, but also as eternal which is future. But if it is not seen in the present, it cannot be seen at all.

This joy which has in itself the depth of blessedness is asked for and promised in the Bible. It preserves in itself its opposite, sorrow. It provides the foundation for happiness and pleasure. It is present in all levels of man's striving for fulfilment. It consecrates and directs them. It does not diminish or weaken them. It does not take away the risks and dangers of the joy of life. It makes the joy of life possible in pleasure and pain, in happiness and unhappiness, in ecstasy and sorrow. Where there is joy, there is fulfilment. And where there is fulfilment, there is joy. In fulfilment and joy the inner aim of life, the meaning of creation, and the end of salvation, are attained.

20. Our Ultimate Concern

Now as they went on their way, he entered a village; and a woman named Martha received him into her house. And she had a sister called Mary, who sat at the Lord's feet and listened to his teaching. But Martha was distracted with much serving; and she went to him and said, 'Lord, do you not care that my sister has left me to serve alone? Tell her then to help me.' But the Lord answered, 'Martha, Martha, you are anxious and troubled about many things; one thing is needful. Mary has chosen the good portion, which shall not be taken away from her.'

LUKE 10:38-42

The words Jesus speaks to Martha belong to the most famous of all the words in the Bible. Martha and Mary have become symbols for two possible attitudes towards life, for two forces in man and in mankind as a whole, for two kinds of concern. Martha is concerned about many things, but all of them are finite, preliminary, transitory. Mary is concerned about one thing, which is infinite, ultimate, lasting.

Martha's way is not contemptible. On the contrary, it is the way which keeps the world running. It is the driving force which preserves and enriches life and culture. Without it Jesus could not have talked to Mary and Mary could not have listened to Jesus. Once I heard a sermon dedicated to the justification and glorification of Martha. This can be done. There are innumerable concerns in our lives and in human life generally which demand attention, devotion, passion. But they do not demand *infinite* attention, *unconditional* devotion, *ultimate* passion. They are important, often very important for you and for me and for the whole of mankind. But they are not *ultimately* important. And therefore Jesus praises not Martha, but Mary. She has chosen the right thing, the one thing man needs, the only thing of ultimate concern for every man.

The hour of a church service and every hour of meditative reading is dedicated to listening in the way Mary listened. Something is being said to us, to the speaker as well as to the listeners, something about which we may become infinitely concerned. This is the meaning of every sermon. It shall awaken infinite concern.

What does it mean to be concerned about something? It means that we are involved in it, that a part of ourselves is in it, that we participate with our hearts. And it means even more than that. It points to the way in which we are involved, namely, *anxiously*. The wisdom of our language often identifies concern with anxiety. Wherever we are involved we feel anxiety. There are many things which interest us, which provoke our compassion or horror. But they are not our real concern; they do not produce this driving, torturing anxiety which is present when we are genuinely and seriously concerned. In our story, Martha was seriously concerned. Let us try to remember what gives us concern in the course of an average day, from the moment of awakening to the last moment before falling asleep, and even beyond that, when our anxieties appear in our dreams.

We are concerned about our work; it is the basis of our existence. We may love it or hate it; we may fulfil it as a duty or as a hard necessity. But anxiety grasps us whenever we feel the limits of our strength, our lack of efficiency, the struggle with our laziness, the danger of failure. We are concerned about our relationships to others. We cannot imagine living without their benevolence, their friendship, their love, their communion in body and soul. But we are worried and often in utter despair when we think about the indifference, the outbursts of anger and jealousy, the hidden and often poisonous hostility we experience in ourselves as well as in those we love. The anxiety about losing them, about having hurt them, about not being worthy of them, creeps into our hearts and makes our love restless. We are concerned about ourselves. We feel responsible for our development towards maturity, towards strength in life, wisdom in mind, and perfection in spirit. At the same time, we are striving for happiness; we are concerned about our pleasures and about 'having a good time', a concern which ranks very high with us. But our anxiety strikes us when we look at ourselves in the mirror of self-scrutiny or of the judgments of others. We feel that we have made the wrong decision, that we have started on the wrong road, that we are failing before men and before ourselves. We compare ourselves with others and feel inferior to them, and we are depressed and frustrated. We believe that we have wasted our happiness either by pursuing it too eagerly and confusing happiness with pleasure or by not being courageous enough to grasp the right moment for a decision which might have brought us happiness.

We cannot forget the most natural and most universal concern of everything that lives, the concern for the preservation of life – for our daily bread. There was a time in recent history in which large groups in the Western world had almost forgotten this concern. Today, the simple concern for food and clothing and shelter is so overwhelming in the greater part of mankind that it has almost suppressed most of the other human concerns, and it has absorbed the minds of all classes of people.

But, someone may ask, do we not have higher concerns than those of our daily life? And does not Jesus himself witness to them? When he is moved by the misery of the masses does he not consecrate the social concern which has grasped many people in our time, liberating them from many worries of their daily lives? When Jesus is moved by pity for the sick and heals them, does he not thereby consecrate the concern shared by medical and spiritual healers? When he gathers around him a small group in order to establish community within it, does he not thereby consecrate the concern about all communal life? When he says that he has come to bear witness to the truth, does he not consecrate the concern for truth, and the passion for knowledge which is such a driving force in our time? When he is teaching the masses and his disciples, does he not consecrate the concern for learning and education? And when he tells the parables, and when he pictures the beauty of nature and creates sentences of classic perfection, does he not consecrate the concern for beauty, and the elevation of mind it gives, and the peace after the restlessness of our daily concerns?

But are these noble concerns the 'one thing' that is needed and the right thing that Mary has chosen? Or are they perhaps the highest forms of what Martha represents? Are we still, like Martha, concerned about many things even when we are concerned about great and noble things?

Are we really beyond anxiety when we are socially concerned and when the mass of misery and social injustice, contrasted with our own favoured position, falls upon our conscience and prevents us from breathing freely and happily while we are forced to heave the sighs of hundreds of people all over the world? And do you know the agony of those who want to heal but know it is too late; of those who want to educate and meet with stupidity, wickedness and hatred; of those who are obliged to lead and are worn out by the people's ignorance, by the ambitions of their opponents, by bad institutions and bad luck? These anxieties are greater than those about our daily life. And do you know what tremendous anxiety is connected with every honest inquiry, the anxiety about falling into error, especially when one takes new and untrod paths of thought? Have you ever experienced the almost intolerable feeling of emptiness when you turned from a great work of art to the demands, ugliness and worries of your daily life? Even this is not the 'one thing' we need as Jesus indicated when he spoke of the beauties of the temple being doomed to destruction. Modern Europe has learned that the millennia of human creativity of which it boasted were not that 'one thing needful', for the monuments of these millennia now lie in ruins.

Why are the many things about which we are concerned connected with worry and anxiety? We give them our devotion, our strength, our passion and we must do so; otherwise we would not achieve anything.

Why, then, do they make us restless in the deepest ground of our hearts, and why does Jesus dismiss them as not ultimately needed?

As Jesus indicates in his words about Mary, it is because they can be taken from us. They all come to an end; all our concerns are finite. In the short span of our lives many of them have already disappeared and new ones have emerged which also will disappear. Many great concerns of the past have vanished and more will come to an end, sooner or later. The melancholy law of transitoriness governs even our most passionate concerns. The anxiety of the end dwells in the happiness they give. Both the things about which we are concerned and we ourselves come to an end. There will be a moment – and perhaps it is not far away – when we shall no longer be concerned about any of these concerns, when their finitude will be revealed in the experience of our own finitude – of our own end.

But we maintain our preliminary concerns as if they were ultimate. And they keep us in their grasp if we try to free ourselves from them. Every concern is tyrannical and wants our whole heart and our whole mind and our whole strength. Every concern tries to become our ultimate concern, our god. The concern about our work often succeeds in becoming our god, as does the concern about another human being, or about pleasure. The concern about science has succeeded in becoming the god of a whole era in history, the concern about money has become an even more important god, and the concern about the nation the most important god of all. But these concerns are finite, they conflict with each other, they burden our consciences because we cannot do justice to all of them.

We may try to dismiss all concerns and to maintain a cynical unconcern. We determine that nothing shall concern us any more, except perhaps casually, but certainly not seriously. We try to be unconcerned about ourselves and others, about our work and our pleasures, about necessities and luxuries, about social and political matters, about knowledge and beauty. We may even feel that this unconcern has something heroic about it. And one thing is true: it is the only alternative to having an ultimate concern. Unconcern or ultimate concern – those are the only alternatives. The cynic is concerned, passionately concerned, about one thing, namely, his unconcern. This is the inner contradiction of all unconcern. Therefore, there is only one alternative, which is ultimate concern.

What, then, is the one thing that we need? What is the right thing that Mary has chosen? Like our story, I hesitate to answer, for almost any answer will be misunderstood. If the answer is 'religion', this will be misunderstood as meaning a set of beliefs and activities. But, as other New Testament stories show, Martha was at least as religious as Mary. Religion can be a human concern on the same level as the others, creating the same anxiety as the others. Every page of the history and psychology of religion demonstrates this. There are even special people who are supposed to cultivate this particular human concern. They are called by a highly blasphemous name: religionists – a word that reveals more about the decay of religion in our time than does anything else. If religion is the special concern of special people and not the ultimate concern of everybody, it is nonsense or blasphemy. So we ask again, what is the one thing we need? And again it is difficult to answer. If we answer 'God', this will also be misunderstood. Even God can be made a finite concern, an object among other objects; in whose existence some people believe and some do not. Such a God, of course, cannot be our ultimate concern. Or we make him a person like other persons with whom it is useful to have a relationship. Such a person may support our finite concerns, but he certainly cannot be our ultimate concern.

The one thing needed – this is the first and in some sense the last answer I can give – is to be concerned ultimately, unconditionally, infinitely. This is what Mary was. It is this that Martha felt and what made her angry, and it is what Jesus praises in Mary. Beyond this, not much has been said or could be said about Mary, and it is less than what has been said about Martha. *But Mary was infinitely concerned*. This is the one thing needed.

If, in the power and passion of such an ultimate concern, we look at our finite concerns, at the Martha sphere of life, everything seems the same and yet everything is changed. We are still concerned about all these things but differently – the anxiety is gone! It still exists and tries to return. But its power is broken; it cannot destroy us any more. He who is grasped by the one thing that is needed has the many things under his feet. They concern him but not ultimately, and when he loses them he does not lose the one thing he needs and that cannot be taken from him.

21. *The Right Time*

Everything has its appointed hour,
    there is a time for all things under heaven:
    a time for birth, a time for death,
    a time to plant and a time to uproot,
    a time to kill, a time to heal,
    a time to break down and a time to build,
    a time to cry, a time to laugh,
    a time to mourn, a time to dance,
    a time to scatter and a time to gather,
    a time to embrace, a time to refrain,
    a time to seek, a time to lose,
    a time to keep, a time to throw away,
    a time to tear, a time to sew,
    a time for silence and a time for speech,
    a time for love, a time for hate,
    a time for war, a time for peace.

ECCLESIASTES 3:1-8

You have read words of a man who lived about two hundred years before the birth of Jesus; a man nurtured in Jewish piety and educated in Greek wisdom; a child of his period – a period of catastrophes and despair. He expresses this despair in words of a pessimism that surpasses most pessimistic writings in world literature. Everything is in vain, he repeats many times. It is vanity, even if you were King Solomon who not only controlled the means for any humanly possible satisfaction but who also could use them with wisdom. But even such a man must say: all is in vain! We do not know the name of the writer of this book who is usually called the Preacher, although he is much more a teacher of wisdom, a practical philosopher. Perhaps we wonder how his dark considerations of man's destiny could become a biblical book. It took indeed a long time and the overcoming of much protest before it was accepted. But finally synagogue and church accepted it; and now this book is in the Bible beside Isaiah and Matthew and Paul and John. The 'all is in vain' has received biblical authority. I believe that this authority is deserved, that it is not an authority produced by a mistake, but that it is the authority of truth. His description of the human situation is truer than any poetry glorifying man and his destiny. His honesty opens our eyes for those things which are overlooked or covered up by optimists of all kinds. So if you meet people who attack Christianity for having too many illusions tell them that their attacks would be much stronger if they allied themselves with the book of the Preacher. The very fact that this book is a part of the Bible shows clearly that the Bible is a most realistic book. And it cannot be otherwise. For only on this background the message of Jesus as the Christ has meaning. Only if we accept an honest view of the human situation, of man's old reality, can we understand the message that in Christ a new reality has appeared. He who never has said about his life 'Vanity of vanities, all is vanity' cannot honestly say with Paul, 'In all these things we are more than conquerors through him who loved us.'

There is a time, an appointed hour, for all things under heaven, says the Preacher. And in fourteen contrasts he embraces the whole of human existence, showing that everything has its time. What does this mean?

When the Preacher says that everything has its time, he does not forget his ever-repeated statement, 'This too is vanity and striving for the wind.' The fact that everything has its appointed time only confirms his tragic view. Things and actions have their time. Then they pass and other things and actions have *their* time. But nothing new comes out of this circle in which all life moves. Everything is timed by an eternal law which is above time. We are not able to penetrate into the meaning of this timing. For *us*, it is mystery and what *we* see is vanity and frustration. God's timing is hidden to us, and our toiling and timing are of no ultimate use. Any human attempt to change the rhythm of birth and death, of war and peace, of love and hate and all the other contrasts in the rhythm of life is in vain.

This is the first but it is not the whole meaning of the statement that everything has its appointed hour. If the Preacher says that there is a time to plant and a time to uproot, a time to kill, a time to heal, a time to break down and a time to build, a time to mourn and a time to dance, a time to speak and a time to be silent, he asks us to be aware of the right time, the time to do one thing and not to do another thing. After he has emphasized that everything is timed by an unsurmountable destiny, he asks us to follow this timing from above and to do our own timing according to it. As a teacher of wisdom who gives many wise rules for our acting, he requests right timing. He knows that all our timing is dependent on the timing from above, from the hidden ruler of time; but this does not exclude our acting at the right and not at the wrong moment. The whole ancient world was driven by the belief that for everything we do there is an adequate hour: if you want to build a house or to marry, if you want to travel or to begin a war – for any important enterprise – you must ask for the right moment. You must ask somebody who knows – the priest or the astrologer, the seer or the prophet. On the ground of their oracles about the good season you may or may not act. This was a belief of centuries and millennia. It was one of the strongest forces in human history, from generation to generation. The greatest men of the past waited for the oracle announcing the appointed hour. Jesus himself says that his hour has not yet come and he went to Jerusalem when he felt that his hour *had* come.

The modern man usually does not ask for oracles. But the modern man knows of the need for timing as much as his predecessors. When in my early years in this country I had to discuss a certain project with an influential American business man he said to me, 'Don't forget that the first step to a successful action is the right timing.' Innumerable times, when reading about political or commercial actions, I was reminded of these words. In many conversations about activities and plans the problem of timing came up. It is one of the most manifest patterns of our culture, of our industrial civilizations. How does it compare with the words of the Preacher?

When the business man spoke to me about timing he thought of what *he* had done and what *he* would do. He betrayed the pride of a man who knows the right hour for his actions, who was successful in his timing, who felt as the master of his destiny, as the creator of new things, as the conqueror of situations. This certainty is not the mood of the Preacher. Even if the Preacher points to the need of right timing he does not give up his great 'All is vanity'. You must do it, you must grasp the right moment, but ultimately it does not matter. The end is the same for the wise and the fool, for him who toils and for him who enjoys himself, the end is even the same for man and for animals.

The Preacher is first of all conscious that he *is* timed; and he points to our timing as a secondary matter. The modern business man is first of all conscious that *he* has to time, and only vaguely realizes that he *is* timed. Of course, he also is aware that he has not produced the right time, that he is dependent on it, that he may miss it in his calculations and actions. He knows that there is a limit to his timing, that there are economic forces stronger than he, that he also is subject to a final destiny which ends all his planning. He is aware of it, but he disregards it when he plans and acts. Quite different is the Preacher. He starts his enumeration of things that are timed with birth and death. They are beyond human timing. They are the signposts which cannot be trespassed. We cannot time them and all our timing is limited by them. This is the reason why in the beginning of our modern era death and sin and hell were removed from the public consciousness. While in the Middle Ages every room, every street, and, more important, every heart and every mind were filled with symbols of the end, of death, it has been today a matter of bad taste even to mention death. The modern man feels that the awareness of the end disturbs and weakens his power of timing. He has, instead of the threatening symbols of death, the clock in every room, on every street, and, more important, in his mind and in his nerves. There is something mysterious about the clock. It determines our daily timing. Without it we could not plan for the next hour, we could not time any of our activities. But the clock also reminds us of the fact that we *are* timed. It indicates the rush of our time towards it. The voice of the clock has reminded many people of the fact that they are timed. In an old German night-watchman's street song every hour is announced with a special reminder. Of midnight it says 'Twelve – that is the goal of time, give us, O God, eternity.' These two attitudes toward the clock indicate two ways of timing – the one as being timed, the other as timing for the next hour, for today and tomorrow. What does the clock tell you? Does it point to the hour of rising and working and eating and talking and going to sleep? Does it point to the next appointment and the next project? Or does it show that another day, another week have passed, that we have become older, that better timing is needed to use our last years for the fulfilment of our plans, for planting and building and finishing before it is too late? Or does the clock make us anticipate the moment in which its voice does not speak any more for us? Have we, the men of the industrial age, the men who are timing every hour from day to day, the courage and the imagination of the Preacher who looks back at all *his* time and all *his* timing and calls it vanity? And if so, what about our timing? Does it not lose any meaning? Must we not say with the Preacher that it is good for man to enjoy life as it is given to him from hour to hour, but that it is better not to be born at all?

There is another answer to the question of human existence, to the question of timing and being timed. It is summed up in the words of Jesus: 'The time is fulfilled and the kingdom of God is at hand.' In these words, God's timing breaks into our human timing. Something new appears, answering the question of the Preacher as well as the question of the business man. We ask with all generations of thinking men: what is the meaning of the flux of time and the passing away of everything in it? What is the meaning of our toiling and planning when the end of all of us and of all our works is the same? Vanity? And this is the answer we get: within this our time something happens that is not of our time but out of eternity, and this times *our* time! The same power which limits us in time gives eternal significance to our timing. When Jesus says that the right hour has come, that the kingdom of God is at hand, he pronounces the victory over the law of vanity. *This* hour is not subject to the circle of life and death and all the other circles of vanity. When God himself appears in a moment of time, when he himself subjects himself to the flux of time, the flux of time is conquered. And if this happens in *one* moment of time, then *all* moments of time receive another significance. When the finger of the clock turns around; not one vain moment is replaced by another vain moment, but each moment says to us: the eternal is at hand in *this* moment. The moment passes, the eternal remains. Whatever in this moment, in this hour, on this day and in this short or long life-time happens has infinite significance. Our timing from moment to moment, our planning today for tomorrow, the toil of our life-time is not lost. Its deepest meaning lies not ahead where vanity swallows it, but it lies above where eternity affirms it. This is the seriousness of time and timing. Through our timing God times the coming of his kingdom; through our timing he elevates the time of vanity into the time of fulfilment. The activist who is timing with shrewdness and intuition what he has to do in his time and for his time, and for our whole activistic civilization cannot give us the answer. And the Preacher, who himself once was a most successful activist, knows that this is not an answer; he knows the vanity of our timing. And let us be honest. The spirit of the Preacher is strong today in our minds. His mood fills our philosophy and poetry. The vanity of human existence is described powerfully by those who call themselves philosophers or poets of existence. They all are the children of the Preacher, this great existentialist of his period. But neither they nor the Preacher know an answer. They know more than the men of mere acting. They know the vanity of acting and timing. They know that we *are* timed. But they do *not* know the answer either. Certainly we must act; we cannot help it. We have to time our lives from day to day. Let us do it as clearly and as successfully as the Preacher when he still followed the example of King Solomon. But let us follow him also when he saw *through* all this and realized its vanity.

Then, and then alone, are we prepared for the message of the eternal appearing in time and elevating time to eternity. Then we see in the movement of the clock not only the passing of one moment after the other, but also the eternal at hand, threatening, demanding, promising. Then we are able to say : 'In spite'! In spite of the fact that the Preacher and all his pessimistic followers today and everywhere and at all times are right, I say yes to time and to toil and to acting. I know the infinite significance of every moment. But again in saying so we should not relapse into the attitude of the activist, not even of the Christian activist – and there are many of them, men and women in Christendom. The message of the fulfilment of time is not a green light for a new, an assumedly Christian activism. But it makes us say with Paul : 'Though our outer nature is wasting away our inner nature is renewed every day – because we look not to the things that are seen but to the things that are unseen. For the things that are seen are transient, but the things that are unseen are eternal.' In these words the message of the Preacher and the message of Jesus are united. All is vanity but through this vanity eternity shines into us, comes near to us, draws us to itself. When eternity calls in time, then activism vanishes. When eternity calls in time, then pessimism vanishes. When eternity times us, then time becomes a vessel of eternity. Then we become vessels of that which is eternal.

22. *Love Is Stronger Than Death*

We know that we have passed out of death into life, because we love the brethren. He who does not love remains in death.

I JOHN 3:14

In our time, as in every age, we need to see something

which is stronger than death. Death has become powerful in our time, in individual human beings, in families, in nations and in mankind as a whole. Death has become powerful – that is to say that the End, the finite, and the limitations and decay of our being have become visible. For nearly a century this was concealed in Western civilization. We had become masters in our earthly household. Our control over nature, and our social planning had widened the boundaries of our being; the affirmation of life had drowned out its negation which no longer dared make itself heard, and which fled into the hidden anxiety of our hearts, becoming fainter and fainter. We forgot that we are finite, and we forgot the abyss of nothingness surrounding us. We had gathered into our barns the fruits of thousands of years of toil. All generations of men had laboured so that we, the generation of fulfilment, might tread death under our feet. It was not death in the sense of the natural end of life which we thought to have destroyed, but death as a power in and over life, as the Lord and master of the soul. We kept the picture of death from our children and when here and there, in our neighbourhood and in the world, mortal convulsions and the End became visible, our security was not disturbed. For us these events were merely accidental and unavoidable, but they were not enough to tear off the lid which we had fastened down over the abyss of our being.

And suddenly the lid was torn off. The picture of Death appeared, unveiled, in a thousand forms. As in the late Middle Ages the figure of Death appeared in pictures and poetry, and the Dance of Death with every living being was painted and sung, so our generation – the generation of world wars, revolutions, and mass migrations – rediscovered the reality of death. We have seen millions die in war, hundreds of thousands in revolutions, tens of thousands in persecutions and systematic purges of minorities. Multitudes as numerous as whole nations still wander over the face of the earth or perish when artificial walls put an end to their wanderings. All those who are called refugees or immigrants belong to this wandering; in them is embodied a part of these tremendous events in which Death has again grasped the reins which we believed it had relinquished forever. Such people carry in their souls, and often in their bodies, the traces of death, and they will never completely lose them. You who have never taken part yourselves in this great migration must receive these others as symbols of a death which is a component element of life. Receive them as people who, by their destiny, shall remind us of the presence of the End in every moment of life and history. Receive them as symbols of the finiteness and transitoriness of every human concern, of every human life, and of every created thing.

We have become a generation of the End and those of us who have been refugees and exiles should not forget this when we have found a new beginning here or in another land. The End is nothing external. It is not exhausted by the loss of that which we can never regain: our childhood homes, the people with whom we grew up, the country, the things, the language which formed us, the goods, both spiritual and material, which we inherited or earned, the friends who were torn away from us by sudden death. The End is more than all this; it is in us, it has become our very being. We are a generation of the End and we should know that we are. Perhaps there are some who think that what has happened to them and to the whole world should now be forgotten. Is it not more dignified, truer and stronger to say 'yes' to that which is our destiny, to refuse to cover the signs of the End in our lives and in our souls, to let the voice of Death be heard? Amid all the new possibilities offered to us, must we not acknowledge ourselves to be that which destiny has made us? Must we not confess that we are symbols of the End? And this End is of an age which was both great and a lie. It is the End for all finitude which always becomes a lie when it forgets that it is finite and seeks to veil the picture of death.

But who can bear to look at this picture? Only he who can look at another picture behind and beyond it – the picture of Love. For love is stronger than death. Every death means parting, separation, isolation, opposition and not participation. So it is, too, with the death of nations, the end of generations, and the atrophy of souls. Our souls become poor and disintegrate insofar as we want to be alone, insofar as we bemoan our misfortunes, nurse our despair and enjoy our bitterness, and yet turn coldly away from the physical and spiritual need of others. Love overcomes separation and creates participation in which there is more than that which the individuals involved can bring to it. Love is the infinite which is given to the finite. Therefore we love in others, for we do not merely love others, but we love the Love that is in them and which is more than their or our love. In mutual assistance what is most important is not the alleviation of need but the actualization of love. Of course, there is no love which does not want to make the other's need its own. But there is also no true help which does not spring from love and create love. Those who fight against death and disintegration through all kinds of relief agencies know this. Often very little external help is possible. And the gratitude of those who receive help is first and always gratitude for love and only afterwards gratitude for help. Love, not help, is stronger than death. But there is no love which does not become help. Where help is given without love, there new suffering grows from the help.

It is love, human and divine, which overcomes death in nations and generations and in all the horror of our time. Help has become almost impossible in the face of the monstrous powers which we are experiencing. Death is given power over everything finite, especially in our period of history. But death is given no power over love. Love is stronger. It creates something new out of the destruction caused by death; it bears everything and overcomes everything. It is at work where the power of death is strongest, in war and persecution and homelessness and hunger and physical death itself. It is omnipresent and here and there, in the smallest and most hidden ways as in the greatest and most visible ones, it rescues life from death. It rescues each of us, for love is stronger than death.

23. Universal Salvation

Now from the sixth hour there was darkness over all the land until the ninth hour. And about the ninth hour Jesus cried with a loud voice, 'Eli, Eli, la'ma sabach-tha'ni?' that is, 'My God, my God, why hast thou forsaken me?'

And Jesus cried again with a loud voice and yielded up his spirit. And behold, the curtain of the temple was torn in two, from top to bottom; and the earth shook, and the rocks were split; the tombs also were opened, and many bodies of the saints who had fallen asleep were raised, and coming out of the tombs after his resurrection they went into the holy city and appeared to many. When the centurion and those who were with him, keeping watch over Jesus, saw the earthquake and what took place, they were filled with awe, and said, 'Truly this was a son of God!'

MATTHEW 27:45-46; 50-54

In the stories of the crucifixion the agony and the death of Jesus are connected with a group of events in nature: darkness covers the land; the curtain of the temple is torn in two; the earth is shaken and the bodies of saints rise out of their graves. Nature, with trembling, participates in the decisive event of history. The sun veils its head; the temple makes the gesture of mourning; the foundations of the earth are moved; the tombs are opened. Nature is in an uproar because something is happening which concerns the universe.

Since the time of the evangelists, wherever the story of Golgotha has been told as the turning event in the world-drama of salvation, the role nature played in this drama has also been told. Painters of the crucifixion have used all their artistic power to express the darkness over the land in almost unnatural colours. I remember my own earliest impression of Good Friday – the feeling of the mystery of the divine suffering, first of all, through the compassion of nature. And so did the centurion, the first pagan who witnessed for the Crucified. Filled with awe, with numinous dread, he understood in a naïve-profound way that something more had happened than the death of a holy and innocent man.

We should *not* ask whether clouds or a dust storm darkened the sun on a special day of a special year, whether an earthquake happened in Palestine just at that hour, whether the curtain before the holy of holies in the temple at Jerusalem had to be repaired or whether the raised bodies of the saints died again. But we *should* ask whether we are able to feel with the evangelists and the painters, with the children and the Roman soldiers, that the event at Golgotha is one which concerns the universe, including all nature and all history. With this question in our mind let us look at the signs reported by our evangelist.

The sun veiled its face because of the depth of evil and shame which it saw under the Cross. But the sun also veiled its face because its power over the world had ceased once and forever in these hours of its darkness. The great shining and burning god of everything that lives on earth, the sun who was praised and feared and adored by innumerable human beings during thousands and thousands of years, had been deprived of its divine power when *one* human being in ultimate agony maintained his unity with that which is greater than the sun. Since those hours of darkness it is manifest that not the sun, but a suffering and struggling soul which cannot be broken by all the powers of the universe is the image of the Highest, and that the sun can only be praised in the way of St Francis, who called it our brother, but not our god.

'The curtain of the temple was torn in two.' The temple tore its gown as the mourners did because he, to whom the temple belonged more than to anybody else, was thrown out and killed by the servants of the temple. But the temple – and with it, all temples on earth – also complained of its own destiny. The curtain which made the temple a holy place, separated from other places, lost its separating power. He who was expelled as blaspheming the temple, had cleft the curtain and opened the temple for everybody, for every moment. *This* curtain cannot be mended any more, although there are priests and ministers and pious people who try to mend it. They will *not* succeed because he, for whom every place was a sacred place, a place where God is present, has been brought on the Cross in the name of the holy place. When the curtain of the temple was torn in two, God judged religion and rejected temples. After this moment temples and churches can only mean places of concentration on the holy which is the ground and the meaning of every place. And like the temple, the earth was judged at Golgotha. Trembling and shaking the earth participated in the agony of the man on the Cross and in the despair of all those who had seen in him the beginning of the new aeon. Trembling and shaking the earth proved that it is not the motherly ground on which we can safely build our houses and cities, our cultures and religious systems. Trembling and shaking the earth pointed to another ground on which the earth itself rests: the self-surrendering love on which all earthly powers and values concentrate their hostility and which they cannot conquer. Since the hour when Jesus uttered a loud cry and breathed his last and the rocks were split, the earth ceased to be the foundation of what we build on her. Only insofar as it has a deeper ground, can it stand; only insofar as it is rooted in the same foundation in which the Cross is rooted, can it last.

And the earth not only ceases to be the solid ground of life; she also ceases to be the lasting cave of death. Resurrection is not something added to the death of him who is the Christ; but it is implied in his death, as the story of the resurrection before the resurrection, indicates. No longer is the universe subjected to the law of death out of birth. It is subjected to a higher law, to the law of life out of death by the death of him who represented eternal life. The tombs were opened and bodies were raised when one man in whom God was present without limit committed his spirit into his Father's hands. Since this moment the universe is no longer what it was; nature has received another meaning; history is transformed and you and I are no more, and should not be any more, what we were before.

ON THE BOUNDARY

*

INTRODUCTION

This autobiographical sketch originally appeared as the first part of Tillich's *Interpretation of History*, a book that is no longer easily obtainable. Of it the psychiatrist, Erik Erikson, has said: 'Paulus Tillich's relation to the study of personality has found its most exquisite expression in some autobiographical notes written with care and charity at about his fiftieth year.' Its publication as a separate volume will earn the gratitude of all those who came to know Tillich either as a writer or a lecturer or a preacher or a friend. His writing and speaking gave a clear picture of a man who scorned the easy method of communication which seeks to simplify the message and who yet was able to speak directly to the minds and hearts of so many people. This is one of the surprising features of Tillich's career. He was at once so difficult a thinker and so successful a communicator. Another is that he was so much a mystery and yet sought on several occasions to lay bare his very soul. I must confess that I have done my share of complaining; and yet when I heard of his death I too mourned the passing of a hero. Now I am all the more conscious of the ambivalent nature of my attitude towards him, but I also know that I have sought to repay the debt I owe him. Several years ago he spoke of me as his 'logical critic' and warned others not to heed my criticism. This was shortly after I had published an article in which I had argued that a major thesis of Tillich's (that philosophy and theology are correlated sciences) was a tautology. The result of this was a violent argument with many of his pupils, for whom this kind of criticism was tantamount to sacrilege, and I think that Tillich himself was led to think that the criticism was malicious. However, his reaction was to invite me to discuss the problem with him – which we did. I argued that you could say nothing about the relation between philosophy and theology by laying down definitions, that definition yielded only tautology. To this Tillich replied that I was a Logical Positivist! I protested and at length he agreed that my criticism was not positivistic, adding that unless I had some metaphysical position there was no point in my criticizing his. The profundity of this reply was not immediately evident to me, but I can now see that the necessity of metaphysics is one of the lessons Tillich taught me. Together with the article there had appeared a review of *The Courage To Be* which I had written. Condensing a fairly long piece into the meagre space which I had at my disposal I had hit on a style which may have seemed impertinent. After an opening sentence or two indicating the richness of the book I had listed several criticisms. Perhaps Tillich thought this sparse style reminiscent of Carnap because he emphasized that the latter's rejection of Heidegger as nonsense was itself non-sensical. When the time came to leave Tillich with characteristic generosity autographed my copy of *The Courage To Be* and wrote on it a quotation from Nietzsche – 'A good fight justifies every cause.' I experienced the same generosity when, shortly before he died, he told me that he valued the way I had approached his work, seeking both to interpret it and to work out an evaluation of it. It is as one who was thus graciously accepted as his pupil but not his follower that I shall always speak of Paul Tillich.

Anyone who comes across this work and has never read any of Tillich's works can quickly and easily form for himself a clear picture of Tillich's achievement and gain a real appreciation of his peculiar style of theological thinking. This is because his thinking was to a remarkable degree autobiographical. The early years in Prussia, the influence of parents, the love of nature, the excitement of living in a city, the intellectual adventure of university life – all these things are part of his most systematic thinking. For instance, he sometimes spoke of his task in theology as the creation of a theology of culture. The roots of such an enterprise are to be found in the culture he imbibed at home, the atmosphere of the old Gothic towns where he grew up, the early intoxicated love of literature and the tremendous discovery of art when he sought relief from the horrors of war in a study of painting. Furthermore, it was due to the circumstances of his career – teaching philosophy first in Dresden and then in Frankfurt – that he came to view his work as a theology of culture, a borderland between philosophy and theology. Because his thought is thus so intimately bound up with his life we are fortunate to have three autobiographical sketches[1] to which we can turn for guidance, and of the three *On the Boundary* is without doubt the most significant. However, before one can speak of this it is necessary to bring Tillich's own unfinished story to its close.

As we leave him in *On the Boundary* he is at the beginning of his new life in an alien continent that was to become very much his home. When I first heard Tillich he impressed me greatly not only because he was obviously a very profound theologian but also because he was so clearly European. This is something I have emphasized in several discussions of Tillich and is, indeed, one more instance of the autobiographical nature of his thinking. Yet, by the same token, he became very much an American theologian. He is unique in the history of twentieth-century thought as a theologian who not only achieved fame by his work in two continents

[1] They are to be found in *The Interpretation of History* (reprinted in this volume), *The Protestant Era*, Nisbet, London, 1951, pp. xxiii-xlv, and *The Theology of Paul Tillich*, Macmillan, N.Y., 1952, pp. 3-21.

but also succeeded in forging a system of thought which
articulated the theological questions of both Europe and
America. His earlier political writings are the expression of a profound consciousness of the Christian obliga-
tion to avert a repetition of the catastrophe of World
War I and to struggle for the realization of justice
and peace. Generalizing from his own experience of disappointment Tillich was able to speak to his fellow
Europeans and for them. He was able also to present a
vision of social justice which, however deficient as a
piece of political science, found echoes in the reaction
of all Christian people to those decisive years. Furthermore, it was this which made Tillich so ready to identify
himself with the United States of America. As he has so
eloquently put in this volume (p. 348-9):

> I was happy to discover on the boundary of this new
> continent where I now live, thanks to American
> hospitality, an ideal which is more consistent with
> the image of one mankind than that of Europe
> in her tragic self-dismemberment. It is the image
> of one nation in whom representatives of all nations
> and races can live as citizens. Although here, too,
> the distance between ideal and reality is infinite
> and the image is often deeply shadowed, nonetheless
> it is a kind of symbol of that highest possibility of
> history which is called 'mankind', and which itself
> points to that which transcends reality – the king-
> dom of God.

It was not surprising, therefore, that Tillich did not
hanker after the old days in his homeland but soon
came to feel at home in the United States and was
able to understand his new cultural milieu and even to
influence it. Tillich really discovered what America is
all about and made definite contact with the people and
their ways of thinking. I have elsewhere commented
on the fact that Tillich, 'unamerican' as he might have
been thought to be, was in fact strangely suited to the

American situation. His philosophical background – that is, Schelling and possibly Hegel – was indeed unfamiliar and even uncongenial. Yet in the American pragmatist tradition he found a real point of contact which made it possible for Americans to understand what he meant when he spoke of Existenz. This rapport enabled him to understand the American phenomenon. *The Courage To Be* contains what is, to my mind, the most penetrating theological analysis of American culture that has been written. Like some Hosea or Jeremiah, Tillich saw clearly the weaknesses of American culture and as he judged them he judged himself. His influence on American culture can be gauged from the interest taken in him by psychiatrists on the one hand and artists on the other. If one looks at the list of papers and lectures which Tillich gave during his last ten years one is surprised not only by the variety but also by the fact that he constantly addressed audiences composed mainly of artists – a lecture here to an orchestral conference and another there to a gathering of poets or painters. More narrowly his influence can be seen in the increasing use made of his theological system by theologians. It has always distressed me that so many of his pupils became 'Tillichians', and this idolizing of a theological genius I shall never cease to attack. However, there are others who have seen his greatness and resisted the temptation to transform his dialectical contribution into a dogma. For all these Reinhold Niebuhr, himself perhaps the greatest American theologian, speaks when he admits his indebtedness to Tillich 'for his creative thrust in the context of the traditional habits of thought in the liberalism of the pre-war culture of the twentieth century'.[2]

Tillich's American career was really a series of careers. When, in 1933, he had been dismissed from his chair in

[2] *Union Theological Seminary Quarterly Review*, November 1965, p. 11.

Frankfurt as a result of his opposition to Hitler, Tillich was asked by Reinhold Niebuhr to come to Union Theological Seminary in New York City. Fleeing from his homeland Tillich was at least assured of a haven. He and his family arrived in New York in November and were made welcome by friends, especially by the Niebuhrs. Quickly winning for himself a place in the intellectual life of New York, Tillich was invited by Union Seminary to join its faculty, first as a visiting professor and then as a member of the permanent staff. So once again he was able to hope that his theological work might be achieved. For a sensitive person like Tillich one necessary condition of work was the friendship and appreciation of colleagues. This he had in Union Seminary – he was admired and liked by both staff and students. So much so that in 1950 he was able to say, 'During sixteen years at Union Seminary I have not had a single disagreeable experience with my American colleagues.'[8] As a result of Union's close co-operation with Columbia University the link Tillich already had with the Department of Philosophy there through Professor Horace Friess became an important part of his life. His stocky figure was often to be seen crossing Broadway either to or from Columbia. He became a member of the Philosophy Club and he also lectured regularly in the Philosophy Department. His interest in politics was still very keen and he joined the Fellowship of Socialist Christians which was led by Reinhold Niebuhr as well as becoming chairman of the Council for a Democratic Germany during the war. His main work, however, was theological – teaching students at Union, giving papers at conferences and lectures at various universities, taking part in church committees and in the ecumenical conference in Oxford. But his establishment as a figure in American theology did not make him forget his homeland. Besides being chairman of the Council for a Democratic Germany he was chairman of the Self-Help

[8] *The Theology of Paul Tillich*, p. 17.

for Emigrés from Central Europe, an organization which sought to assist refugees with advice and help. Most of these who came in their thousands every year were Jews, and the organization helped them to make a new life for themselves in the United States. When he visited England to deliver the First Lectures in Nottingham (1950) and later to deliver the Gifford Lectures in Aberdeen (1953-54) he was sought out by German refugees and he was very kind to them.

The story of his second and third American careers can be told briefly, for it is a story of increasing popularity and fame and the achievement of a life-work. When, in 1955, he had retired from his Chair of Philosophical Theology at Union, Tillich was invited by Harvard University to become University Professor, a distinction which is accorded only to outstanding academic figures. Being University Professor Tillich was not responsible for teaching any particular course and could lecture on any subject he chose. He had become a legend in New York and his fame was such that students flocked to hear him. Several hundreds of students crowded the lecture hall when he gave his final series of lectures at Harvard in 1962. Their enthusiasm was immense, and Tillich loved this extension of his academic career. After Harvard came Chicago where he enjoyed similar status and a similar success. One of the attractions of Chicago was the proximity of the Chicago University Press which had published the first two volumes of *Systematic Theology* and was to publish the third. If it had taken a long time to produce volume two it was to take longer to produce volume three. The Press was anxious to have the manuscript but Tillich was loath to let it go. After several revisions it was finally published in 1963 (1964 in Britain). However, when I saw Tillich in the summer of 1965, he told me that he was not satisfied and asked me to give him a list of passages which I thought ought to be changed. He was planning a further revision of this and several other of his works. Yet he must have felt that his life-work was now almost finished. He had achieved what it is given to very few people to achieve – he had lived fully and he had more or less finished what he had begun. Together with his lectures at Chicago and his completion of *Systematic Theology* Tillich was busy during those last four years literally going all over the world giving lectures. When I last saw him in New York in 1965 I commented on his healthy appearance, saying that he seemed to have recovered from the illness of the previous year. He replied that he had never felt better and was working happily. As we parted he said to me, 'Why don't you ask me to give a lecture in Durham? If you do I will come.' Preparations for this were being made when the news came that he had died. He had suffered a heart attack in the middle of October and within a day or two seemed to be on the mend. Then suddenly his condition deteriorated and the end came quickly on October 24. His ashes were interred in Paul Tillich Park, New Harmony, Indiana. This village was founded by a group of religious German refugees in 1814 and subsequently purchased from them by the philanthropist, Robert Owen. The park is planted with trees and has quotations from various sermons by Tillich engraved in granite. It was donated by a former pupil of his, Mrs Kenneth Dale Owen. A bronze portrait bust of Tillich by James Rosati is to be placed in the park, and on the bust are to be inscribed verses 3 and 4 of Psalm 1:

And he shall be like a tree planted by the streams of water
That bringeth forth its fruit in its season,
Whose leaf also doth not wither;
And whatsoever he doeth shall prosper.
The wicked are not so;
But are like the chaff which the wind driveth away.

I have spoken of the last time I saw Tillich. I believe the first time I saw him was when he preached a sermon at the beginning of the academic year in Union Seminary in 1952. His text, I recall, was: 'A man shall leave his father and mother.' The message he proclaimed to students who had left their homes to come to university was particularly relevant to someone like myself who had left not only home but his homeland and his home-continent. I was profoundly moved. It was not homiletic skill nor any technique but the sheer piety of the man that moved me. And this is why so many people have found Tillich a relevant and a persuasive preacher. Much has been said about his attempt to communicate to modern man in his own language. It seems to me that all this kind of talk misunderstands Tillich's success as a preacher. It was the transparent honesty of the preacher that won your heart – not his language. Indeed, it was not because of his highly abstract and classical language but despite it that he managed to make one aware of the fact that he understood what one felt and what one feared and to speak directly to one's need. He never tired of saying that man was a question to himself and that this was the reason why he was a theologian. But I should say that successful though Tillich always was as a preacher he was most successful in his preaching to students, and this because he had chosen to stand at the boundary.

Probably when the history of twentieth-century theology is written it will be as a boundary-theologian that Tillich will be considered important. He sought to express anew what had been expressed before but he was very much aware of the need to do this in new and appropriate ways. To this end he quarried for theological gold in the most unlikely places as well as in familiar and some-times forgotten mines. A generation which had grown accustomed to the profound estrangement of philosophy from theology was surprised that a philosophical theology should be attempted once more. Tillich began his academic work as a philosopher and remained convinced of the need to do philosophy in the context of theology. He was ever conscious of a metaphysical frisson as he contemplated the existence of anything. Like the poet Tillich would say, '*nihil humanum a me alienum puto*', and he turned in humility and gratitude to the psychologist, the sociologist, the poet, the novelist, the dramatist and the painter to sharpen and deepen his theological understanding. The portrait of a man whose very life and theological task were acted out on the boundary is what he has himself given us in these pages. To read them is to hear him again and to realize once more how great a man one had the privilege of knowing.

J. Heywood Thomas

In the introduction to my *Religiöse Verwirklichung* (Religious Realization),[1] 'The boundary is the best place for acquiring knowledge.' When I was asked to give an account of the way my ideas have developed from my life, I thought that the concept of the boundary might be the fitting symbol for the whole of my personal and intellectual development. At almost every point, I have had to stand between alternative possibilities of existence, to be completely at home in neither and to take no definitive stand against either. Since thinking presupposes receptiveness to new possibilities, this position is fruitful for thought; but it is difficult and dangerous in life, which again and again demands decisions and thus the exclusion of alternatives. This disposition and its tension have determined both my destiny and my work.

Between Two Temperaments

In the shaping of a child's character, one should not ascribe too much importance to the characters of its parents. There are, however, parental and ancestral traits that do recur rather strikingly in children and later descendants, and perhaps cause deep conflicts in them. Whether this is more a matter of heredity or of the impressions of early childhood is an open question. Nevertheless, I have never doubted that the union of a father from Brandenburg and a mother from the Rhineland implanted in me the tension between eastern and western Germany. In eastern Germany, an inclination to meditation tinged with melancholy, a heightened consciousness of duty and personal sin, and a strong regard for authority and feudal traditions are still alive. Western Germany is characterized by a zest for life, love of the concrete, mobility, rationality and democracy. Though neither set of characteristics was the exclusive property of either parent, it was through my parents that these conflicting traits influenced the course of my inner and outer life. The importance of such parental legacies is not that they determine the course of one's life, but that they define the scope and supply the substance out of which critical decisions are drawn.

Without this double inheritance my position on the boundary would be hard to understand. My father's influence was dominant, in part because of the early death of my mother. Consequently the character of my mother's world asserted itself only through constant and deep struggle with that of my father. In order for the maternal side of my makeup to express itself, outbreaks, often extreme, were necessary. Classical composure and harmony were not part of my heritage. This may explain why Goethe's classical traits were alien to me, and why the pre- and post-classical periods of Greek antiquity were more assimilable than the classical. This tension also accounts in part for certain premises underlying my interpretation of history: the choice of the line moving forward and towards a goal rather than the classical premise of the self-enclosed circle; the idea that the struggle between two opposing principles constitutes the content of history; the theory of dynamic truth, which holds that truth is found in the midst of struggle and destiny, and not, as Plato taught, in an unchanging 'beyond'.

Between the ages of four and fourteen I lived in a small town near the Elbe, where my father was the leading minister and the superintendent of the church district. In the small towns of many parts of Germany, the typical resident is the 'farmer-burgher' – a townsman, usually well-to-do, who manages a fairly good-sized farm from his town residence. Towns of this kind have a decidedly rustic character. Many of the houses have yards, barns, and gardens attached to them, and it is only a few minutes' walk out into the fields. Cattle and sheep are herded through the streets morning and evening. Nevertheless, these are real towns with civic rights and traditions as old as the Middle Ages. The gates of the town wall open on to narrow streets with serried rows of houses and shops. The sheltered, protective quality of the town with its hustle and bustle, in contrast to the eeriness of the forest at night and the silent fields and sleepy hamlets, is one of the earliest and strongest of my childhood impressions. Visits to Berlin, where the railroad itself struck me as something half-mythical, heightened these memories and developed in me an often overpowering longing for the big city. This affected me later in many ways; it came to philosophical expression in the essays 'Logos und Mythos der Technik'[2] and 'Die technische Stadt als Symbol' (The Technical City as Symbol).[3]

This attraction to the city saved me from a romantic rejection of technical civilization and taught me to appreciate the importance of the city for the development of the critical side of intellectual and artistic life. Later on, I arrived at a vital and sympathetic understanding of Bohemianism, a movement that is possible only in large cities. I also learned to appreciate aesthetically both the fantastic inner activity and the physical size of a city. Finally, I acquired firsthand knowledge of the political and social movements concentrated in a large city. These experiences and their lasting effect on me – the myth of the city, so to speak – are largely responsible for the popularity of my book *The Religious Situation*.[4]

My ties to the country, however, are even stronger. Nearly all the great memories and longings of my life are interwoven with landscapes, soil, weather, the fields of grain and the smell of the potato plant in autumn, the shapes of clouds, and with wind, flowers and woods. In all my later travels through Germany and southern and western Europe, the impression of the land remained strong. Schelling's philosophy of nature, which I read enthusiastically while surrounded by the beauty of nature, became the direct expression of my feeling for nature.

The weeks and, later, months that I spent by the sea every year from the time I was eight were even more important for my life and work. The experience of the infinite bordering on the finite suited my inclination toward the boundary situation and supplied my imagination with a symbol that gave substance to my emotions and creativity to my thought. Without this experience it is likely that my theory of the human boundary situation, as expressed in *Religiöse Verwicklichung*, might not have developed as it did.

There is another element to be found in the contemplation of the sea: its dynamic assault on the serene firmness of the land and the ecstasy of its gales and waves. My theory of the 'dynamic mass' in the essay 'Masse und Geist' (Mass and Spirit),[5] was conceived under the immediate influence of the turbulent sea. The sea also supplied the imaginative element necessary for the doctrines of the Absolute as both ground and abyss of dynamic truth, and of the substance of religion as the thrust of the eternal into finitude. Nietzsche said that no idea could be true unless it was thought in the open air. Many of my ideas were conceived in the open and much of my writing done among trees or by the sea. Alternating regularly between the elements of town and country always has been and still is part of what I consider indispensable and inviolable in my life.

Between Social Classes

The particular nature of small-town life made the boundary between social classes visible to me at an early age. I attended the local school, made my friends in it, and shared their animosity toward the upper class represented by my parents and the families of the mayor, the doctor, the druggist, some merchants, and a few others. Although I took private lessons in Latin with some of the children of this select group, and later on attended the *Gymnasium* in a near-by city with them, my real friends were the boys of the local school. This led to a great deal of tension with the children of my own social level, and we remained strangers throughout our schooldays. Belonging to the privileged class, therefore, aroused in me very early the consciousness of social guilt that later became very important in my life and work. There seem to be only two possible outcomes when a sensitive upper-class child has an early and intimate encounter with children of the lower classes: one is the development of a consciousness of social guilt; the other – a response to the lower-class children's aggressive resentment – is class hatred. I have met both types frequently.

But my situation on the boundary with regard to social issues extends further. My father's church district included many people from the old landed nobility. Because these people were church patrons, my parents had professional and social contact with them. I was proud that I could visit their manor houses and play with their children. A descendant of one of these families, a man of rare intellectual ability, has been my life-long friend. As a result of this borderline situation, my later opposition to the bourgeoisie (my own social class) did not itself become bourgeois, as so often happened in socialism. Instead I attempted to incorporate into socialism those elements of the feudal tradition that have an inward affinity with the socialist principle. The particular outline of religious socialism that I attempted to develop first in 'Grundlinien des religiösen Sozialismus' (Principles of Religious Socialism)[6] and later in my book *Die sozialistische Entscheidung* (Socialistic Decision)[7] is rooted in this attitude. Hence it was with difficulty, and only because of the political situation of the time, that I was able to bring myself to join a party that had become as bourgeois as the Social Democrats in Germany. The essay 'Das Problem der Macht: Versuch einer philosophischen Grundlegung',[8] which concerns these experiences of my youth, has been misunderstood even by some of my friends because their bourgeois pacifism lacks this particular boundary situation.

I should say something here about the civil service which, in Germany more than anywhere else, forms a separate group with its own peculiar traditions. In the narrowest sense I belong to it, both as the son of a minister who was also a school functionary and as a former professor at a Prussian university. What Prussian bureaucracy means is most clearly expressed in Kant's *Critique of Practical Reason*. It holds the primacy of the idea of duty above everything else, the valuation of law and order as the highest norm, the tendency to centralize the power of the state, a subjection to military and civil authorities, and a conscious subordination of the individual to the 'organic whole'. It is quite justifiable to ascribe to this very ideology the preference of much German philosophy for highly developed systems in philosophical theory and political practice. This Prussian ideology is reflected in my own life and work in several places: in my *Entwurf eines Systems der Wissenschaften* (Outline of a System of the Sciences),[9] in my readiness to subordinate myself to military and civil authorities during peace and war, and finally in my support of a political party whose programme I largely opposed. To be sure, I am conscious of the limitations of this attitude. These include the tremendous burden upon my conscience, which accompanies every personal decision and every violation of tradition, an indecisiveness in the face of the new and unexpected, and a desire for an all-embracing order that would reduce the risk of personal choice.

The deep-seated aversion I felt against a distinctly bourgeois life was expressed in my preference for the small social group called 'Bohemia'. Artists, actors, journalists and writers were very influential within this group, which combined intellectual ferment with a genuinely non-bourgeois outlook. As a theologian and academician, I was once more on the boundary. The hallmarks of this group were an obvious lack of certain bourgeois conventions in thought and behaviour, an intellectual radicalism, and a remarkable capacity for ironical self-criticism. The bohemians met at cafés, ateliers and resorts not frequented by the middle class. They were inclined toward radical political criticism and felt closer to the communist workers than to members of their own class. They followed international artistic and literary movements; they were sceptical, religiously radical, and romantic; they were anti-militaristic and influenced by Nietzsche, expressionism, and psychoanalysis.

Neither the members of the feudal order nor the well-to-do bourgeois opposed the 'bohemian' groups; and conversely both were always able to gain admittance in the bohemian group. In exchange for membership, they offered the bohemians social and economic privileges. Opposition came from the petit bourgeoisie, the lower middle class, with its prejudices and pretensions, its unconcern for intellectual and especially artistic problems, its need for security, and its distrust of the intelligentsia.

The fact that I was never seriously involved in the life of the petit bourgeoisie but rather, like many from its ranks, repudiated it with an apparent, if only half-conscious, arrogance was to shape both my intellectual and my personal destiny. Intellectually, the struggle to overcome the narrowness of the petit bourgeoisie constantly opened up new vistas which in turn made it difficult for me to find any intellectual or social resting place. I came under personal attack from the reactionary revolution of the middle class, which hit the intelligentsia hard and finally destroyed it. The spiteful persecution of the German intelligentsia by representatives of a romantic middle-class ideology (Nazism) was in response to the intelligentsia's partially justified and partially unjustified repudiation of the middle class.

Between Reality and Imagination

The difficulties I experienced in coming to terms with reality led me into a life of fantasy at an early age. Between fourteen and seventeen, I withdrew as often as possible into imaginary worlds which seemed to be truer than the world outside. In time, that romantic imagination was transformed into philosophical imagination. For good and for ill, the latter has stayed with me ever since. It has been good in that it has given me the ability to combine categories, to perceive abstractions in concrete terms (I would almost say 'in colour') and to experiment with a wide range of conceptual possibilities. It has been of doubtful value insofar as such imaginative ability runs a risk of mistaking the creations of the imagination for realities, that is, of neglecting experience and rational critique, of thinking in monologues rather than dialogues, and of isolating itself from co-operative scientific effort. Whether good or bad, this imaginative tendency (plus certain other circumstances), prevented me from becoming a scholar in the accepted sense of the word. Amongst intellectuals of the twenties there was a kind of aversion against the scholar in the restricted sense of 'expert'.

Imagination manifests itself, among other ways, in a delight in play. This delight has accompanied me all my life, in games, in sports (which I never took as more than play), in entertainment, in the playful emotion that accompanies productive moments and makes them expressions of the sublimest form of human freedom. The romantic theory of play, Nietzsche's preference for play as opposed to 'the spirit of gravity', Kierkegaar's 'aesthetic sphere', and the imaginative element in mythology were always both attractive and dangerous to me. Perhaps it was an awareness of this danger that drove me more and more to the uncompromising seriousness of prophetic religion. My comments in *Die sozialistische Entscheidung* (Socialistic Decision)[10] about the mythological consciousness were a protest not only against the ultimate lack of seriousness in nationalistic paganism, but also against the mythical-romantic element not conquered in myself.

Art is the highest form of play and the genuinely creative realm of the imagination. Though I have not produced anything in the field of the creative arts, my love for the arts has been of great importance to my theological and philosophical work. At home my father maintained the musical traditions associated with the evangelical ministry. He himself wrote music. Like most German Protestants, however, he cared little for architecture and the fine arts. Since I am not artistically inclined and only later gained an appreciation of the visual arts, my longing for art was directed toward literature. This was in line with the humanist tradition in education at the *Gymnasium*. Schlegel's classical German translation of Shakespeare became particularly important for me. I identified myself (almost dangerously) with figures like Hamlet. My instinctive sympathy to-day for what is called existentialism goes back in part to an existential understanding of this great work of literature. Neither Goethe nor Dostoevsky had a similar effect on me. I came to know Dostoevsky too late in my life. Goethe's work seemed to express too little of the boundary situation in the Kierkegaardian sense; it did not then seem to be existential enough, although I have revised this judgment in my maturity. Even after my infatuation with Hamlet, which lasted for some time, I preserved the capacity for complete identification with other creatures of poetic fancy. The specific mood, the colour as it were, of certain weeks or months of my life, would be determined by one literary work or the other. Later this was especially true of novels which I read infrequently but with great intensity.

Literature, however, contains too much philosophy to be able to satisfy fully the desire for pure artistic contemplation. The discovery of painting was a crucial experience for me. It happened during World War I, as a reaction to the horror, ugliness and destructiveness of war. My delight even in the poor reproductions obtainable at the military bookstores developed into a systematic study of the history of art. And out of this study came the experience of art; I recall most vividly my first encounter – almost a revelation – with a Botticelli painting in Berlin during my last furlough of the war. Out of the philosophical and theological reflection that followed these experiences, I developed some fundamental categories of philosophy of religion and culture, viz., form and substance. It was the expressionist style emerging in Germany during the first decade of this century and winning public recognition following the war and the bitter struggle with an uncomprehending lower middle-class taste that opened my eyes to how the substance of a work of art could destroy form and to the creative ecstasy implied in this process. The concept of the 'breakthrough', which dominates my theory of revelation, is an example of the use of this insight.

Later, when expressionism gave way to a new realism, I developed my concept of 'belief-ful realism' from a study of the new style. The idea of 'belief-ful realism' is the central concept of my book, *The Religious Situation*,[11] which for that reason is dedicated to an artist friend. My impressions of various representations of individuals and groups in Western art gave me the inspiration and material for a lecture, 'Masse und Persönlichkeit' (Mass and Personality).[12] My growing preference for the old Church and her solutions to such theological problems as 'God and the World', 'Church and State', was nourished by the deep impression made on me by early Christian art in Italy. The mosaics in the ancient Roman basilicas accomplished what no amount of studying church history could have done. My interest in painting is directly reflected in the article, 'Stil und Stoff in der bildenden Kunst' (Style and Material in Plastic Art), in my address at the opening of an exhibition of religious art in Berlin in 1930, in the pertinent sections of *Das System der Wissenschaften nach Gegenständen und Methoden* (System of the Sciences),[13] in my 'Religionsphilosophie' (Philosophy of Religion),[14] and in *The Religious Situation*.

This vital experience of modern painting also opened the way for an appreciation of modern German literature, as represented by Hofmannsthal, George, Rilke, and Werfel. I was most deeply impressed by the later poetry of Rilke. Its profound psychoanalytical realism, mystical richness, and a poetic form charged with metaphysical content made this poetry a vehicle for insights that I could elaborate only abstractly through the concepts of my philosophy of religion. For myself and my wife, who introduced me to poetry, these poems became a book of devotions that I read again and again.

I never doubted – nor did anyone else – that I was destined to a life devoted to intellectual rather than practical matters. I was about eight when I first wrestled with the idea of the Infinite. In school and in my pre-confirmation instruction, I was fascinated with Christian dogmatics; I devoured popular books on philosophy. My education in the humanistic tradition and my enthusiasm for the language and literature of the Greeks strengthened this disposition toward the theoretical. I fully agreed with Aristotle's contention, as expressed in the *Nichomachean Ethics*, that pure contemplation alone offers pure happiness. My inward struggles with the truth of traditional religion also helped keep me within the domain of the speculative. In the religious life, however, contemplation implies something other than philosophical intimations of Being. In religious truth, one's very existence is at stake. The question is: to be or not to be. Religious truth is existential truth; to this extent it cannot be separated from practice. Religious truth is *acted*, as the Gospel of John says.

It soon became clear, though, that a one-sided devotion to contemplation was based on the same escape from reality as my flight into literary fantasy. As soon as I recognized this danger and was confronted with practical tasks, I threw myself into them with complete ardour – partly to the advantage and partly to the disadvantage of my intellectual pursuits. The first example of this plunge into day-by-day affairs was my active participation in a student organization called *Wingolf*. The tensions between its Christian principles and modern liberal ideas and practices, as well as those personal tensions that readily flare up in groups of young students, gave rise to many questions of practical policy, especially during the time when I was a leader of the organization. The question of the principles of a Christian community was so thoroughly argued out in the group that all who were active in the struggle profited a great deal by it. During that time I came to understand the value of objective statements like denominational creeds. If a community gives general recognition to a confessional foundation whose meaning transcends subjective belief or doubt, it will hold together even while allowing room for tendencies toward doubt, criticism, and uncertainty.

My university studies were followed by two years of parish work and four years as a field chaplain on the Western front. After the war I spent a brief period in church administrative work. My theoretical studies were severely restricted, though not entirely interrupted, during these years of practical activity. This time of immersion in practical problems, however, did not shake my basic devotion to the theoretical life.

The tension between theory and practice was heightened at the outbreak of the revolution. For the first time, I became very much alive to the political situation. Like most German intellectuals before 1914, I had been rather indifferent to politics. Our consciousness of social guilt had not expressed itself politically. It was during the collapse of imperial Germany and the revolution of the last year of World War I that I began to understand such issues as the political background of the war, the interrelation of capitalism and imperialism, the crisis of bourgeois society, and the schisms between classes. The tremendous pressure of the war, which had threatened to obscure the idea of God or to give it demonic colouration, found an outlet in the discovery of the human responsibility for the war and the hope for a refashioning of human society. When the call to a religious socialist movement was sounded, I could not and would not refuse to heed it. At first we worked only on theoretical problems of 'religion and socialism'. The working circle to which I belonged was a group of professors, Mennicke, Heimann, Löw and others, all explicitly concerned with theory. But the goal of our work was political, and we were thus inevitably faced with problems of practical politics which often conflicted with theoretical positions. This conflict was reflected in our discussion of the influence of religious socialism on the churches, the political parties and, insofar as we were professors, the universities.

In the Evangelical Church a league of religious socialists had been formed with the aim of closing the gap between the Church and the Social Democratic Party through changes in church policy and also through theoretical discussion. Believing that its theoretical foundations were inadequate, I kept aloof from the group, perhaps unjustifiably, and thus missed an opportunity for being active in ecclesiastical politics. This time the tension between theory and practice was resolved wholly in favour of theory, though perhaps not for its benefit.

So too it was with my relations to the Social Democratic Party. I became a member in order to influence it by contributing to the elaboration of its theoretical base. For this purpose I joined with my friends of the religious-socialist group to found the magazine *Neue Blätter für den Sozialismus*.[15] Through it we hoped to revitalize the rigid theology of German socialism and to remould it from a religious and philosophical standpoint. I myself did not engage in practical politics, but since many of my co-workers were very active politically, our magazine was drawn into the problems of the existing political situation. Of course, I did not refuse specific tasks. But I did not look for them, perhaps once more to the detriment of theoretical work that was intended to serve a political end and to supply the conceptual form of a political movement. On the other hand, even those comparatively rare contacts with practical politics interrupted the concentration that my professional work so urgently required.

The tension between theory and practice came to a head in the post-war discussion about the reorganization of the German universities. In the course of the nineteenth century, the old humanistic ideal of classicism was undermined by the specialization of the sciences and by an increased demand, quantitative and qualitative, for professional training. With the heavy influx of students we could no longer even pretend to uphold the classical ideal of the 'well rounded' man. Weak compromises were invented to cover up the discrepancy between the ideal and reality. In an essay published in the *Frankfurter Zeitung*, 22 November 1931, I proposed a plan for a twofold educational programme that prompted a storm of approval and protest. On the one hand, I advocated the establishment of professional schools and, on the other, a liberal arts faculty that would be freed from the tasks of professional training to represent the old idea of the university. Both were to be interrelated yet different in aim and method. The liberal arts faculty was to be permeated by the spirit of that philosophy whose task is the illumination of the question of human existence by means of the Logos. There was to be radical questioning without regard for political or religious allegiances. At the same time, the educational philosophy of the faculty was to be fully informed by the spiritual and social problems of contemporary life. Any great creative philosophy must meet these demands. It was an indication of weakness when, in the nineteenth century, philosophy became, with few exceptions, more and more a tool of the schools and of the 'professors of philosophy'. It is, however, no less destructive of philosophy whenever our own century endeavours to suppress radical questions by political means and to dictate a political world view. The 'political university' of today sacrifices theory to practice. This, like its opposite, is fatal to both types of university. At present the boundary between theory and practice has become a battlefield on which the fate of the university of the future, and with it the fate of humanist culture in a civilized world, will be decided.

Between Heteronomy and Autonomy

I was able to reach intellectual and moral autonomy only after a severe struggle. My father's authority, which was both personal and intellectual and which, because of his position in the Church, I identified with the religious authority of revelation, made every attempt at autonomous thinking an act of religious daring and connected criticism of authority with a sense of guilt. The age-old experience of mankind, that new knowledge can be won only by breaking a taboo and that all autonomous thinking is accompanied by a consciousness of guilt, is a fundamental experience of my own life. As a result, every theological, ethical, and political criticism encountered inner obstacles that were overcome only after lengthy struggles. This heightened for me the significance, seriousness, and weight of such insights. When I would belatedly arrive at a conclusion that had long since become commonplace to the average intelligence, it still seemed to me to be shocking and full of revolutionary implications. Free-wheeling intelligence was suspect to me. I had scant confidence in the creative power of purely autonomous thought. In this spirit I delivered a series of university lectures dealing specifically with the catastrophic failures, past and present, of autonomous thought, e.g., the development of Greek philosophy from the emergence of rational autonomy and its decline into scepticism and probabilism to the return to the 'new archaism' of late antiquity. It constituted for me conclusive historical evidence of the inability of autonomous reason to create by itself a world with real content. In lectures on medieval philosophy, on the intellectual history of Protestantism, and in my essay *The Religious Situation*, I applied this idea to the history of Western thought and derived from it the need for a theonomy, that is, an autonomy informed by a religious substance.

The critique of pure autonomy was not meant to ease the way to a new heteronomy. Submission to divine or secular authorities, i.e., heteronomy, was precisely what I had rejected. I neither can nor want to return to it. If the existing trend of events in Europe is moving toward a return to both old and new heteronomies, I can only protest passionately, even while I understand the motives for the trend. An autonomy won in hard struggle is not surrendered so readily as one that always has been accepted as a matter of fact. Once a man has broken with the taboos of the most sacred authorities, he cannot subject himself to another heteronomy, whether religious or political. That such submission has become so easy for so many in our day is a consequence of the emptiness and scepticism surrounding most traditional authority. Freedom that has not been fought for and for which no sacrifices have been made is easily cast aside. It is only thus that we can understand the desire for a new bondage among European youth (leaving sociological factors aside).

I have long been opposed to the most expressly heteronomous religious system, Roman Catholicism. This protest was both Protestant and autonomous. It was never directed, in spite of theological differences, against the dogmatic values or liturgical forms in the Roman Catholic system but rather against Catholicism's heteronomous character with its assertion of a dogmatic authority that is valid even when submission to it is only superficial. Only once did I with any seriousness entertain the idea of becoming a Catholic. In 1933, before the awakening of German Protestantism to the meaning of Nazism, I seemed to have only two alternatives: either the Roman Church or a nationalist paganism in Protestant dress. In deciding between these two heteronomies, I would have had to choose Catholicism. I did not have to make that choice because German Protest-antism remembered its Christian foundation.

The struggle between autonomy and heteronomy re-appears at another level in Protestantism. It was pre-cisely through my protest against Protestant orthodoxy, even in its moderate nineteenth-century form, that I found my way to autonomy. For this reason, my fun-damental theological problem arose in applying the re-lation of the Absolute, which is implied in the idea of God, to the relativity of human religion. Religious dog-matism, including that of Protestant orthodoxy and the most recent phase of what is called dialectical theology, comes into being when a historical religion is cloaked with the unconditional validity of the divine, as when a book, person, community, institution, or doctrine claims absolute authority and demands the submission of every other reality; for no other claim can exist be-side the unconditioned claim of the divine. But that this claim can be grounded in a finite, historical reality is the root of all heteronomy and all demonism. The demonic is something finite and limited which has been invested with the stature of the infinite. Its demonic character becomes clear as, sooner or later, another finite reality also claiming infinitude opposes it so that human con-sciousness is severed between the two.

Karl Barth has said that my negative attitude toward heteronomy and my use of the word demonic to de-scribe it represents a struggle against the Grand Inquis-itor (as portrayed in Dostoevsky's *The Brothers Kar-amazov*) that is no longer necessary today. I think that the development of the German Confessional Church in the last years proves how necessary the struggle re-mains. The Grand Inquisitor is now entering the Con-fessional Church wearing the strong but tight-fitting armour of Barthian supranaturalism. The extremely narrow position of the Barthians may save German Pro-testantism, but it also creates a new heteronomy, an anti-autonomous and anti-humanistic attitude that I must regard as a denial of the Protestant principle. For Protestantism will continue to be something more than a weakened version of Catholicism only so long as the protest against every one of its own realizations remains alive within it. This Protestant protest is not rational criticism but prophetic judgment. It is not autonomy but theonomy, even when it appears, as often happens, in rationalistic and humanistic forms. In the theonomous, prophetic word, the contradiction between autonomy and heteronomy is overcome.

But if protest and prophetic criticism are necessary elements of Protestantism, the question arises as to how Protestantism can be embodied in the world. Worship, preaching, and instruction presuppose expressions of the substance that can be handed on. The institutional church and even the prophetic word itself require a sacramental basis, an incarnate life to draw upon. Life cannot stand only on its own boundaries; it must also live at its centre, out of its own abundance. The Protestant principle of criticism and protest is a necessary corrective, but is not in itself constructive. In co-operation with others, I contributed an essay to the book, *Protestantismus als Kritik und Gestaltung* (Protestantism as Criticism and Construction),[16] dealing with the question of the realization of Protestantism. The title of my first large theological work, *Religiöse Verwirklichung* (Religious Realization),[17] was prompted by this problem. Protestantism must live within the tension between the sacramental and the prophetic, between the constitutive and the corrective. If these elements were to separate, the former would become heteronomous and the latter empty. Their unity, as symbol and as reality, seems to me to be given in the New Testament picture of the crucified Christ. There the highest human religious possibility is manifested and sacrificed at the same time.

The events of the last few years in German Protestantism and the emergence of neo-paganisms on Christian soil have given new importance to the problem of religious autonomy and heteronomy. The question of the final criterion for human thought and action has become acute today as never before since the struggle between Roman paganism and early Christianity. The Nazi attack on the Cross as the criterion of every human creation has renewed our understanding of the meaning of the Cross. The question of heteronomy and autonomy has become the question of the final criterion of human existence. In this struggle, the destiny of German Christendom, of the German nation, and of Christian nations in general is being decided.

Every political system requires authority, not only in terms of possessing instruments of force but also in terms of the silent or express consent of the people. Such consent is possible only if the group in power stands for an idea that is powerful and significant for all. Thus, in the political sphere there is a relationship of authority and autonomy which in my essay, 'Der Staat als Erwartung und Aufgabe' (The State as Promise and Task)[18] I have characterized as follows: 'Every political structure presupposes power and, consequently, a group in power. Since a power group is also a cluster of interests opposed to other units of interest, it is always in need of a corrective. Democracy is justifiable and necessary insofar as it is a system that incorporates correctives against the misuse of political authority. It becomes untenable as soon as it hinders the emergence of a power group. This occurred in the Weimar Republic, whose particular democratic form made it impossible from the start for any group to gain power. On the other hand, the corrective against the abuse of authority by the power group is lacking in dictatorial systems. The result is the enslavement of the entire nation and the corruption of the ruling class.' Since making my first political decision a few years before World War I, I have stood with the political left, even to opposing very strong conservative traditions. This was a protest against political heteronomy, just as my earlier protest against religious heteronomy led me to side with liberal theology. In spite of all my subsequent criticism of economic liberalism, it was and is impossible for me to join the all-too-common depreciation of 'liberal thinking'. I would rather be accused of being 'liberalistic' than of ignoring the great, and truly human, liberal principle of autonomy.

Nevertheless, the question of political power remained urgent during a period in which one of our most difficult political problems was reintegrating the disintegrated masses of modern capitalism. I dealt with this problem in connection with recent events in German history in an essay, 'The Totalitarian State and the Claims of the Church'.[19] In it I stressed that an authoritarian engulfment of the masses is inevitable when they have been deprived of all meaningful existence. There are also important reflections on this problem in my book, *Masse und Geist* (Mass and Spirit),[20] which appeared soon after the war. In the chapter, 'Mass and the Personality', I argued that only specialized esoteric groups should strive for an autonomous position. The retreat to an esoteric autonomy seemed to me to be demanded by the forces of history operating in the present (which are roughly comparable to those of late antiquity). Just how this retreat is to be accomplished without too great a sacrifice of truth and justice is a strategic problem for future generations. It will be both a political and religious problem. I am determined to stand on the boundary between autonomy and heteronomy, in principle and in fact. I intend to remain on this boundary even if the coming historical era should fall under the sway of heteronomy.

Between Theology and Philosophy

The boundary situation from which I am trying to explain my life and thought is most clearly seen at this point. Ever since the last years of my secondary education, I wanted to be a philosopher. I used every free hour to read those philosophical books that came by chance into my hands. I found Schwegler's *Geschichte der Philosophie* (History of Philosophy) in the dusty corner of a country preacher's bookshelf, and Fichte's *Wissenschaftslehre* (Theory of Science) on top of a wagon load of books on a Berlin street. In a state of boyish excitement, I bought Kant's *Critique of Pure Reason* from a bookstore for the immense price of fifty cents. These works, especially that of Fichte, introduced me to the most difficult aspects of German philosophy. Discussions with my father, who was an examiner in philosophy on the committee which examined students for the ministry, enabled me from the beginning of my university career to carry on discussions with older students and young instructors about idealism and realism, freedom and determinism, God and the world. Fritz Medicus, who was philosophy professor at Halle and later at Zürich, was my teacher in philosophy. His work on Fichte initiated the rediscovery of Fichte's philosophy at the turn of the century that ultimately led to a general renaissance of German idealism. Partly through the accident of a bargain purchase, and partly through an inner affinity for his work, I came under the influence of Schelling. I read through his collected works several times, and eventually made his work the subject of my dissertations for the degrees of doctor of philosophy and licentiate of theology. The latter dissertation was published in book form as *Mystik und Schuldbewusstsein in Schelling's philosophischer Entwicklung* (Schelling's Philosophical Development).

During this time I also studied Protestant theology, and at the conclusion of my studies I became an assistant pastor in various parishes of the 'Old Prussian United Church'. My most important theological teachers were Martin Kähler and Wilhelm Lütgert, both of Halle. Kähler was a man whose intellectual ability and moral and religious power were overwhelming. As a teacher and writer he was difficult to understand. In many respects he was the most profound and most modern representative of the nineteenth-century theology of mediation. He was an opponent of Albrecht Ritschl, a proponent of the theological doctrine of justification, and a critic of the idealism and humanism from which he was himself intellectually descended.

I am indebted to him primarily for the insight that he gave me into the all-embracing character of the Pauline-Lutheran idea of justification. On the one hand, the doctrine of justification denies every human claim before God and every identification of God and man. On the other hand, it declares that the estrangement of human existence, its guilt and despair, are overcome through the paradoxical judgment that before God the sinner is just. My Christology and dogmatics were informed by the interpretation of Christ's crucifixion as the event in history through which the divine judgment against the world becomes concrete and manifest. Thus it was easy for me to make a connection between my theology and that of Karl Barth, and to accept the analysis of human existence given by Kierkegaard and Heidegger. However, it was difficult and even impossible for me to reconcile my thinking with liberal dogmatics, which replaces the crucified Christ with the historical Jesus and dissolves the paradox of justification into moral categories.

In spite of my negative attitude toward liberal dogmatics, I am deeply appreciative of the liberal movement's historical accomplishments. I soon parted company with the Halle theologians over this issue, and I found myself less and less in accord with the Barthian neo-supranaturalism that wishes to resurrect the dogmatic doctrines of the Reformation by bypassing the scientific work of the last two hundred years. The historical interpretation of the Old Testament developed by Wellhausen and Gunkel, the so-called *religionsgeschichtliche* method, caught my interest and helped me to understand the fundamental significance of the Old Testament for Christianity and for mankind. An enthusiasm for the Old Testament has stayed with me, and through its bearing on my political positions it has decisively shaped my life and thought.

I owe my historical insights into the New Testament principally to Schweitzer's *The Quest of the Historical Jesus* and Bultmann's *The Synoptic Tradition*. When I read the work of Ernst Troeltsch I finally shed the last remnants of my interest in the theology of mediation and its apologetics and turned to church history and the problem of historical criticism. The documentary proof of this change of interest is a set of propositions which I presented to a group of theological friends in 1911. I asked how Christian doctrine might be understood if the non-existence of the historical Jesus were to become historically probable, and then attempted to answer my own question. Even now I insist on raising this question radically rather than falling back on the kind of compromises that I encountered then and that Emil Brunner is now offering. The foundation of Christian belief is the biblical picture of Christ, not the historical Jesus. The criterion of human thought and action is the picture of Christ as it is rooted in ecclesiastical belief and human experience, not the shifting and artificial construct of historical research. Because I took this position I was called a radical theologian in Germany, whereas Americans call me a Barthian. But agreement with the Barthian paradox, the mystery of justification, does not mean agreement with Barthian supranaturalism; and agreement with the historical and critical achievement of liberal theology does not mean agreement with liberal dogmatics.

I managed to reconcile the doctrine of justification with radical historical criticism by developing an interpretation of the idea of justification that has been of the greatest importance to me, both personally and professionally. I applied the doctrine of justification to the sphere of human thought. Not only human acts but human thinking as well stand under the divine 'No'. No one, not even a believer or a Church, can boast of possessing truth, just as no one can boast of possessing love. Orthodoxy is intellectual pharisaism. The justification of the doubter corresponds to the justification of the sinner. Revelation is just as paradoxical as the forgiveness of sins. Neither can become an object of possession. I developed these ideas in the essays, 'Rechtfertigung und Zweifel' (Justification and Doubt)[21] and 'Die Idee der Offenbarung' (The Idea of Revelation).[22]

It was the work of Schelling, particularly his late thought, which helped me relate these basic theological ideas to my philosophical development. Schelling's philosophical interpretation of Christian doctrine opened the way, I thought, to a unification of theology and philosophy. His development of a Christian philosophy of existence, as opposed to Hegel's humanistic philosophy of essence, and his interpretation of history as *Heilsgeschichte*, moved in the same direction. I confess that even today I find more 'theonomous philosophy' in Schelling than in any of the other German idealists. But not even he was able to achieve a unity of theology and philosophy. World War I was disastrous for idealistic thought in general. Schelling's philosophy was also affected by this catastrophe. The chasm that he had seen but soon covered up again opened itself anew. The experience of those four years of war revealed to me and to my entire generation an abyss in human existence that could not be ignored. If a reunion of theology and philosophy is ever to be possible it will be achieved only in a synthesis that does justice to this experience of the abyss in our lives. My philosophy of religion has attempted to meet this need. It consciously remains on the boundary between theology and philosophy, taking care not to lose the one in the other. It attempts to express the experience of the abyss in philosophical concepts and the idea of justification as the limitation of philosophy. A lecture which I delivered before the Kant Society of Berlin, 'Die Uberwindung des Religionsbegriffs in der Religionsphilosophie' (The Elimination of the Concept Religion in the Philosophy of Religion),[23] reflects this paradoxical attempt even in its title.

A philosophy of religion, however, is shaped by philosophical concepts as well as by religious reality. My own philosophical position developed in critical dialogue with neo-Kantianism, the philosophy of value, and phenomenology. I accepted their common rejection of positivism, especially in the psychologistic guise that it assumed in philosophy of religion. Husserl's *Logische Untersuchungen* (Studies in Logic) in which psychologism is most forcefully rejected, confirmed what I had learned from Kant and Fichte. But I could not attach myself to any of the three positions. Because of its pan-logistical tendency, neo-Kantianism could not comprehend the experience of the abyss and the paradox. I could not accept the philosophy of value because it too is neo-Kantian and because its attempt to understand religion as a realm of value contradicts the transcendence of values which is assumed in the experience of the abyss. Phenomenology lacks the element of dynamism and also furthers Catholic-conservative tendencies, as can be seen from the biographies of the bulk of its proponents.

Nietzsche, whom I did not read until I was thirty, made a tremendous impression on me. Nietzschean vitalism expresses the experience of the abyss more clearly than neo-Kantianism, value-philosophy, or phenomenology. The ecstatic affirmation of existence so prevalent after the war as a reaction to the wartime years of death and hunger made Nietzsche's affirmation of life very attractive. Because it is, at least partly, historically rooted in Schelling's thought, I could readily accept it. I might well have developed my philosophy along these lines, incorporating pagan elements instead of Jewish and Catholic motifs; but the experience of the

German revolution of 1918 decisively redirected my concerns toward a sociologically based and politically ori-
ented philosophy of history. My study of Troeltsch had
paved the way for this change of direction. I clearly remember the statement he made during his first Berlin
lecture on the philosophy of history, claiming that his
was the first philosophical treatment of this subject at
the University of Berlin since Hegel's death. Although
we were to a great extent agreed about the problems involved, I repudiated his idealistic point of departure.
Troeltsch's idealism made it impossible for him to overcome what he called historicism, against which he
fought. Historicism could be overcome only by a generation that had been forced to make fundamental historical decisions. In light of the necessity of facing history squarely – a demand that is both grounded in and
limited by the Christian paradox – I sought to develop a
philosophy of history that could become also a philosophy of religious socialism.

Anyone standing on the boundary between theology
and philosophy must necessarily develop a clear conception of the logical relation between them. I attempted to do this in my book *Das System der Wissenschaften* (System of the Sciences).[24] My ultimate concern
there was with the questions: How can theology be a
science in the sense of *Wissenschaft*? How are its several
disciplines related to the other sciences? What is distinctive about its method?

I answered by classifying all of the methodological
disciplines as sciences of thinking, being, and culture; by
maintaining that the foundation of the whole system of
sciences is the philosophy of meaning (*Sinnphilosophie*);
by defining metaphysics as the attempt to express the
Unconditioned in terms of rational symbols, and by defining theology as theonomous metaphysics. In this way
I attempted to win a place for theology within the
totality of human knowledge. The success of this analysis presupposes that the theonomous character of know-

ledge itself must be acknowledged; that is to say, we must understand that thought itself is rooted in the Absolute as the ground and abyss of meaning. Theology takes as its explicit object that which is the implicit presupposition of all knowledge. Thus theology and philosophy, religion and knowledge, embrace one another. In light of the boundary position, this appears as their real relationship.

When existential philosophy was introduced into Germany, I came to a new understanding of the relationship between theology and philosophy. Heidegger's lectures at Marburg, the publication of his *Sein und Zeit* (Being and Time), and also his interpretation of Kant were significant in this connection. Both to the followers and to the opponents of existential philosophy, Heidegger's work is more important than anything since Husserl's *Logische Untersuchungen* (Studies in Logic). Three factors prepared the ground for my acceptance of existential philosophy. The first was my close knowledge of Schelling's final period, in which he outlined his philosophy of existence in response to Hegel's philosophy of essence. The second was my knowledge, however limited, of Kierkegaard, the real founder of existential philosophy. The final factor was my enthusiasm for Nietzsche's 'philosophy of life'. These three elements are also present in Heidegger. Their fusion into a kind of mysticism tinged with Augustinianism accounts for the fascination of Heidegger's philosophy. Much of its terminology is found in the sermon literature of German Pietism. His interpretation of human existence implies and develops, however unintentionally, a doctrine of man that is one of human freedom and finitude. It is so closely related to the Christian interpretation of human existence that one is forced to describe it as 'theonomous philosophy' in spite of Heidegger's emphatic atheism. To be sure, it is not a philosophy which presupposes the theological answer to the question of human finitude and then explains it in philosophical terms. That would be a variant of idealism and the opposite of a philosophy of existence. Existential philosophy asks in a new and radical way the question whose answer is given to faith in theology.

These ideas, which I developed in my Yale University lectures, led to a sharper distinction between theology and philosophy than my earlier philosophy of religion had made. But I have never denied their mutual relatedness.

My professional career has also been 'on the boundary' between the two disciplines. I received the degrees of Doctor of Philosophy in Breslau and Licentiate in Theology and later Doctor of Theology (*honoris causa*) in Halle; I was Lecturer in Theology in Berlin, Professor of the Science of Religion in Dresden and Professor Honorarius of Theology in Leipzig, Professor Ordinarius of Philosophy in Frankfurt-on-Main, and Visiting Professor of Philosophical Theology at Union Theological Seminary in New York. A constant change of faculties and yet no change in subject matter! As a theologian I have tried to remain a philosopher, and vice versa. It would have been easier to abandon the boundary and to choose one or the other. Inwardly this course was impossible for me. Fortunately, outward opportunities matched my inward inclinations.

Between Church and Society

Although I have often criticized Church doctrine and practice, the Church has always been my home. This became very clear to me at the time when neo-pagan ideas were making their way into it and when I feared that I would lose my religious as well as my political home. The peril made me conscious of the fact that I belonged to the Church. This feeling grew out of the experiences of my early years – the Christian influence of a Protestant minister's home and the relatively uninterrupted religious customs of a small east-German city at the close of the nineteenth century. My love for church buildings and their mystic atmosphere, for liturgy and music and sermons, and for the great Christian festivals that moulded the life of the town for days and even weeks of the year left an indelible feeling in me for the ecclesiastical and sacramental. To these must be added the mysteries of Christian doctrine and their impact on the inner life of a child, the language of the Scriptures, and the exciting experiences of holiness, guilt, and forgiveness. All this played a crucial part in my decision to become a theologian and to remain one. My ordination, my pastoral activities, the interest in sermons and liturgy that persisted long after I moved into a university environment, were all outgrowths of the realization that I belonged within the Church.

But here, too, I was on the boundary. A sense of alienation accompanied my increasing criticism of the doctrines and institutions of the Church. My contact with the intelligentsia and the proletariat outside the Church was crucial in this connection. I did not encounter the intelligentsia outside the Church until rather late, after finishing my theological studies. In this encounter my attitude was apologetic in accordance with my borderline position. To be apologetic means to defend oneself before an opponent with a common criterion in view. When apologists of the ancient Church were vindicating themselves before an aggressive paganism, the commonly acknowledged criterion was the Logos — theoretical and practical reason. Because the apologists equated Christ with the Logos, and the divine commands with the rational law of nature, they could plead the cause of Christian doctrine and practice before their pagan opponents. In our day, apologetics does not mean erecting a new principle in opposition to existing intellectual and moral standpoints. Its task is to defend the Christian principle against emerging rival positions. The decisive question for both ancient and modern apolo-

getics is that of the common criterion, the court of judgment where the dispute can be settled.

In my search for this common criterion I discovered
that the modern trends of thought which are rooted in
the Enlightenment are substantially Christian, in spite
of their critical attitude toward ecclesiastical Christianity. They are not, as they are often called, pagan. Paganism, especially in nationalistic garb, first appeared after
World War I in connection with the complete disintegration of Christian humanism. There is no such thing
as apologetics in the face of this kind of paganism. The
only question is survival or extinction. This is the same
struggle that prophetic monotheism has always carried
on against demonic polytheism. Apologetics was possible
in antiquity only because polytheism was suffused with
humanism, and in humanism Christianity and antiquity
had a common criterion at their disposal. But while ancient apologetics was confronted with a humanism that
was pagan in substance, the distinctive factor in modern
apologetics is its confrontation with a humanism that is
Christian in substance. I have discussed this problem in
my essay, 'Lessing und die Idee der Erziehung des Mens-
chengeschlechts'.[25] With this viewpoint in mind, I con-
ducted lectures and discussions on apologetics in various
private residences in Berlin. The results of these gather-
ings were summarized in a report to the governing body
of the Evangelical Church; this action later led to the
establishment of a commission for apologetics in home
missions.

It was only after the war that the reality and nature
of this Christian humanism were brought fully home to
me. My contact with the Labour Movement, with the
so-called dechristianized masses, showed me clearly that
here too, within a humanistic framework, the Christian
substance was hidden, even though this humanism
looked like a materialistic philosophy that had long since
been discredited by art and science. An apologetic message to the masses was even more necessary and more

difficult than to the intelligentsia since the former's opposition to religion was heightened by class antagonism.
The Church's attempt to frame an apologetic message
without considering the class struggle was doomed to
complete failure at the outset. Defending Christianity in
this situation required active participation in the class
struggle. Only religious socialism could carry the apologetic message to the proletarian masses. Religious socialism, not 'inner mission', is the necessary form of Christian activity and apologetics among the working classes.
The apologetic element in religious socialism has often
been obscured by its political aspects so that the Church
failed to understand the indirect importance of religious
socialism for its work. It was understood much better
by the socialists themselves, who often expressed to me
their fear that religious socialism would bring the masses
under the Church's influence and thus alienate them
from the struggle to achieve a socialist government.

The Church also repudiated religious socialism because the movement either had to discard the traditional
symbols and concepts of ecclesiastical thought and practice, or to use them only after a certain amount of
groundwork had been laid. Had they been used indis-
criminately, the proletariat would have automatically
rejected them. The task of religious socialism was to
demonstrate that implicit in the Christian humanism of
the Labour Movement was the same substance as in the
entirely different sacramental forms of the Church. A
number of young theologians shared this understanding
of Christian humanism; they accepted non-ecclesiastical
positions, especially in the social services, for the express purpose of influencing religiously those whom no
church official could have reached in any way. Unfortunately, such opportunities were available only to a
few. And since the problems of 'Church and humanist
society' and 'Church and proletariat' were of little significance to the younger theologians of the Barthian
school, the chasm was never bridged by the Church. A

disintegrated humanist society thus fell victim, in large measure, to neo-pagan tendencies. The Church was compelled to fight these tendencies and thus to appear even more anti-humanist. The proletariat sank back into religious passivity. Though the intelligentsia came to admire the Church for its stand against nationalistic paganism, they were not drawn to it. The dogma defended by the Church did not and could not appeal to them. In order to reach this group, the Church must proclaim the gospel in a language that is comprehensible to a non-ecclesiastical humanism. It would have to convince both the intellectuals and the masses that the gospel is of absolute relevance for them. But this conviction cannot be imparted by the pointedly anti-humanist paradoxes that are used in confessional theology. The reality which gives rise to such paradoxes must first be illuminated. But theologians like Brunner and Gogarten do not attempt the illumination. They feed on humanism by negating it, for their descriptions of the positive content of the Christian proclamation consist of using and, at the same time, negating that which they are opposing.

Grave problems arise whenever the question of the language of the Christian gospel is taken seriously, as it was by the *Neuwerkkreis* and in the magazine of the same name which was edited by my old friend and comrade in this struggle, Hermann Schafft. It is certain that the original religious terminology of the Scriptures and the liturgies of the ancient Church cannot be supplanted. Mankind does have religious, archetypal words, as Martin Buber once remarked to me. But these archetypal words have been robbed of their original power by our objectifying way of thinking and by our scientific conception of the world. Rational criticism is powerless before the meaning of the archetypal word 'God'; but atheism is a correct response to the 'objectively' existing God of literalistic thought. A hopeless situation arises when a speaker uses a word in its original symbolic sense but the listener understands the word in a contemporary scientific sense. This is why I once proposed, for the sake of provocation, that the Church impose a thirty-year moratorium on all of its archetypal language. Were this to happen, as it did in a few instances, the Church would have to develop a new terminology. But attempts made thus far to translate the archaic language of liturgy and Scripture into contemporary idiom have been deplorable failures. They represent a depletion of meaning, not a new creation. Even using the terminology of the mystics, especially in sermons – as I have sometimes done – is dangerous. A different content is conveyed by these words, a content that hardly covers all the substance of the Christian gospel. The only solution is to use the archetypal religious words while at the same time making their original meaning clear by disavowing their distorted usage. One must stand between the archaic and contemporary terminologies to recapture, on the boundary, the original archetypal language. The present peril of society has driven many to this boundary where the language of religion can be heard again in its original meaning. It would be regrettable if a blind and arrogant orthodoxy should monopolize these words and thus frighten away those who are sensitive to religious reality, either forcing them into some modern paganism or conclusively driving them out of the Church.

The problem of Church and Society prompted me, in an essay entitled 'Kirche und humanistische Gesellschaft' (Church and Humanistic Society),[26] to draw a distinction between a 'manifest' and a 'latent' Church. This was not the old Protestant distinction between the visible and the invisible Church, but was concerned with a duality within the visible churches. The kind of distinction I suggested in that essay seems to be necessary in order to take into account the Christian humanism which exists outside the churches. It is not permissible to designate as 'unchurched' those who have become alienated from organized denominations and traditional creeds. In living among these groups for half a generation I learned how much of the latent Church there is within them. I encountered the experience of the finite character of human existence, the quest for the eternal and unconditioned, an absolute devotion to justice and love, a hope that lies beyond any Utopia, an appreciation of Christian values and a very sensitive recognition of the ideological misuse of Christianity in the interpenetration of Church and State. It has often seemed to me that the 'latent Church', as I call what I found among these groups, was a truer Church than the organized denominations, if only because its members did not presume to possess the truth. The last few years have shown, however, that only the organized Church is capable of maintaining the struggle against the pagan attacks on Christianity. The latent Church has neither the religious nor the organizational weapons necessary for this struggle. But it is also true that the use of these weapons within the manifest Church threatens to deepen the chasm between Church and Society. The concept of the latent Church is a concept of the boundary on which countless Protestants in our day are fated to stand.

Between Religion and Culture

If a person who had been deeply moved by the mosaics of Ravenna, the ceiling paintings of the Sistine Chapel, or the portraits of the older Rembrandt, were asked whether his experience had been religious or cultural, he would find the question difficult to answer. It might be correct to say that the experience is cultural in form and religious in substance. It is cultural because it is not attached to a specific ritual act; but it is religious because it touches on the question of the Absolute and the limits of human existence. This is as true of music, poetry, philosophy and science as it is of painting. And whatever is true in this intuition and understanding of the world remains true in the practical work of shaping laws and customs, in morality and education, in community and state. Culture is religious wherever human existence is subjected to ultimate questions and thus transcended; and wherever unconditioned meaning becomes visible in works that have only conditioned meaning in themselves. In experiencing the substantially religious character of culture I came to the boundary between religion and culture, and I have never left it. My philosophy of religion is chiefly concerned with the theoretical aspects of this boundary.

The relationship between religion and culture must be defined from both sides of the boundary. Religion cannot relinquish the absolute and, therefore, universal claim that is expressed in the idea of God. It cannot allow itself to become a special area within culture, or to take a position beside culture. Liberalism has tended to interpret religion in one or the other of these ways. In either case, religion becomes superfluous and must disappear because the structure of culture is complete and self-contained without religion. It is also true, however, that culture has a claim on religion that it cannot surrender without surrendering its autonomy and therefore itself. It must determine the forms through which every content, including the 'absolute' content, expresses itself. Culture cannot allow truth and justice to be sacrificed in the name of the religious absolute. As religion is the substance of culture, so culture is the form of religion. Only one difference must be noted: religion's intentionality is toward substance, which is the unconditioned source and abyss of meaning, and cultural forms serve as symbols of that substance. Culture's intentionality is toward the form, representing conditioned meaning. The substance, representing unconditioned meaning, can be glimpsed only indirectly through the medium of the autonomous form granted by culture. Culture attains its highest expression where human existence is comprehended in its finitude and its quest for the Infinite within the framework of a complete, autonomous form. Conversely, religion in its highest expression must include the autonomous form, the Logos, as the ancient Church called it, within itself.

These ideas constituted the basic principles of my philosophy of religion and culture and provided a framework for discussing the history of culture from a religious point of view. This explains why my book, *The Religious Situation*,[27] is concerned with the full range of intellectual and social movements in the immediate past, while religious questions, in the narrower sense, occupy less space. I have no doubt that this approach corresponds to the actual religious situation of the present. Political and social concerns have absorbed the energies of religion to such a degree that for great numbers of Europeans and Americans religious and political ideals coincide. The myths of the nation and of social justice are widely replacing Christian doctrine and have had effects that can be regarded only as religious even though they appear in cultural forms. The outline for a theological analysis of culture that I developed in my lecture, 'Über die Idee einer Theologie der Kultur' (On the Idea of a Theology of Culture),[28] takes into consideration the course of recent history.

I sketched the theological consequences of these reflections in an article concerning the relation of Protestantism to Secularism. In it I argue that if Protestantism has any ruling passion it is toward the 'profane'. Such an idea rejects in principle the Catholic separation of the sacred and the profane. In the presence of the Unconditioned (the Majesty of God, in the traditional language of Christianity), there is no preferred sphere. There are no persons, scriptures, communities, institutions, or actions that are holy in themselves, nor are there any that are profane in themselves. The profane can profess the quality of holiness, and the holy does not cease to be profane. The priest is a layman, and the layman can become a priest at any time. To me this is not only a theological principle, but also a position I have maintained professionally and personally. As a clergyman and theologian, I cannot be anything other than a layman and philosopher who has tried to say something about the limits of human existence. Nor have I any intention of concealing my theological endeavours. On the contrary, I have aired them where, for example, in my work as a professor of philosophy, they could easily have been concealed. But I did not want to develop a theological habitude that would set me apart from profane life and earn me the label 'religious'. It seems to me that the unconditioned character of religion becomes far more manifest if it breaks out from within the secular, disrupting and transforming it. I likewise believe that the dynamic dimension of the religious is betrayed when certain institutions and personalities are considered to be religious in themselves. To think of the clergyman as a man whose faith is a professional requirement borders on blasphemy.

My response to efforts at reforming the ritual of the German Church stems from this conviction. I joined the so-called *Berneuchen* movement which was led by Wilhelm Stählin and Karl Ritter. This group urged more rigorous reforms than all other reforming groups, and it did not limit itself to matters of ritual. These men sought first of all to formulate a clearly defined theological basis for reform. Thus I had an opportunity for fruitful theological collaboration. Ritual acts, forms and attitudes do not contradict a 'passion for the secular' if they are understood for what they are: symbolic forms in which the religious substance that supports our entire existence is represented in a unique way. The meaning of a ritual or sacramental act is not that the act is holy in itself, but that it is a symbol of the Unconditioned which alone is holy and which is, and is not, in all things at the same time.

In a lecture entitled 'Natur und Sakrament' (Nature and Sacrament),[29] delivered at a conference of the

Berneuchen group, I tried to explain the distinction between the non-sacramental, intellectualistic thinking of Protestantism and humanism and the original meaning of sacramental thinking, which was lost in the late medieval period. Within the framework of Protestantism, this is a difficult but necessary task. No Church is possible without a sacramental representation of the holy. It was this conviction that bound me to the Berneuchen group. However, I could not go along with them when they moved away from our mutual concern with the boundary between the secular and the sacred, to an exclusive preoccupation with (often archaic) liturgical forms. Here again, I am convinced that I must stay on the boundary.

Between Lutheranism and Socialism

It is comparatively easy to move into socialism from Calvinism, especially in the more secularized forms of later Calvinism. By way of Lutheranism, the road to socialism is very difficult. I am a Lutheran by birth, education, religious experience, and theological reflection. I have never stood on the boundary between Lutheranism and Calvinism, not even after I experienced the disastrous consequences of Lutheran social ethics and came to recognize the inestimable value of the Calvinistic idea of the kingdom of God in the solution of social problems. The substance of my religion is and remains Lutheran. It includes a consciousness of the 'corruption' of existence, a repudiation of every kind of social Utopia (including the metaphysics of progressivism), an awareness of the irrational and demonic nature of existence, an appreciation of the mystical element in religion, and a rejection of Puritanical legalism in private and corporal life. My philosophical thinking also expresses this unique content. Up to now, only Jacob Boehme, the philosophical spokesman for German mysticism, has attempted a specifically philosophical elaboration of Lutheranism. Through Boehme, Lutheran mysticism influenced Schelling and German idealism, and through Schelling it in turn influenced the philosophies of irrationalism and vitalism that emerged in the nineteenth and twentieth centuries. To the extent that much anti-socialist ideology has been based on irrationalism and vitalism, Lutheranism has worked indirectly through philosophy, as well as directly, to check socialism.

The course of German theology after the war shows very clearly that it is practically impossible for a people educated as Lutherans to move from religion to socialism. Two theological movements, both Lutheran, were opposed to religious socialism. The first was the religious nationalism which called itself 'young Lutheran' theology; its chief proponent was Emmanuel Hirsch, a one-time fellow student and friend who was to become my theological and political opponent. The second was Barthian theology, which is wrongly called 'dialectical theology'. Although Barth's theology has many Calvinistic elements, his strongly transcendent idea of the kingdom of God is definitely Lutheran. Both Barthian theology's indifference to social questions and Hirsch's sanctification of nationalism are so consistent with religious, social and political traditions in Germany that it was futile for religious socialism to oppose them. But the fact that religious socialism had no future on German soil did not imply that it was theologically wrong or politically unnecessary. The impossibility of uniting religion and socialism will be recognized in the near or distant future as a tragic element in German history.

Standing on the boundary between Lutheranism and religious socialism requires first of all a critical confrontation with the problem of Utopianism. The Lutheran doctrine of man, even in the naturalistic form it takes in vitalism, negates all Utopianism. Sin, cupidity, the will to power, the unconscious urge, or any other word used to describe the human situation is so bound up with the existence of man and nature (not, of course, with their essence or creaturely endowment) that establishing the kingdom of justice and peace within the realm of estranged reality is impossible. The kingdom of God can never be fulfilled in time and space. Every Utopianism is doomed to metaphysical disappointment. However changeable human nature may be, it is not amenable to fundamental moral correction. Improvements in education and environment may serve to raise the general ethical level of a people and to polish its original crudeness, but such improvements do not affect the freedom to do good and evil as long as man is man. Mankind does not become better; good and evil are merely raised to a higher plane.

With these considerations, which are drawn directly from the Lutheran understanding of human existence, I have touched on a problem which has become more and more important to socialist thinking and which is of particular concern to religious socialism – the problem of the doctrine of man. I am convinced that a false anthropology has robbed religious socialism of its persuasive force, particularly in Germany. A politician who does not admit the truth about man (in Luther's phrase, 'what there is in man') cannot be successful. On the other hand, I do not believe that the Lutheran conception, especially in its naturalistic versions, i.e., in vitalism and fascism, has the last word to say about man. The prophetic message may point the way here as elsewhere. The prophetic message is that human nature shall be transformed together with all nature. Even though this belief implies a miracle, it is more realistic than those views which leave nature unchanged while striving to transform man. They represent Utopianism, not the paradox of prophetic expectation.

Long before the anthropological implications of Utopianism were clearly understood, the utopian problem was the central issue in the religious socialist movement. We met shortly after the Russian Revolution of 1917 to discuss religion and socialism. In these first meetings, it became clear that our basic issue was the relationship of religion to some kind of social Utopianism. It was then that I first used the New Testament concept of the Kairos, the fullness of time, which as a boundary concept between religion and socialism has been the hallmark of German religious socialism. The concept of the fullness of time indicates that the struggle for a new social order cannot lead to the kind of fulfilment expressed by the idea of the kingdom of God, but that at a particular time particular tasks are demanded, as one particular aspect of the kingdom of God becomes a demand and an expectation for us. The kingdom of God will always remain transcendent, but it appears as a judgment on a given form of society and as a norm for a coming one. Thus, the decision to be a religious socialist may be a decision for the kingdom of God even though the socialist society is infinitely distant from the kingdom of God. I edited and contributed to two volumes, *Kairos*: Vol. 1. *Zur Geisteslage und Geisteswendung*[30] and Vol. 2. *Protestantismus als Kritik und Gestaltung*,[31] in which the idea of the Kairos is explored in its theological and philosophical presuppositions and implications.

A very important concept related to the 'Kairos' idea is that of the demonic. I have discussed it in the essay 'On the Demonic'.[32] This concept could not have been developed without the groundwork laid by Lutheran mysticism and philosophical irrationalism. The demonic is a power in personal and social life that is creative and destructive at the same time. In the New Testament, men possessed by demons are said to know more about Jesus than those who are normal, but they know it as a condemnation of themselves because they are divided against themselves. The early Church called the Roman Empire demonic because it made itself equal to God, and yet the Church prayed for the emperor and gave thanks for the civic peace he assured. Similarly, religious socialism tries to show that capitalism and nationalism are demonic powers, insofar as they are simultaneously destructive and creative, and attribute divinity to their system of values. The course of European nationalism and Russian communism and their quasi-religious self-justification has fully confirmed this diagnosis.

It is not surprising that my earlier ideas regarding the relations between religion and culture, the sacred and the secular, heteronomy and autonomy, were incorporated into my reflections on religious socialism, which thus became the focal point for all my thinking. Above all, socialism provided a theoretical foundation and practical impetus as I attempted to evolve a theonomous philosophy of history. By analysing the character of 'historical' time, as distinguished from physical and biological time, I developed a concept of history in which the movement toward the new, which is both demanded and expected, is constitutive. The content of the new, toward which history moves, appears in events in which the meaning and goal of history become manifest. I called such an event the 'centre of history'; from the Christian viewpoint the centre is the appearance of Jesus as the Christ. The powers struggling with one another in history can be given different names, according to the perspective from which they are viewed: demonic-*divine*-human, sacramental-*prophetic*-secular, heteronomous-*theonomous*-autonomous. Each middle term represents the synthesis of the other two, the one toward which history is always extending itself – sometimes creatively, sometimes destructively, never completely fulfilled, but always driven by the transcendent power of the anticipated fulfilment. Religious socialism should be understood as one such move toward a new theonomy. It is more than a new economic system. It is a comprehensive understanding of existence, the form of the theonomy demanded and expected by our present Kairos.

Between Idealism and Marxism

I grew up in the atmosphere of German idealism, and doubt that I can ever forget what I learned from it. Above all I am indebted to Kant's critique of knowledge, which showed me that the question of the possibility of empirical knowledge cannot be answered merely by pointing to the realm of objects. Every analysis of experience and every systematic interpretation of reality must begin at the point where subject and object meet. It is in this sense that I understand the idealist principle of identity. It is not an example of metaphysical speculation, but a principle for analysing the basic character of all knowledge. To date no critique of idealism has convinced me that this procedure is incorrect. By taking this principle as my point of departure, I have been able to avoid all forms of metaphysical and naturalistic positivism. Thus I am epistemologically an idealist, if idealism means the assertion of the identity of thought and being as the principle of truth. Furthermore, it seems to me that the element of freedom is given expression in the idealistic conception of the world in a way that best corresponds to subjective and objective experience. The fact that man asks questions, his recognition of absolute demands (the categorical imperative) in thought and action, his perception of meaningful forms in nature, art, and society (as in modern *Gestalt* theories) – all these have convinced me that a doctrine of man must be a philosophy of freedom. Nor can I deny that there is a correspondence between reality and the human spirit which is probably expressed most adequately in the concept of 'meaning'. It led Hegel to speak of the unity of objective and subjective spirit in an Absolute Spirit. When idealism elaborates the categories that give meaning to the various realms of existence, it seeks to fulfil that task which alone is the justification for philosophy.

It was an altogether different issue that led me to the boundary of idealism. The idealists claim that their system of categories portrays reality as a whole, rather than being the expression of a definite and existentially limited encounter with reality. Only Schelling in his second period was conscious of the limitation of idealistic or essentialist systems. He recognized that reality is not only the manifestation of pure essence but also its contradiction and, above all, that human existence itself is an expression of the contradiction of essence. Schelling realized that thought is also bound to existence and shares its contradiction of essence (which does not necessarily imply that it is defective). Schelling did not develop this seminal idea. Like Hegel, he believed that he and his philosophy stood at the end of a historical process through which the contradictions within existence had been overcome and an absolute standpoint attained. Schelling's idealism triumphed over his initial efforts at existential thinking.

Kierkegaard was the first to break through the closed system of the idealist philosophy of essence. His radical interpretation of the anxiety and despair of life led to a philosophy that could really be called existentialist. The importance of his work for post-war German theology and philosophy can hardly be over-estimated. As early as in my last student years (1905-1906), I came under the influence of his aggressive dialectics.

During this same period, opposition to the idealist philosophy of being flared up from another direction. Hegel's radical followers, who came out against their teacher and 'turned idealism on its head', proclaimed a theoretical and practical materialism in idealist categories. Karl Marx, who was a member of this group, went even further. He rejected both the idealist categories and their materialistic inversion (cf. his *Theses against Feuerbach*), and advocated a position that was directed against philosophy as such. This new position was 'not to explain, but to change the world'. According to Marx, philosophy – which he identified with the philosophy of essence – seeks to obscure the contradictions within existence, to abstract from that which is really important to human beings, namely the social contradictions that determine their lives in the world. These contradictions, or more specifically the conflict of the social classes, show that idealism is an ideology, that is, a system of concepts whose function is to veil the ambiguities of reality. (Analogously, Kierkegaard showed that the philosophy of essence tended to conceal the ambiguities within individual existence.)

First and foremost I owe to Marx an insight into the ideological character not only of idealism but also of all systems of thought, religious and secular, which serve power structures and thus prevent, even if unconsciously, a more just organization of reality. Luther's warning against the self-made God is the religious equivalent of what ideology means for philosophy.

A new definition of truth follows from the repudiation of the closed system of essentialism. Truth is bound to the situation of the knower: to the situation of the individual for Kierkegaard, and to that of society for Marx. Knowledge of pure essence is possible only to the degree in which the contradictions within existence have been recognized and overcome. In the situation of despair (the condition of every human being according to Kierkegaard), and in the situation of class struggle (the historical condition of humanity according to Marx), every closed and harmonious system is untrue. Both Kierkegaard and Marx, therefore, seek to associate truth with a particular psychological or social situation. For Kierkegaard truth is subjectivity which does not deny its despair and its exclusion from the world of essence, but which passionately affirms truth within this condition. For Marx, the locus of truth is the class-interest of the class that becomes aware of its destiny to overcome class conflict, that is, the non-ideological class. In both instances we learn, amazingly – though understandably from the Christian standpoint – that the highest possibility for achieving non-ideological truth is given at the point of profoundest meaninglessness, through the deepest despair, in man's greatest estrangement from his own nature. In an essay entitled *Das Protestantische Prinzip und die proletarische Situation* (The Protestant Principle and the Proletarian Situation),[35] I have related this idea to the Protestant principle and its doctrine concerning the human boundary situation. Of course, this is possible only if the notion of proletariat is used typologically. The actual proletariat at times corresponds to the proletarian type even less than some of the non-proletarian groups do – such as, for example, those intellectuals who have broken through their class situation to a boundary situation from which they are able to bring the proletariat to self-consciousness. One should not identify the proletarian masses with the typological concept of the proletariat as used by Marx.

Commonly understood, the word Marxism implies 'economic materialism'. But, intentionally or not, this combination of words overlooks the ambiguity in the term materialism. If materialism could mean only 'metaphysical materialism', I should never have found myself on the boundary of Marxism, and Marx himself, who struggled against both materialism and idealism, would have been no Marxist. We should remember that economic materialism is not a metaphysics but a method of historical analysis. It does not imply that the 'economic', which itself is a complex factor relating to all sides of human existence, is the sole principle for interpreting history. That would be a meaningless assertion. Economic materialism, however, does show the fundamental significance of economic structures and motives for the social and intellectual forms and changes in a historical period. It denies that there can be a history of thought and religion independent of economic factors, and thereby confirms the theological insight, neglected by idealism, that man lives on earth and not in heaven

for, in philosophical terms, that man lives within existence and not in the realm of essence).

Marxism can be understood as a method for unmasking hidden levels of reality. As such, it can be compared
with psychoanalysis. Unmasking is painful and, in certain circumstances, destructive. Ancient Greek tragedy,
e.g., the Oedipus myth, shows this clearly. Man defends
himself against the revelation of his actual nature for
as long as possible. Like Oedipus, he collapses when he
sees himself without the ideologies that sweeten his life
and prop up his self-consciousness. The passionate rejection of Marxism and pychoanalysis, which I have frequently encountered, is an attempt made by individuals
and groups to escape an unmasking that can conceivably
destroy them. But without this painful process the ultimate meaning of the Christian gospel cannot be perceived. The theologian, therefore, should use these means
for exposing the true condition of man as often as he
can rather than propagating an idealism that smoothes
over the ambiguities of existence. He can do so from
his position on the boundary – he can, as I have tried to
do myself, criticize the partially obsolete terminology
of psychoanalysis; he can reject the utopian and dogmatic elements in Marxism; and he can dispense with the
many individual theories of both psychoanalysis and
Marxism that lack scientific validity. The theologian
can and must resist metaphysical and ethical materialism, whether or not it is a legitimate interpretation of
Freud or Marx. But he must not deprive himself of either
movement's efficacy in shattering ideologies and revealing the realities of human existence.

But Marxism has not only an 'unmasking' effect; it involves also demand and expectation, and, as such, it has
had and continues to have a tremendous impact on history. There is prophetic passion in it, whereas idealism,
insofar as it has been moulded by the principle of
identity, has mystical and sacramental roots. In the
central section of my book *Die socialistische Entscheid-*

ung (Socialist Decision),[34] I tried to distinguish the prophetic elements in Marxism from its rational-scientific terminology and thus to make more comprehensible its far-reaching religious and historical implications. I also tried to gain a new understanding of the socialist principle by comparing it with the tenets of Judeo-Christian prophecy. Marxists may accuse me of idealism and idealists may complain of my materialism, but I am actually on the boundary between the two.

Marxism has become a slogan for defaming political opponents. Admitting that I stand on the boundary of Marxism adds nothing new politically to what I have said about my relationship to religious socialism. It does not commit me to any political party. Were I to say that I have stood between two political parties, the 'between' would have to be interpreted differently than it has been elsewhere in these pages. It would mean that I do not inwardly belong to any party and never have, because what seems to me most important in the political realm is something that is never fully manifest in political parties. I desire and always have desired a fellowship that is bound to no party, although it may be nearer to one than to another. This group should be the vanguard for a more righteous social order, established in the prophetic spirit and in accord with the demand of the Kairos.

Between Native and Alien Land

My writing this self-portrait in an alien country is a destiny that, like all true destiny, represents freedom at the same time. The boundary between native land and alien country is not merely an external boundary marked off by nature or by history. It is also the boundary between two inner forces, two possibilities of human existence, whose classic formulation is the command to Abraham: 'Go from your home . . . to the land that I will show you'. He is bidden to leave his native soil, the community of his family and cult, his people and state, for the sake of a promise that he does not understand. The God who demands obedience of him is the God of an alien country, a God not bound to the local soil, as are pagan deities, but the God of history, who means to bless all the races of the earth. This God, the God of the prophet and of Jesus, utterly demolishes all religious nationalism – the nationalism of the Jews, which he opposes constantly, and that of the pagans, which is repudiated in the command to Abraham. For the Christian of any confession, the meaning of this command is indisputable. He must ever leave his own country and enter into a land that will be shown to him. He must trust a promise that is purely transcendent.

The real meaning of 'homeland' varies according to the situation of the individual. It may be the land of his birth and his national community. Occasionally, 'physical emigration' may be demanded. But the command to go from one's country is more often a call to break with ruling authorities and prevailing social and political patterns, and to resist them passively or actively. It is a demand for 'spiritual emigration' – the Christian community's attitude toward the Roman Empire. The path into an alien country may also signify something wholly personal and inward: parting from accepted lines of belief and thought; pushing beyond the limits of the obvious; radical questioning that opens up the new and uncharted. In Nietzsche's words, it means moving into 'the land of our children' and out of 'the land of our fathers and mothers'. It is a temporal, not a geographical, emigration. The alien land lies in the future, the country 'beyond the present'. And when we speak of this alien country we also point to our recognition that even what is nearest and most familiar to us contains an element of strangeness. This is the metaphysical experience of being alone in the world that existentialism takes as its expression of human finitude.

In every sense of the word, I have always stood between native and alien land. I have never decided exclusively for the alien, and I have experienced both types of 'emigration'. I began to be an 'emigrant' personally and spiritually long before I actually left my homeland.

My attachment to my native land in terms of landscape, language, tradition and mutuality of historical destiny has always been so instinctive that I could never understand why it should have to be made an object of special attention. The over-emphasis of cultural nationalism in national education and intellectual productivity is an expression of insecurity about national ties. I am convinced that this over-emphasis occurs in individuals who come from the boundary – either externally or internally – and who feel obligated, therefore, to justify their patriotism to themselves and to others. They are also afraid to return to the boundary.

I have always felt so thoroughly German by nature that I could not dwell on the fact at length. Conditions of birth and destiny cannot really be questioned. We should instead ask : What shall we do with this which is given in our lives? What should be our criterion for evaluating society and politics, intellectual and moral training, cultural and social life? Accidents of birth do not constitute answers to such questions, because the questions presuppose them. If the presuppositions are mistaken for the answers we find ourselves caught in the vicious circle that today is praised as national feeling, although it testifies to a lack of confidence in the strength of our national substance and leads to a terrible emptiness of national life. I expressed my opposition to such nationalistic tendencies in my Frankfurt lectures on public education : 'Sozialpädagogik' (Social Education).

Today, however, the problem of nationalism is primarily an economic and political problem. I have held varying attitudes toward it. In an article on the totalitarian state and the claims of the Church, I discussed the causes of militant totalitarianism in Europe and its relationship to the disintegration of capitalism. My essay, 'Das Problem der Macht' (On the Philosophy of Power),[35] deals with the meaning and limits of power as it is related to the general problem of Being, that is, ontology. In *Die socialistische Entscheidung*,[36] I tried to lay bare the anthropological roots and political consequences of nationalism. The experience of World War I was crucial for my position. It revealed the demonic and destructive character of the national will to power, particularly for those who went to war enthusiastically and with a firm belief in the justice of their national cause. Consequently, I can only view European nationalism as an instrument for the tragic self-destruction of Europe even though – or perhaps because – I realize that nationalism is inevitable. But this insight never made me a pacifist, in the strict sense of the word. One type of pacifism is suspect to me because of the effeminate character of its representatives. The kind of pacifism advocated by victorious and self-satisfied nations has an ideological and pharisaic taint. For such nations pacifism is too useful to be honest. Legalistic pacifism, in my opinion, ends in consequences which are opposite from those intended. In this world, national as well as international peace depends on the power to restrain the violators of peace. I am not speaking in justification of a national will to power; but I recognize the necessity for inter-connected forces, behind which there must be a power capable of preventing the self-destruction of mankind. Today the idea of 'mankind' is more than an empty notion. It has become an economic and political reality; for the fate of every part of the world depends on the fate of every other part. The increasing realization of a united mankind represents and anticipates, so to speak, the truth implicit in a belief in the kingdom of God to which all nations and all races belong. Denying the unity of mankind as aim includes, therefore, denying the Christian doctrine that the kingdom of God is 'at hand'. I was happy to discover on the boundary of this new continent where I now live, thanks to American hospitality, an ideal which is more consistent with the image of one mankind than that of Europe in her tragic self-dismemberment. It is the image of one nation in whom representatives of all nations and races can live as citizens. Although here too the distance between ideal and reality is infinite and the image is often deeply shadowed, nonetheless it is a kind of symbol of that highest possibility of history which is called 'mankind', and which itself points to that which transcends reality – the kingdom of God. In that highest possibility, the boundary between native and alien land ceases to exist.

Retrospect: Boundary and Limitation

Many possibilities of human existence, both physical and spiritual, have been discussed in these pages. Some things have not been mentioned, although they are part of my biography. Many more things have been left untouched, because they do not belong to the story of my life and thought. Each possibility that I have discussed, however, I have discussed in its relationship to another possibility – the way they are opposed, the way they can be correlated. This is the dialectic of existence; each of life's possibilities drives of its own accord to a boundary and beyond the boundary where it meets that which limits it. The man who stands on many boundaries experiences the unrest, insecurity, and inner limitation of existence in many forms. He knows the impossibility of attaining serenity, security, and perfection. This holds true in life as well as in thought, and may explain why the experiences and ideas which I have recounted are rather fragmentary and tentative. My desire to give definitive form to these thoughts has once again been frustrated by my boundary-fate, which has cast me on the soil of a new continent. Completing such a task to the best of my ability is a hope that becomes more uncertain as I approach fifty. But whether or not it is to be fulfilled, there remains a boundary for human activity which is no longer a boundary between two possibilities but rather a limit set on everything finite by that which transcends all human possibilities, the Eternal. In its presence, even the very centre of our being is only a boundary and our highest level of accomplishment is fragmentary.

NOTES

1. *Religiöse Verwirklichung*. Berlin: Furche, 1929.
2. 'Logos und Mythos der Technik'. *Logos* (Tübingen), XVI, No. 3 (November, 1927).
3. Die technische Stadt als Symbol'. *Dresdner Neueste Nachrichten*, No. 115 (17 May, 1928).
4. *The Religious Situation*. New York: Henry Holt, 1932.
5. 'Masse und Geist'. *Studien zur Philosophie der Masse*. 'Volk und Geist', No. 1 Berlin/Frankfurt a.M.: Verlag der Arbeitsgemeinschaft, 1922.
6. 'Grundlinien des religiösen Sozialismus. Ein systematischer Entwurf'. *Blätter für Religiösen Sozialismus* (Berlin), IV, No. 8/10 (1923).
7. *Die sozialistische Entscheidung*. Potsdam: Alfred Protte, 1933.
8. 'Das Problem der Macht. Versuch einer philosophischen Grundlegung'. *Neue Blätter für den Sozialismus* (Potsdam), II, No. 4 (April, 1931).
9. *Das System der Wissenschaften nach Gegenständen und Methoden. Ein Entwurf*. Göttingen: Vandenhoeck & Ruprecht, 1923.
10. *Die sozialistische Entscheidung*. Potsdam: Alfred Protte, 1933.
11. *The Religious Situation*. New York: Henry Holt, 1932.
12. 'Masse und Persönlichkeit'. Göttingen: Vandenhoeck & Ruprecht, 1920.
13. *Das System der Wissenschaften nach Gegenständen und Methoden. Ein Entwurf*. Göttingen: Vandenhoeck & Ruprecht, 1923.
14. 'Religionsphilosophie'. *Lehrbuch der Philosophie*, ed. Max Dessoir. Vol. II: *Die Philosophie in ihren Einzelgebieten*. Berlin: Ullstein, 1925.
15. *Neue Blätter für den Sozialismus*. Potsdam: Alfred Protte, 1931.
16. *Protestantismus als Kritik und Gestaltung*. Darmstadt: Otto Reichl, 1929.
17. *Religiöse Verwirklichung*. Berlin: Furche, 1929.
18. 'Der Staat als Erwartung und Forderung'. In: *Religiöse Verwirklichung*. Berlin: Furche, 1929.

19. 'The Totalitarian State and the Claims of the Church'. *Social Research* (New York) I, No. 4 (November, 1934).

20. 'Masse und Geist'. *Studien zur Philosophie der Masse*. Berlin/Frankfurt a.M.: Verlag der Arbeitsgemeinschaft, 1922.

21. 'Rechtfertigung und Zweifel'. *Vorträge der theologischen Konferenz zu Giessen*, 39. Folge, Giessen: Alfred Töpelmann, 1924.

22. 'Die Idee der Offenbarung'. *Zeitschrift für Theologie und Kirche* (Tübingen), N.F., VIII, No. 6 (1927).

23. 'Die Überwindung des Religionsbegriffs in der Religionsphilosophie'. *Kant-Studien* (Berlin), XXVII, No. 3/4 (1922).

24. *Das System der Wissenschaften nach Gegenständen und Methoden. Ein Entwurf.* Göttingen. Vandenhoeck & Ruprecht, 1923.

25. *Religiöse Verwirklichung.* Berlin: Furche, 1929.

26. 'Kirche und humanistische Gesellschaft'. *Neuwerk* (Kassel), XIII, No. 1 (April-May, 1931).

27. *The Religious Situation.* New York: Henry Holt, 1932.

28. 'Über die Idee einer Theologie der Kultur'. *Religions-philosophie der Kultur.* Berlin: Reuther & Reichard, 1919.

29. 'Natur und Sakrament'. In: *Religiöse Verwirklichung.* Berlin: Furche, 1929.

30. *Kairos: Zur Geisteslage und Geisteswendung.* Darmstadt: Otto Reichl, 1926.

31. *Protestantismus als Kritik und Gestaltung.* Darmstadt: Otto Reichl, 1929.

32. *The Interpretation of History.* New York: Scribner's, 1936.

33. *Das Protestantische Prinzip und die proletarische Situation.* Bonn: F. Cohen, 1931.

34. *Die sozialistische Entscheidung.* Potsdam: Alfred Protte, 1933.

35. 'Das Problem der Macht. Versuch einer philosophischen Grundlegung'. *Neue Blätter für den Sozialismus* (Potsdam), II, No. 4 (April, 1931).

36. *Die sozialistische Entscheidung.* Potsdam: Alfred Protte, 1933.